DK ESSENTIAL
GUIDE TO
WORD

DK ESSENTIAL
GUIDE TO
WORD

LONDON, NEW YORK, MUNICH, MELBOURNE, DELHI

SENIOR EDITOR Amy Corzine
SENIOR ART EDITOR Sarah Cowley
DTP DESIGNER Julian Dams
PRODUCTION CONTROLLER Michelle Thomas

MANAGING EDITOR Adèle Hayward
SENIOR MANAGING ART EDITOR Nigel Duffield

Produced for Dorling Kindersley Limited by
Design Revolution Limited, Queens Park Villa,
30 West Drive, Brighton, East Sussex BN2 0QW
EDITORIAL DIRECTOR Ian Whitelaw
SENIOR DESIGNER Andrew Easton
PROJECT EDITOR John Watson
DESIGNER Paul Bowler

First published in Great Britain in 2001 by
Dorling Kindersley Limited,
80 Strand, London WC2R 0RL

A Penguin Company

2 4 6 8 10 9 7 5 3 1

A CIP catalogue record for this book is available from the British Library.

ISBN 0-7513-3540-1

Colour reproduced by Colourscan, Singapore
Printed and bound in Italy by Graphicom

For our complete catalogue, visit
www.dk.com

ABOUT THIS BOOK

The *Essential Word 2000 Guide* is an easy-to-follow guide to using Microsoft® Word 2000 to create professional-quality documents, complete with illustrations, charts, and graphs.

A S ONE OF THE MOST FLEXIBLE AND feature-filled word-processing programs available, Microsoft Word is now among the most widely used applications available for the PC. Each of the five sections in this book concentrates on one aspect of Word and helps to show the range of text- and graphic-based output that can be produced with relative ease. The first section concentrates on the basic uses of text in Word. The second section builds on the first by showing the wide variety of ways in which text can be styled and documents designed. The third section moves into the areas of handling and representing data in tables and charts. This is followed by the use of Word to create graphics, and the book ends with a section on how Word can be customized and used more efficiently, introducing a wide range of keyboard shortcuts.

The information is presented in easily understood step-by-step sequences. Virtually every step is accompanied by an illustration to show how your screen should look at each stage.

The book's features help you understand what you need to do. Command keys, such as ENTER and CTRL, are shown in these rectangles: Enter↵ and Ctrl, so that there's no confusion, for example, over whether you should press that key or type the letters "ctrl."

Cross-references are shown in the text as left- or right-hand page icons: ◁ and ▷. The page number and the reference are shown at the foot of the page.

There are also boxes that explain a feature in detail and tip boxes that provide alternative methods. Finally, at the back, there is a glossary of common terms and a comprehensive index.

CONTENTS

LETTERS
& MAILING

WORD'S ESSENTIAL FEATURES are presented in separate chapters within this first section of the *Essential Guide to Word*. The tasks that are covered include launching the program on your PC, understanding the Word window and the toolbars, keying in text, and changing its appearance. This section also shows you how to save your documents and organize them in folders, print them, improve them using Word's tools, templates, and wizards, and how to carry out a mail merge.

MICROSOFT WORD

Microsoft Word has been around for well over a decade and, with each new release, adds to its reputation as the world's leading word-processing program.

WHAT CAN WORD DO?

The features contained in Word make it one of the most flexible word-processing programs available. Word can be used to write anything from shopping lists to large publications that contain, in addition to the main text, illustrations and graphics, charts, tables and graphs, captions, headers and footers, cross references, footnotes, indexes, and glossaries – all of which are easily managed by Word. Word can check spelling and grammar, check text readability, search and replace text, import data, sort data, perform calculations, and provide templates for many types of documents from memos to web pages. The comprehensive and versatile design, formatting, and layout options in Word make it ideal for desktop publishing on almost any scale. In short, there's very little that Word cannot do.

WHAT IS A WORD DOCUMENT?

In its simplest form, a Word document is a sequence of characters that exists in a computer's memory. Using Word, a document can be edited, added to, and given a variety of layouts. Once the document has been created, there are a large number of actions that can be carried out, such as saving, printing, or sending the document as an email.

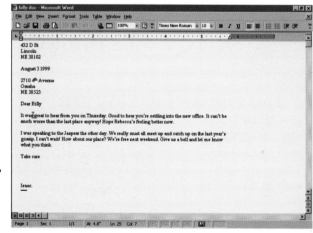

LAUNCHING WORD

Word launches just like any other program running in Windows. With the Windows desktop on-screen, you can launch Word as the only program running, or you can run Word alongside other software to exchange data with other applications.

1 LAUNCHING BY THE START MENU

● Place the mouse cursor over the **Start** button on the Taskbar and click with the left mouse button.
● Move the cursor up the pop-up menu until **Programs** is highlighted. A submenu of programs appears to the right.
● Move the cursor down the menu to **Microsoft Word** and left-click again. (If **Microsoft Word** is missing from the **Programs** menu, it may be under **Microsoft Office**.)
● The Microsoft Word window opens ⬜.

2 LAUNCHING BY A SHORTCUT

● You may already have a Word icon on-screen, which is a shortcut to launching Word. If so, double-click on the icon.
● The Microsoft Word window opens ⬜.

THE WORD WINDOW

At first, Word's document window may look like a space shuttle computer display. However, you'll soon discover that similar commands and actions are neatly grouped together. This "like-with-like" layout helps you quickly understand where you should be looking on the window for what you want. Click and play while you read this.

THE WORD WINDOW

1 Title bar
2 Menu bar
Contains the main menus.
3 Standard toolbar
Buttons for frequent actions.
4 Formatting toolbar
Main layout options.
5 Tab selector
Clicking selects type of tab.
6 Left-indent buttons
Used to set left indents.
7 Ruler
Displays margins and tabs.
8 Right-indent button
Used to set right indent.
9 Insertion point
Shows where typing appears.
10 Text area
Area for document text.
11 Split box
Creates two text panes.
12 Scroll-up arrow
Moves up the document.
13 Scroll-bar box
Moves text up or down.
14 Vertical scroll bar
Used to move through text.

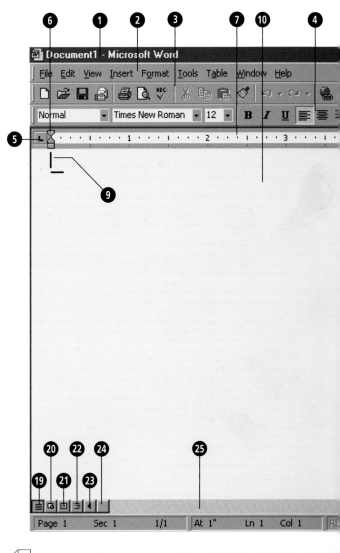

34 Indenting the Address

16 Insertion Point

TOOLBAR LAYOUT

If Word doesn't show the Formatting toolbar below the Standard toolbar, first place the cursor over the Formatting toolbar "handle." When the four-headed arrow appears, (right) hold down the mouse button and "drag" the toolbar into position.

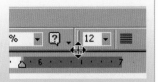

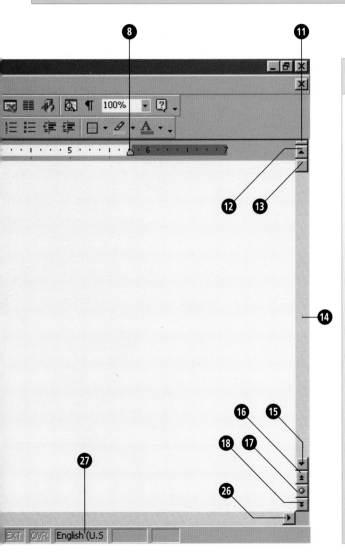

THE WORD WINDOW

⓯ Scroll-down arrow
Moves down the document.
⓰ Page-up button
Shows previous page of text.
⓱ Select browse object
Opens browse options menu.
⓲ Page-down button
Displays next page of text.
⓳ Normal view
Default document view.
⓴ Web layout view
Web-browser page view.
㉑ Page layout view
Printed-page view of text.
㉒ Outline view
Shows document's structure.
㉓ Left-scroll arrow
Shows the text to the left.
㉔ Scroll-bar box
Moves text horizontally.
㉕ Horizontal scroll bar
To view wide documents.
㉖ Right-scroll arrow
Shows the text to the right.
㉗ Language
Spelling, thesaurus, and proofing settings.

THE WORD TOOLBARS

Word provides a range of toolbars where numerous commands and actions are available. The principal toolbars are the Standard toolbar and the Formatting toolbar, which contain the most frequently used features of Word. There are also more than 20 other toolbars available for display. Click on **Tools** in the Menu bar, move the cursor down to **Customize**, and click the mouse button. The **Customize** dialog box opens. Click the **Toolbars** tab to view the variety of toolbars available.

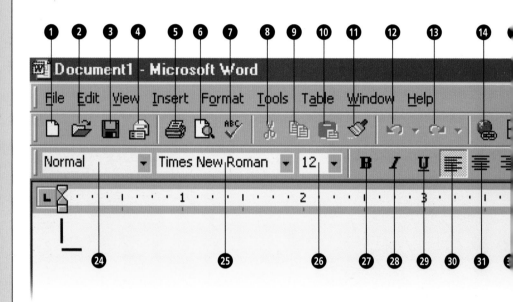

THE STANDARD TOOLBAR

1. New document
2. Open folder or file
3. Save
4. Email
5. Print
6. Print preview
7. Spelling and grammar
8. Cut text
9. Copy text
10. Paste text
11. Format painter
12. Undo action(s)
13. Redo action(s)
14. Insert hyperlink
15. Tables and borders
16. Insert table
17. Insert Excel worksheet
18. Columns
19. Drawing toolbar
20. Document map
21. Show/hide formatting marks
22. Zoom view of text
23. Microsoft Word help

| 19 | Formatting Marks | 50 | Print Preview | 53 | Printing Quickly |

CUSTOMIZING A TOOLBAR

To add a **Close** button to a toolbar, click on the **Commands** tab of the **Customize** box (see left). Place the cursor over the **Close** icon, hold down the mouse button, drag the icon to the toolbar, and release the mouse button.

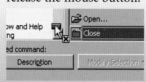

ScreenTips

It isn't necessary to memorize all these buttons. Roll the cursor over a button, wait for a second, and a ScreenTip appears telling you the function of the button.

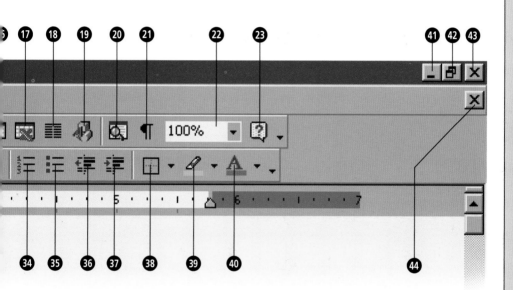

THE FORMATTING TOOLBAR

- ㉔ Style selector
- ㉕ Font selector
- ㉖ Font size selector
- ㉗ Bold
- ㉘ Italic
- ㉙ Underline
- ㉚ Left-aligned text
- ㉛ Centered text
- ㉜ Right-aligned text
- ㉝ Justified text
- ㉞ Numbered list
- ㉟ Bulleted list
- ㊱ Decrease indent
- ㊲ Increase indent
- ㊳ Outside border
- ㊴ Highlight color
- ㊵ Font color
- ㊶ Minimize Word
- ㊷ Restore Word
- ㊸ Close Word
- ㊹ Close document

39	Quick Ways to Align Text

40	Font and Font Size

40	Quick Ways to Format Fonts

YOUR FIRST LETTER

Microsoft Word makes the process of writing a letter and printing it out easier than ever. This chapter takes you through the few simple steps involved in creating your first letter.

TYPING THE LETTER

The first image on your screen when you start Microsoft Word is a blank area with a blinking cursor, surrounded by buttons and symbols that may mean nothing to you. Don't worry about them for now. To begin with, the only thing you need to concentrate on is to start writing your letter on that blank screen.

1 BEGINNING TYPING

● Type the first line of your address. As you type, the insertion point moves with your text. Don't worry about mistakes – they are easily corrected.

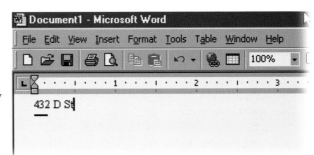

2 STARTING A NEW LINE

● Press the [Enter←] button.
● The insertion point has now moved to the beginning of a new line.

Insertion point ●

INSERTION POINT

This is a blinking upright line that precedes your text as you type. If you are ever unsure about where your typing will appear on the page, check where the insertion point is.

| 18 | **Correcting Errors as You Type** |

3 COMPLETING THE ADDRESS

● Finish typing your address, pressing Enter↵ at the end of each line.

● At the end of the last address line, press Enter↵ twice to leave a line space.

432 D St
Lincoln
NE 38102

4 STARTING THE LETTER

● Now type the date, leave another line space, then type the recipient's address.

● Leave two lines (by pressing Enter↵ three times) and type your greeting.

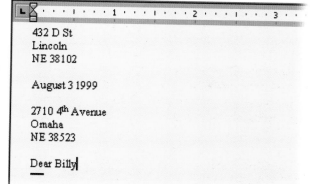

432 D St
Lincoln
NE 38102

August 3 1999

2710 4th Avenue
Omaha
NE 38523

Dear Billy

5 CREATING PARAGRAPHS

● Leave another line and start your first paragraph. When typing paragraphs in Word, just keep typing until the end of the paragraph, and only then press Enter↵. At the end of each line, Word "wraps" your text around to start a new line.

● To start a new paragraph, press Enter↵ to end the first paragraph, and press Enter↵ again to leave a line space. You are ready to start the new paragraph.

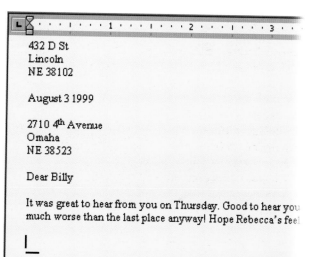

432 D St
Lincoln
NE 38102

August 3 1999

2710 4th Avenue
Omaha
NE 38523

Dear Billy

It was great to hear from you on Thursday. Good to hear you much worse than the last place anyway! Hope Rebecca's feel

6 FINISHING THE LETTER

● If your letter is longer than can fit on the screen, Word moves the text up as you type. If you need to go back to it, simply hold down the ⬆ arrow key. The insertion point moves up the text to the top of your letter.

● Type a sign-off after the last paragraph. Press Enter↵ a few times to leave room for your signature. Then type your name.

● You have now typed your first letter using Word.

It was great to hear from you on Thursday. Good to hear yo
much worse than the last place anyway! Hope Rebecca's fee

I was speaking to the Jaspers the other day. We really must a
gossip. How about our place? We're free next weekend. Giv
think.

Take care

Isaac

Page 1	Sec 1	1/1	At 4.8"	Ln 25	Col 7

Start | Document1 - Microso... | Paint Shop Pro

CORRECTING ERRORS AS YOU TYPE

1 REMOVING THE ERROR

● You have misspelled a word as you are typing.

● To remove the misspelled word, first press the Backspace (← Bksp) key. This removes text one letter at a time to the left of the insertion point.

● Keep tapping ← Bksp until the word is gone.

Dear Billy

It was great to hear from you on Thursday. Good to hear you
much worse than the last place anyway! Hope Rebecca's fee

I was speaking to the Jaspers the other day. We really must a
gossip. How aubot

Dear Billy

It was great to hear from you on Thursday. Good to hear you
much worse than the last place anyway! Hope Rebecca's fee

I was speaking to the Jaspers the other day. We really must a
gossip. How

2 REPLACING THE ERROR

• Now type the word again. Remember to leave a space before it – ← Bksp also removes spaces and line spaces if they are immediately to the left of the insertion point.

• You have corrected the error and you can continue typing your letter.

Dear Billy

It was great to hear from you on Thursday. Good to hear you much worse than the last place anyway! Hope Rebecca's feel

I was speaking to the Jaspers the other day. We really must a gossip. How about

FORMATTING MARKS

Word uses invisible markers (called formatting marks) within your text to mark the spaces between words, and where you have decided to leave line spaces. Formatting marks do not appear on paper when you print out the text. Initially you don't see them on your screen, which makes the text on the screen appear exactly how it will print out. However, you may want to see the formatting marks so that you can see double spaces and control where you want the line spaces to be placed. To see the formatting marks, click on the small, down-arrow button in the middle of your toolbar. A menu drops down. Click on the button with the paragraph mark. You are now able to see the formatting marks. Click the button again when you want to turn off the formatting marks. You won't need to drop down the menu again – after the first use, Word adds the button to your toolbar.

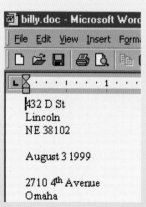

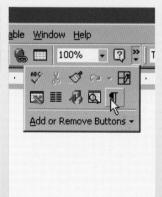

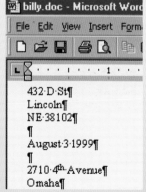

CORRECTING ERRORS FROM EARLIER IN THE TEXT

It is inevitable that errors are made as you type, such as misspellings and duplicate words. If you notice an error higher up in your letter than where you are currently typing, you can move the insertion point back to the error and easily correct it.

1 MOVING TO THE ERROR

● The misspelled word is higher in the text than the insertion point. You may be familiar with using the mouse to relocate the insertion point, but you may be less familiar with using the arrow keys.

● Move the insertion point up to the line containing the error by using the ⬆ arrow key.

● Use the ⬅ and ➡ arrow keys until you've placed the insertion point at the end of the misspelled word.

> It was great to hear from you on Thursday. Good to hear you
> much worse than the last place anyway! Hope Rebecca's fee
>
> I was spaeking to the Jaspers the other day. We really must a
> gossip. How about our place? We're free next weekend. Giv
> think|
> ▬

> It was great to hear from you on Thursday. Good to hear you
> much worse than the last place anyway! Hope Rebecca's fee
>
> I was spaeking|to the Jaspers the other day. We really must a
> gossip. How about our place? We're free next weekend. Giv
> think.
> ▬

2 CORRECTING THE ERROR

● Remove the misspelled word and type it in with the correct spelling.

● You have now corrected the error. Use the ⬇ arrow key to return the insertion point to where you left off. You can now continue with your typing.

> It was great to hear from you on Thursday. Good to hear you
> much worse than the last place anyway! Hope Rebecca's fee
>
> I was speaking|to the Jaspers the other day. We really must a
> gossip. How about our place? We're free next weekend. Giv
> think.
> ▬

ADDING WORDS IN THE MIDDLE OF THE TEXT

Word makes it easy for you to change your text at any time while writing your letter. If you decide to add something further, or suddenly realize that an important point has been left out, you can type it in by first using the insertion point.

1 POSITIONING THE INSERTION POINT

● Move the insertion point to the place in the text where you want to add words. Use the arrow keys on your keyboard again for further practice. Remember, you can only move to where text has already been typed.

Insertion point ●

Omaha
NE 38523

Dear Billy

It was great to hear from you on Thursday. Good to hear you much worse than the last place anyway! Hope Rebecca's fee

I was speaking to the Jaspers the other day. We really must a gossip. How about our place? We're free next weekend. Giv think.

Take care

Isaac.

2 ADDING THE WORDS

● Start typing the new text. If the insertion point is in the middle of a paragraph, you'll notice that Word automatically moves text along to accommodate what you are adding.
● Use the arrow keys to return to the place where you left off typing.

Omaha
NE 38523

Dear Billy

It was great to hear from you on Thursday. Good to hear you much worse than the last place anyway! Hope Rebecca's fee

I was speaking to the Jaspers the other day. We really must a gossip. I can't wait! How about our place? We're free next w what you think.

Take care

MANIPULATING PARAGRAPHS

Paragraphs organize your text, help with the sense of your document, and make your document more readable. With Word, it's easy to create a new paragraph when another is needed, and to combine them when two paragraphs aren't required.

1 SPLITTING A PARAGRAPH

● To split a paragraph into two, move the insertion point to the start of the sentence that will begin the new second paragraph. Then press Enter⏎ twice. You now have two paragraphs.

> I was speaking to the Jaspers the other day. We really must a gossip. I can't wait! How about our place? We're free next w what you think.
>
> Take care

> I was speaking to the Jaspers the other day. We really must a gossip. I can't wait!
>
> How about our place? We're free next weekend. Give us a b
>
> Take care

2 COMBINING PARAGRAPHS

● If you want to join two paragraphs together to make one, place the insertion point at the beginning of the second paragraph. Then press ←Bksp twice to remove the line spaces. Your two paragraphs now form one larger paragraph.

> It was great to hear from you on Thursday. Good to hear you're settling into the new office. It c much worse than the last place anyway! Hope Rebecca's feeling better now.
>
> I was speaking to the Jaspers the other day. We really must all meet up and catch up on the last gossip. I can't wait! How about our place? We're free next weekend. Give us a bell and let me k what you think.
>
> Take care

3 PARAGRAPH MARKS

Pressing the [Enter ←] key ends a paragraph and inserts a paragraph mark. You can see these marks by turning on the formatting marks ⬚. Deleting the line space between paragraphs is just a matter of deleting the paragraph mark just like any other character.

> It was great to hear from you on Thursday. Good to hear you're settling into the new office. It c
> much worse than the last place anyway! Hope Rebecca's feeling better now. I was speaking to
> Jaspers the other day. We really must all meet up and catch up on the last year's gossip. I can't
> wait! How about our place? We're free next weekend. Give us a bell and let me know what you
>
> Take care

USING WORD TO START A NEW PAGE

If you want to begin a new page, before the text has reached the end of the current page, you can use Word to split the page into two.

Move the insertion point to the position in your letter where you want the new page to start. Hold down the [Ctrl] key and press [Enter ←]. Word inserts a "manual" page break. You can delete this page break by placing the insertion point at the top left of the second page and pressing [← Bksp].

> Dear Billy
>
> It was great to hear from you on Thursday. Good to hear you're settling into the new office. I
> much worse than the last place anyway! Hope Rebecca's feeling better now.
> |
> I was speaking to the Jaspers the other day. We really must all meet up and catch up on the l
> gossip. I can't wait! How about our place? We're free next weekend. Give us a bell and let m
> what you think.

> Dear Billy
>
> It was great to hear from you on Thursday. Good to hear you're settling into the new office. I
> much worse than the last place anyway! Hope Rebecca's feeling better now.
> ················Page Break················
> |
> I was speaking to the Jaspers the other day. We really must all meet up and catch up on the l
> gossip. I can't wait! How about our place? We're free next weekend. Give us a bell and let m
> what you think.

19 **Formatting Marks**

SAVING YOUR LETTER

Now that your letter is finished and correct, you should save it as a file on your computer's hard disk so that if you need to find it later, or make changes after you have printed it out, you will be able to bring it back up on the screen.

1 SAVING THE FILE

● Move your mouse pointer over the word **File** in the Menu bar at the top of the screen. Click on **File** and the File menu drops down. Move the mouse pointer down and click on **Save**.

● The **Save As** dialog box pops up in the middle of your screen. In this box you are able to give your letter a file name and decide where you want to save it on the hard disk.

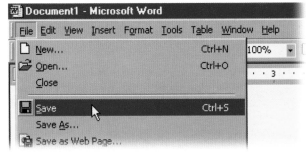

2 NAMING AND SAVING

● Choose a file name that identifies the letter for you and type it into the **File name** box.

● Select a folder in the **Save in** box and click on the **Save** button. The dialog box closes and your letter is saved to disk.

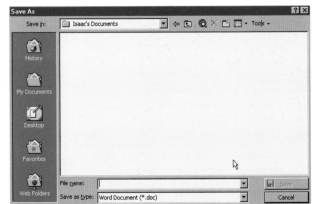

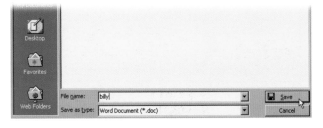

PRINTING YOUR LETTER

1 FILE PRINT

● Click on the **File** menu. The **File** menu drops down.
● This time choose **Print** from the File menu by clicking once on **Print**.

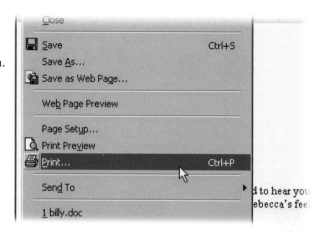

2 PRINT YOUR LETTER

● The **Print** dialog box pops up. Don't worry about any of the features here at this stage. Just make sure that the printer is plugged into the computer and is switched on.
● Click on the **OK** button at the bottom of the dialog box and your letter begins to print.

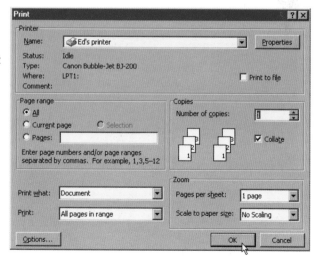

Very good...
You have now typed, corrected, saved, and printed your first letter using Word. These simple steps have shown you the basic process that you use to create a letter with Microsoft Word. Now we go into more detail and explore each step of the process in detail.

WORKING WITH TEXT

This section deals with methods of working with text: moving around text, shifting text from one place to another, deleting text, and copying text.

MOVING AROUND YOUR TEXT

There are many different ways to move around and see different parts of your letter. Here are some techniques to move through your letter that make use of either the mouse or the different actions that are available through the keyboard.

1 GET TO THE START OF THE LETTER

● The insertion point is midway through or at the end of the letter.
● Hold down the [Ctrl] key and press the [Home] key on your keyboard.
● The screen now shows the top of the letter. The insertion point is at the very beginning of the text.

The insertion point ● ── *moves to the start of the letter*

Dear Billy

It was great to hear from you on Thursday. Good to hear you much worse than the last place anyway! Hope Rebecca's fee

I was speaking to the Jaspers the other day. We really must a gossip. I can't wait! How about our place? We're free next v what you think.

Take care

L ⸱ ⸱ ⸱ I ⸱ ⸱ ⸱ 1 ⸱ ⸱ ⸱ I ⸱ ⸱ ⸱ 2 ⸱ ⸱ ⸱ I ⸱ ⸱ ⸱ 3 ⸱ ⸱

432 D St
Lincoln
NE 38102

August 3 1999

2710 4th Avenue
Omaha
NE 38523

Dear Billy

2 GET TO THE END OF THE TEXT

- Hold down the Ctrl key and press the End key on your keyboard.
- The screen now shows the foot of the letter. The insertion point is at the very end of the text.

I was speaking to the Jaspers the other day. We really must a gossip. I can't wait! How about our place? We're free next w what you think.

Take care

Isaac|

3 SCROLLING THROUGH TEXT

- If you can't see the part of the letter you want, position the mouse cursor over the sliding box in the scroll bar.

Hold down the left mouse button and move the box up and down the bar to scroll through the text.

- Alternatively, use the buttons at the top and

bottom of the scroll bar. Click on them to scroll the text up and down.

- Stop when the section of the text appears that you want to work on.

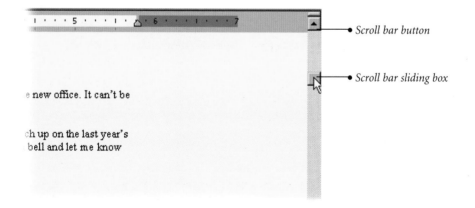

• Scroll bar button

• Scroll bar sliding box

e new office. It can't be

ch up on the last year's
bell and let me know

MOVING AROUND WITHOUT THE MOUSE

If you want to move quickly around your letter without using the mouse, you can use the PgUp and PgDn keys on your keyboard to move up or down your letter one screen at a time. This method moves the insertion point directly. You can use the arrow keys to place the insertion point in the exact position in the text where you need to make your changes.

4 CLICKING ON TEXT

● Move the mouse pointer to the exact point in the text where you want the insertion point to go.
● Left-click once. The insertion point appears.

Dear Billy

It was great to hear from you on Thursday. Good to hear you
much worse than the last place anyway! Hope Rebecca's fee

I was speaking to the Jaspers the other day. We really must a
gossip. I can't wait! How about our place? We're free next w
what you think.

Take care

SELECTING TEXT

Before Word can carry out any changes that you want to make, you first need to tell Word what parts of the text you want it to work on. This is done by selecting text, which is one of the most frequently used operations when using Word.

1 USING THE KEYBOARD

● Move the insertion point to the start of the text you want to select.
● Hold down the ⬆ Shift key and press the → arrow key. This has the effect of creating a block of selected text one letter at a time.

It was great to hear from you on Thursday. Good to hear you
much worse than the last place anyway! Hope Rebecca's fee

I was speaking to the Jaspers the other day. We really must a
gossip. I can't wait! How about our place? We're free next w
what you think.

Take care

It was great to hear from you on Thursday. Good to hear you
much worse than the last place anyway! Hope Rebecca's fee

I was speaking to the Jaspers the other day. We really must a
gossip. I can't wait! How about our place? We're free next w
what you think.

Take care

● If the block you want to select extends over more than one line, keep the `⇧ Shift` key held down, and press the `↓` key to select whole lines at a time. Then use the `←` and `→` keys to choose the end of the block. Don't release the `⇧ Shift` key until you have selected the entire block of text that you want.

Dear Billy

It was great to hear from you on Thursday. Good to hear you much worse than the last place anyway! Hope Rebecca's fee

I was speaking to the Jaspers the other day. We really must gossip. I can't wait! How about our place? We're free next w what you think.

Take care

Vanishing Point

You will notice that when you have selected and highlighted a block of text, there is no longer an insertion point in your Word window. What has happened is that the block of selected text becomes one very large insertion point. It is important to be careful here because if you press any character key on the keyboard while your block is selected, your entire block will vanish and be replaced by whatever you type.

2 USING THE MOUSE

● Move the mouse pointer to the precise point where you want to start your selected block of text.
● Hold down the left mouse button and move the mouse pointer to the position that marks the end of the block that you want.
● Release the mouse button. Your block of text is now selected.
● If you make a mistake, simply click outside the selection and go through the process again.

Dear Billy

It was great to hear from you on Thursday. Good to hear you much worse than the last place anyway! Hope Rebecca's fee

I was speaking to the Jaspers the other day. We really must gossip. I can't wait! How about our place? We're free next w what you think.

Dear Billy

It was great to hear from you on Thursday. Good to hear you much worse than the last place anyway! Hope Rebecca's fee

I was speaking to the Jaspers the other day. We really must gossip. I can't wait! How about our place? We're free next w what you think.

3 SELECTING ALL THE TEXT

● Click on **Edit** on the menu bar. The **Edit** menu drops down.

● Now click on **Select All** in the **Edit** menu.

● The whole of your letter is now selected.

● Alternatively, you can move the mouse cursor to the left of your text where it changes from pointing left to pointing to the right. Hold down the Ctrl key and click on the left mouse button. The whole of your text is now selected.

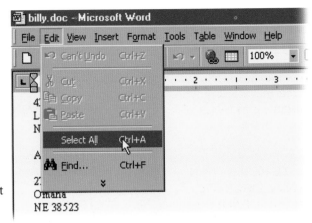

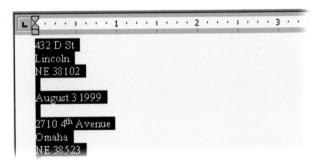

4 SELECTING LINES AT A TIME

● Selecting blocks of text by lines can save time. Move the mouse pointer to the left of the first line that you want to select. Hold down the left mouse button and move the mouse pointer to the last line of your chosen block. Release the mouse button and the block is selected.

MOVING TEXT – CUT AND PASTE

You can move whole blocks of text either within your document or between documents when using Word. The easiest way to do this is by "cutting" selected blocks of text from your letter and "pasting" them back into a different place.

1 CUTTING TEXT

- Select a block of text ↰.
- Click on **Edit** on the menu bar. The **Edit** menu drops down.
- Click on **Cut** in the **Edit** menu. Your block of text will disappear, but it is not lost. The rest of the text will move back into place around it.

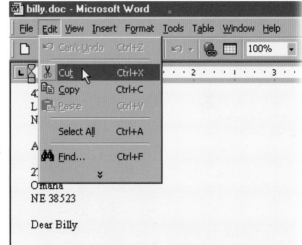

Block of text to be cut ●————

Cutting has removed the text ●————

Selecting Text

2 PASTING TEXT

- Position the insertion point where you want the text to reappear.
- Click on **Edit** in the Menu bar, then on **Paste** in the drop down menu.
- The text is pasted back into your letter exactly where you want it.

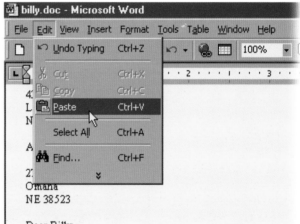

Dear Billy

It was great to hear from you on Thursday. Good to hear you
much worse than the last place anyway! Hope Rebecca's fee

I was speaking to the Jaspers the other day. We really must a
gossip. How about our place? We're free next weekend. Giv
think.

Take care

COPYING TEXT

You may want to copy a block of text to a new location while leaving the original block in its old position. Simply go through the cut and paste procedures detailed on these pages, but when you come to cut the text, select **Copy** instead of **Cut** on the **Edit** menu. The block will stay where it is, but you will be able to paste copies of it whenever you want.

Dear Billy

It was great to hear from you on Thursday. Good to hear you
much worse than the last place anyway! Hope Rebecca's fee

I was speaking to the Jaspers the other day. We really must a
gossip. How about our place? We're free next weekend. Giv
think. I can't wait!

Take care

Moving Text – Drag and Drop

This method is a quicker way of moving text around and uses only the mouse. Once you've told Word what part of the text you want to move, you can then "drag" it to the position where you want to move it, and "drop" it into place.

1 SELECTING THE TEXT

● Select a block of text using one of the methods that you have already learned.

> Dear Billy
>
> It was great to hear from you on Thursday. Good to hear you
> much worse than the last place anyway! Hope Rebecca's fee
>
> I was speaking to the Jaspers the other day. We really must a
> gossip. How about our place? We're free next weekend. Giv
> think. I can't wait!
>
> Take care

2 MOVING THE TEXT

● Place the mouse cursor over the block of selected text. Hold down the left mouse button and move, or "drag," the mouse cursor to the position in your letter where you want the text to appear. Don't release the mouse button until the mouse pointer is in exactly the right place.

● Now release the mouse button and the text appears in the new location.

> Dear Billy
>
> It was great to hear from you on Thursday. Good to hear you
> much worse than the last place anyway! Hope Rebecca's fee
>
> I was speaking to the Jaspers the other day. We really must a
> gossip. How about our place? We're free next weekend. Giv
> think. I can't wait!
>
> Take care

> Dear Billy
>
> It was great to hear from you on Thursday. Good to hear you
> much worse than the last place anyway! Hope Rebecca's fee
>
> I was speaking to the Jaspers the other day. We really must a
> gossip. We're free next weekend. How about our place? Giv
> think. I can't wait!
>
> Take care

28 Selecting Text

CHANGING THE LAYOUT

In this section we deal with how to lay your text out on the page in the way you want it. The most common layout changes that you'll be making are indenting and aligning.

INDENTING THE ADDRESS

1 SELECTING YOUR ADDRESS

● Using either the mouse or the keyboard, select the lines of your address as a block of text ◫.

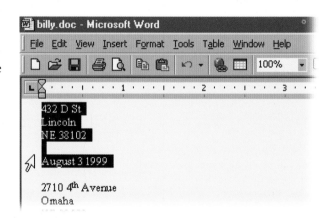

2 CHANGING THE INDENT

● Directly above the text on the screen is a numbered line. This is the ruler.

● Move your mouse pointer to the small symbol called the left indent marker shown at right.

● Click on the box at the base of the left indent marker, and hold down the left mouse button.

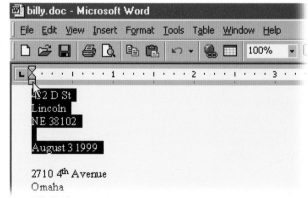

Selecting Text

- Drag the left indent marker, by using the box, across the ruler however far you want your address to be indented.
- Now release the mouse button. Your address has moved across the screen.

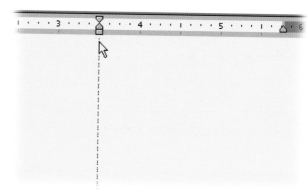

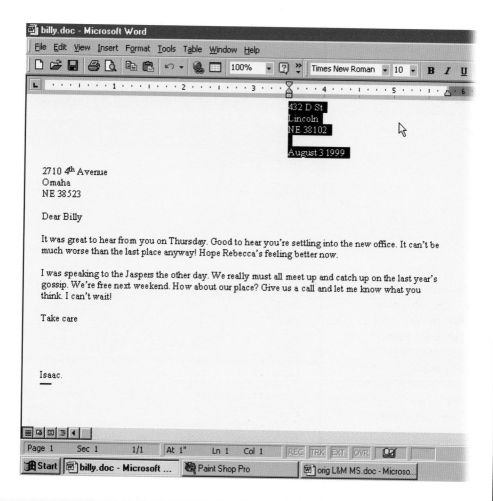

432 D St
Lincoln
NE 38102

August 3 1999

2710 4th Avenue
Omaha
NE 38523

Dear Billy

It was great to hear from you on Thursday. Good to hear you're settling into the new office. It can't be much worse than the last place anyway! Hope Rebecca's feeling better now.

I was speaking to the Jaspers the other day. We really must all meet up and catch up on the last year's gossip. We're free next weekend. How about our place? Give us a call and let me know what you think. I can't wait!

Take care

Isaac.

INDENTING PARAGRAPHS

You may want to make each of your paragraphs begin a little further into the page than the main text (a "first line indent"). Or you may want the body of text indented except for the lines beginning each paragraph (a "hanging indent"). These steps take you through how to do each of these procedures.

1 SELECT THE PARAGRAPHS

● Select only the paragraphs of text in your letter and not the addresses, date, greeting, and sign-off.

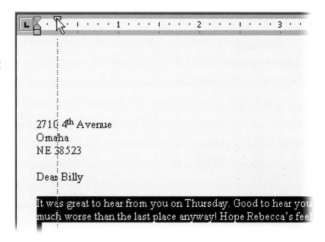

2710 4ᵗʰ Avenue
Omaha
NE 38523

Dear Billy

It was great to hear from you on Thursday. Good to hear you much worse than the last place anyway! Hope Rebecca's fee

I was speaking to the Jaspers the other day. We really must a gossip. We're free next weekend. How about our place? Giv think. I can't wait!

Take care

2 FIRST LINE INDENT

● Move your mouse pointer over the left indent marker on the ruler.
● When the pointer is on the top part of the left indent marker, hold down the left mouse button.
● Drag the pointer along the ruler to however far in you want the indent.

2710 4ᵗʰ Avenue
Omaha
NE 38523

Dear Billy

It was great to hear from you on Thursday. Good to hear you much worse than the last place anyway! Hope Rebecca's fee

● Release the mouse button. The first lines of each of your paragraphs are now indented.

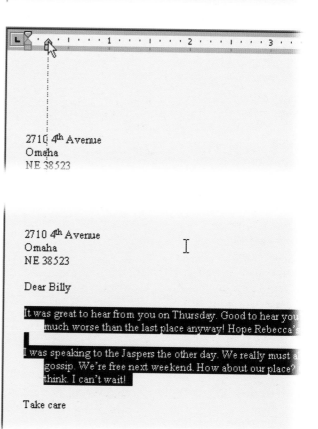

3 HANGING INDENT

● For a hanging indent, go through Step 1 (opposite) to select the text.
● Now, move the mouse pointer until it is over the left indent marker ⌷.
● Position the pointer over the middle part of the left indent marker, (avoiding the other two parts of the left indent marker may need some practice).
● Hold down the left mouse button and drag the pointer over to the right as far as you want the paragraphs to be indented.
● Release the mouse button. Your paragraphs are now formatted with a hanging indent.

34 Indenting the Address

ALIGNMENT

At the moment all your text except for your address is aligned to the left – the left side is straight while the right is ragged, like text created with a typewriter. Word can make the right side straight as well, like text in a book (this is called "justified text"). Other possibilities include aligning your text to the right, which leaves the left side ragged, or centering the text exactly down the middle of the page.

1 JUSTIFIED TEXT

● Select the text you want to realign.

● Drop down the **Format** menu from the menu bar at the top of the screen.

● Click on **Paragraph** in the Format menu and the **Paragraph** dialog box opens on-screen.

● Click on the drop-down button next to the **Alignment** option. A small menu will drop down.

● Click on the word **Justified** in this menu.

● Click on **OK** and the dialog box closes.

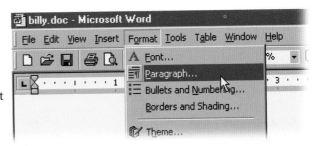

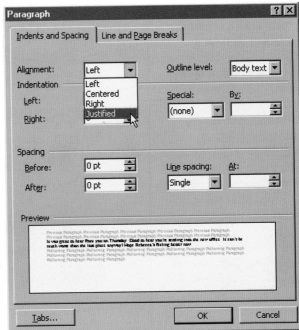

● Your text is now justified with the left- and right-hand sides both straight.

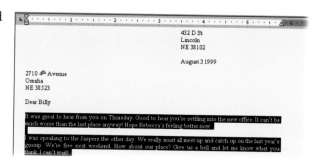

2 RIGHT-ALIGNED TEXT

● Follow Step 1 (opposite) until you get to the **Alignment** drop-down menu in the **Paragraph** dialog box.
● This time click on **Right** and then on **OK**.
● Your text has been aligned to the right.

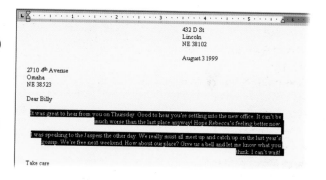

3 CENTERED TEXT

● Follow Step 1 until you get to the **Alignment** drop-down menu in the **Paragraph** dialog box.
● Click on **Center** this time, then on **OK**.
● Your text has been centered on the page.

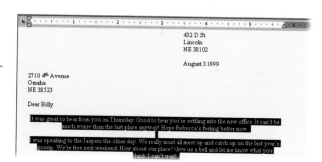

QUICK WAYS TO ALIGN TEXT

You are also able to realign text by using the alignment buttons (shown at left) on the toolbar at the top of the screen. First select the text and click on the button you need. From left to right, the buttons mean: left-align, center, right-align, and justify.

APPEARANCE

Your letter now looks better than it did before. However, there are many other Word features that can transform your text, so that it appears just as you want it to.

FONT AND FONT SIZE

The font is the kind of lettering that Word uses to display your text. You may wish to use different fonts in different kinds of letter: a stern, professional-looking font

for business letters, and a lighter, friendlier font for your personal letters. You may also wish either to increase or decrease the size of the font that you use.

1 THE FONT DIALOG BOX

- Select all the text in the document.
- Drop down the **Format** menu from the menu bar.
- Choose **Font** in the **Format** menu. The **Font** dialog box opens.

QUICK WAYS TO FORMAT FONTS

B *I* <u>U</u> You may have noticed that the font, font size, and the buttons for bold, italic, and underline are included in the Formatting toolbar (just above the ruler). To format fonts without using the **Font** dialog box, you can select the text and use these tools to format it. The font and font size are drop-down menus. The font style buttons (shown left) click in or out to show if, say, Bold is on or off in a selected block of text.

28 **Selecting Text**

2 CHANGING THE FONT

● The **Font** menu is displayed under the **Font** tab in the **Font** dialog box. Scroll up and down it using the scroll bar at the side of the menu. Your text is probably in Times New Roman at the moment.

● As you click on different fonts, the appearance of the selected font is shown in the **Preview** box in the **Font** dialog box.

● Keep scrolling through the fonts until you find one you want to use.

Preview Box •

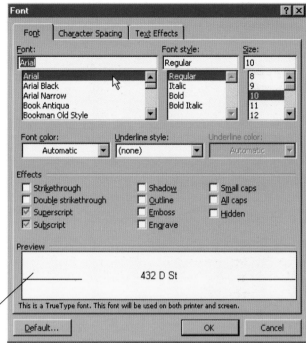

3 FONT SIZE

● Now check the **Size** menu at top right of the **Font** dialog box.

● The font size is probably set to 10. This is quite small. Try clicking on **12** or any font size you want – 10 and 12 are the most often used in plain text.

● The **Preview** box will show the new font in its new size.

4 APPLYING YOUR CHANGES

- When you are satisfied with the font and font size, click on the **OK** button.
- The **Font** dialog box will close. Your text is now formatted in the new font and font size.

FONT STYLE

In addition to the regular font, there are three other font styles – bold, italic, and underline – that can be used to emphasize individual words, phrases, or any other block of text. They can also be used in combination for extra effect.

1 BOLD TEXT

- Select the text □ you want to make bold.
- Open the **Font** dialog box from the **Format** menu.
- In the **Font style** menu click on **Bold**.
- Click **OK** to close the **Font** dialog box.
- Your selected text now appears in bold.

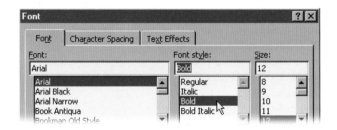

Bold text ●

2 ITALIC TEXT

● Follow Step 1 (opposite), but click on **Italic** in the **Font Style** menu of the **Font** dialog box.

● Click **OK** to close the **Font** dialog box.

● Your selected text is now displayed in italics.

Italicized text •

Dear Billy

It was great to hear from you on Thursday. the new office. It can't be much worse tha Rebecca's feeling better now.

I was speaking to the Jaspers the other day catch up on the last year's gossip. We're fre place? Give us a call and let me know what you

Take care

3 UNDERLINED TEXT

● Select the text and open the **Font** dialog box in the usual way.

● Drop down the **Underline** menu (below the **Font** menu in the dialog box).

● There are many underline options, but the most useful is **Single** – a single line under the selected text. An alternative is **Words only** – each word is underlined, but not the spaces separating them. Click on your choice.

● Click **OK** to close the **Font** dialog box.

● The selection is now emphasized by underlining.

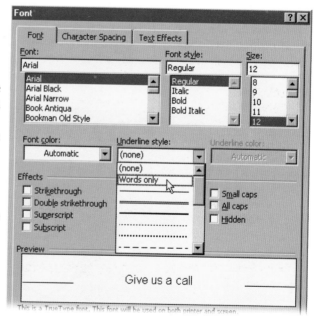

Words only •
underlined text

I was speaking to the Jaspers the other day catch up on the last year's gossip. We're fre place? Give us a call and let me know what you

Take care

LINE SPACING

You may want to increase the spacing between the lines of your letter – some find it easier to read. For example, double line spacing creates a space the height of one line between each line of the text. Other options are also available.

1 SELECT THE ENTIRE LETTER

● Click on **Format** on the menu bar to drop down the **Format** menu.
● Click on **Paragraph** from the **Format** menu to open the **Paragraph** dialog box.

2 LINE SPACING SELECTION

● Click the small down arrow on the right of the **Line spacing** box. The **Line spacing** menu drops down.
● Choose **Double** line spacing from the menu.

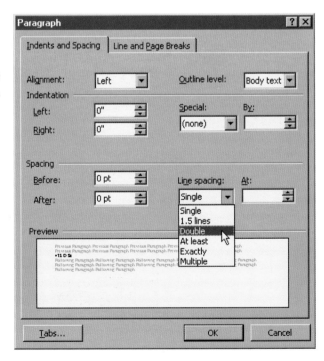

● Click on the **OK** button. Your selected text now appears with the chosen line spacing.

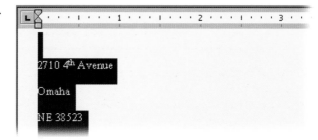

3 MULTIPLE LINE SPACING

You are not limited only to single, 1.5, and double line spacing when using Word.
● Select part of your text and click the down arrow in the **Line spacing** box. The **Line spacing** menu drops down.
● Click on **Multiple** at the foot of the menu.
● In the **At:** box the figure 3 appears. Three-line spacing is the default selection for multiple line spacing. If you want a different number, highlight the 3, type the number of line spaces, and click on **OK**.
● The lines of your selected text are now separated by your chosen line spacing.

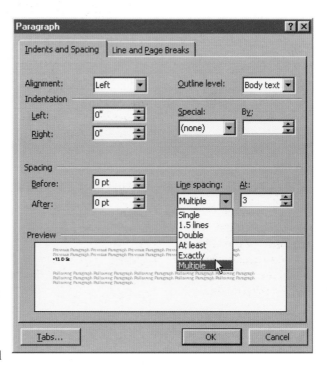

STORING YOUR LETTERS

It is usually essential to save your letters on your hard disk so that you can refer to them at a later date. This section provides an overview of how to store and recall your text.

WORKING WITH FILES

A file is what we call any piece of data that is stored on a computer's hard disk. This could be a spreadsheet, a program, or your letter that you have created using Word. Not only can you store (save) your documents when you have completed them, it is important that you also save your files as you work, especially if they are long and you have put a lot of work into them. If your computer suddenly crashes you could lose everything you have done since you last saved your work.

1 CREATING A NEW FILE

● When you open Word, a new file is automatically created in which you can begin typing.

● You may want to create other new files later on. Drop down the **File** menu and click on **New**.

● Click on **Blank Document** to select it and click on **OK**.

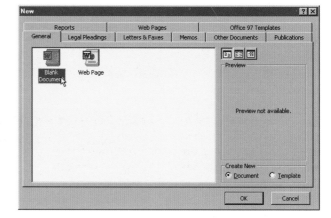

2 SAVING A FILE

● Drop down the **File** menu from the menu bar. Click on **Save**.

● If the file has already been saved, the **Save** command will simply save the new version and you may continue typing. If you are saving the file for the first time, the **Save As** dialog box appears and you can assign the document a name and a location.

3 OPENING A FILE

● Drop down the **File** menu from the menu bar. Click on **Open**. The **Open** dialog box appears.

● The **Open** dialog box shows the files you have already saved. Click on the file you want and then click on **Open**.

● The file opens and you may begin working on it.

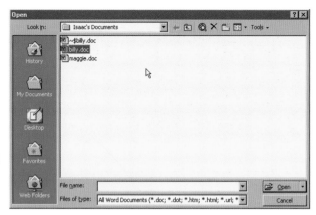

4 CLOSING A FILE

● You usually close a document when you have finished working on it. Drop down the **File** menu and click on **Close**.

● If you have not saved your text, or if you have changed it since you last saved, you are asked if you want to save the file.

● Click on Yes if you have forgotten to save your work. Click on No if you're absolutely sure that you don't want to save either the document or the changes you have made since you last saved. If in doubt, click on Cancel and return to the document.

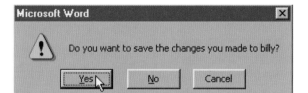

5 SAVING THE FILE TO FLOPPY DISK

● Click on **Save As** in the **File** menu to open the **Save As** dialog box.

● Drop down the Save In menu in the dialog box.

● Click on **3½ Floppy (A:)** in the **Save In** menu.

● Click **OK** and your file is saved to the floppy disk.

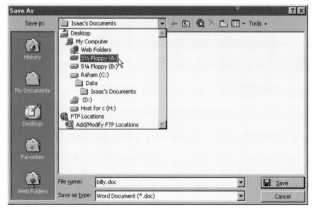

WORKING WITH FOLDERS

As you create more files, your hard disk may begin to look cluttered. When you want to open a file, you may not be able to find it because the list of files is so long.

The way to avoid this is to use folders, which can be given names, such as Personal and Finance, so that you know where to store and find your files.

1 CREATE A NEW FOLDER

● When you want to save a document in a new folder, begin by dropping down the **File** menu and click on **Save As**. The **Save As** dialog box appears.

● Click on the button showing a sparkling folder – this is the **Create New Folder** button.

● The **New Folder** dialog box opens. Type in a name for your new folder and click the **OK** button.

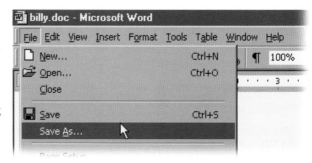

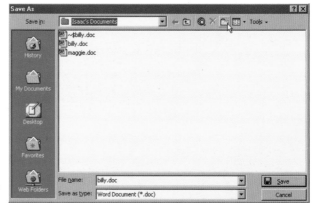

● The **New Folder** dialog box closes. The **Save As** dialog box reappears, this time showing your new, and empty, folder.

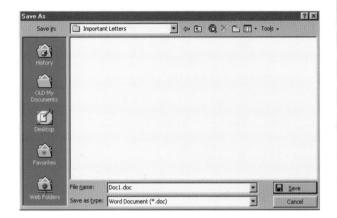

2 SAVING INTO YOUR FOLDER

● Type a name for your file in the **File** name text box and click on **Save**. The **Save As** dialog box closes and your file has been saved in the new folder.

3 MOVING WITHIN FOLDERS

● To open the folder containing the current folder, click on the folder icon that contains the right-angled arrow in the **Save As** dialog box – this icon is also in the **Open** dialog box.

So many folders…
You can have as many folders as you want within a single folder, but again, this may become unwieldy. So it might be better to split your folders according to type. You could have a Work folder with a Customer folder and a Supplier folder to divide two different kinds of letters; and a Personal folder with a Friends folder and a Family folder within it. You can of course further subdivide. Utility is the key – create folders only when you think they'll be helpful.

PRINTING

You will want your letter to appear on paper looking as neat as possible. Word has features that let you preview the printout of your letter, make improvements, and finally print your letter.

PRINT PREVIEW

Print Preview lets you see how the printed version of your letter will appear. This is done by showing each page as a scaled-down version of the specified paper size – usually 8½ x 11. The changes you can make in Print Preview include adjusting the margins, but it's not possible to edit the text when previewing. You can preview one page at a time or view several pages at once. Seeing more than one page lets you compare how they look and see how your changes affect your letter.

1 PREVIEW YOUR TEXT

● Open a file that you want to print out.
● Go to the top of the text with the insertion point ⌐.
● Click on **File** in the Menu bar and click on **Print Preview** in the **File** drop-down menu.
● Your screen now shows a print preview of your letter.

12 **Insertion Point**

2 SHOWING MULTIPLE PAGES

- If your letter has more than one page, you may want to see them all on one screen. Look at the Print Preview toolbar (now the only toolbar at the top of the screen). There is a rounded box containing four small rectangles (shown at right). This is the **Multiple Pages** icon.
- Click on the **Multiple Pages** icon, a menu of gray pages appears.
- Move the mouse pointer over the menu to choose

how many pages you want to view. In the example shown, **1 x 2 Pages** is selected. The first number is the number of rows in which your pages appear, the second number is the number of pages to be shown. The maximum is 3 x 8, which is selected by holding down the left mouse button and moving the mouse pointer right.

- Release the mouse button over the required display.
- You can now see how your letter will appear on the printed page.

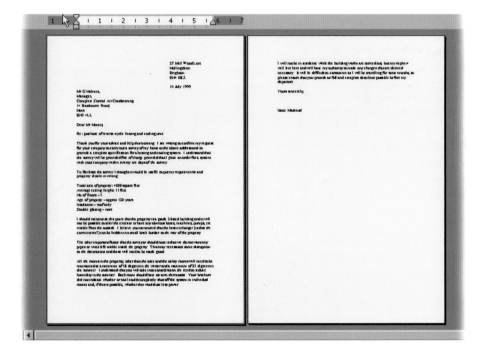

3 PAGE SETUP

● You may want to improve the look of your letter. Perhaps there is not enough room between the text and the edge of the paper. Or maybe a couple of lines spill onto a new page that could fit on the previous page. Both of these problems can be solved by changing the margins.

● Begin by dropping down the **File** menu and click on **Page Setup**.

● The **Page Setup** dialog box appears.

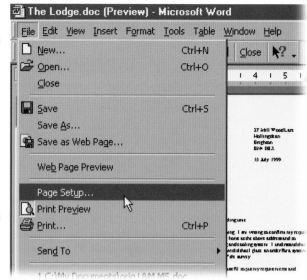

4 CHANGING THE MARGINS

● There are four boxes in the **Page Setup** dialog box to control the top, bottom, left, and right margins.

● You can increase or decrease the margins by increments of one-tenth of an inch by clicking the up and down arrow buttons to the right of each margin control box. Or click inside a box to enter a size.

● When you have selected the margin sizes, click the **OK** box to see your results.

● When you are satisfied with your changes, click on **Close** in the Print Preview toolbar to return to the normal view of your letter.

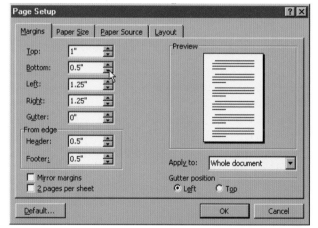

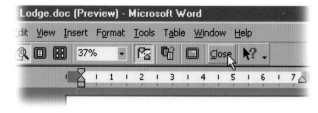

PRINTING YOUR LETTER

The actual process of printing out your letter is very simple. The Print Preview feature makes it unnecessary to print a number of draft versions of your letter because you now know how it will appear on the page. All that is left to do now is to use the very simple Print command to produce a hard copy of your letter.

1 THE PRINT DIALOG BOX

● Drop down the **File** menu and click on Print to open the **Print** dialog box.

● You can print selected pages of your letter if you want. Enter the numbers of the pages into the **Pages** box under **Page range**.

● You can also print more than one copy of your letter. Enter the number you want into the **Number of copies** box at the right of the **Print** dialog box.

● Check that your printer is connected to your computer and that it is switched on.

● Click on **OK** and your letter begins to be printed.

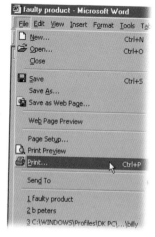

PRINTING QUICKLY

In most cases, you will not need to "customize" your printing because you simply need one copy of all the pages of your letter. Click on the printer icon in the toolbar at the top of the screen. Your letter is printed without using the Print dialog box.

Enter the number of copies required ●

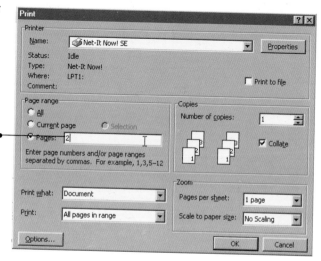

LET WORD HELP

Word has many helpful features including a spelling checker, a grammar checker, a thesaurus, templates on which to base your documents, and wizards that produce customized documents.

SPELLING CHECKER

However good your letter looks on paper, it can be let down by typing errors. Even if your spelling is impeccable it is inevitable that some incorrect keystrokes are made.

Word can check your spelling for you as you type, or you can have Word check the spelling of your whole document when you've finished writing it.

1 CHECKING AS YOU TYPE

● Try typing a deliberate mistake into your letter.
● A wavy red line appears below the incorrect word.
● Move the mouse pointer over the word containing the error and click with the right mouse button (right click). A pop up menu appears near the word.
● Word lists alternative words that you could have intended to type instead of the mistake. Left-click on the correct word.

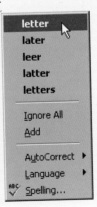

Dear Margaret

Thanks for your leter

Thanks for your leter

| letter |
| later |
| leer |
| latter |
| letters |
| Ignore All |
| Add |
| AutoCorrect ▶ |
| Language ▶ |
| Spelling... |

● The mistake is replaced by the correct word and the pop up closes.

Dear Margaret

Thanks for your letter |

2 ADDING WORDS

● Now type something that is correct but obscure and which the spelling checker is unlikely to recognize, such as a foreign word or an unusual name.

● The word, though not a mistake, is underlined by the wavy red line.

● Right click the word. The menu drops down.

● Click on **Add**. The spelling checker adds the word to its dictionary and will no longer underline the word as a "mistake."

● The wavy red line disappears because the spelling is now accepted as being correct.

Dear Margaret

Thanks for your letter. I've made some calls to but so far no luck. C'est la vie. |

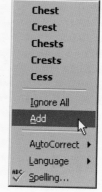

Thanks for your letter. I've made some calls to but so far no luck. C'est la vie.

| Chest |
| Crest |
| Chests |
| Crests |
| Cess |
| Ignore All |
| Add |
| AutoCorrect ▶ |
| Language ▶ |
| ✓ Spelling... |

Dear Margaret

Thanks for your letter. I've made some calls to but so far no luck. C'est la vie.

GRAMMAR CHECKER

Word's automatic grammar checker works very much like the spelling checker. The obvious difference is that Word marks what it believes to be grammatical errors with a wavy green line, not a red line. The grammar checker cannot offer perfect advice due to the complexities of English. So accept its suggestions carefully.

CORRECTING GRAMMAR

● Word has detected a clumsy sentence structure.
● Right-click the sentence and a menu pops up.
● Choose the suggestion or click on **About this Sentence** to have the problem explained. Click on **Ignore** if you think the grammar checker is itself making a mistake.
● If you click on **About this Sentence**, the office assistant, which can be switched on by using the **Help** menu, pops up and explains what Word thinks is the problem.
● Click with the mouse button away from the advice to close the panel.

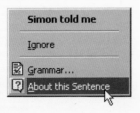

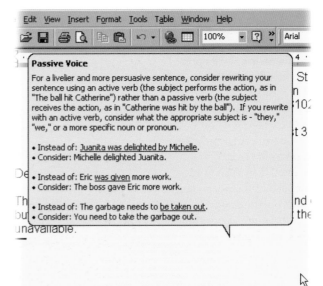

● Right-click the sentence again to display the pop up menu and click on the suggested correction.

The grammar of the sentence has been revised

THESAURUS

You may want to find an alternative word to express what you mean. The thesaurus feature in Word lists possible words in the same way as the paper-based thesaurus except that it works directly on the word for which you require a synonym.

SYNONYMS

● Place the insertion point in the word for which you want to find a synonym.

● Drop down the **Tools** menu from the menu bar. Click on **Language**.

● A submenu appears, click on **Thesaurus**.

- The **Thesaurus** dialog box appears. Synonyms are listed on the right-hand side.
- Click on a synonym. It appears in the **Replace with Synonym** box.
- Click on the **Replace** button.
- The word is replaced with the synonym.

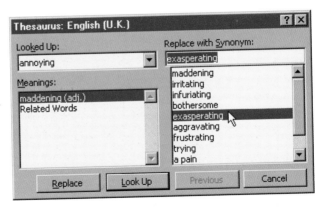

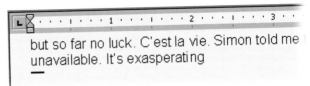

CHECKING AFTER YOU HAVE FINISHED TYPING

Some people find that having Word checking their spelling and grammar as they type is distracting and intrusive. If you would prefer not to have the wavy red and green underlines appearing below your text, you can turn these functions off.

1 TURNING OFF CHECKING

- To turn off the spelling checker while you type, drop down the **Tools** menu from the toolbar.
- Click on **Options** and the **Options** dialog box opens on screen.

● There are a number of tabs at the top of the **Options** dialog box for altering different aspects of Word. Click on the **Spelling & Grammar** tab to display the available options under **Spelling** and **Grammar**.

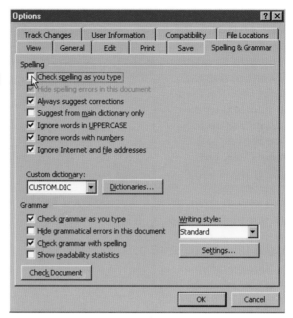

● Click once in the **Check spelling as you type** tick box. The tick disappears.

● Click on the **OK** button. Word will now no longer check your spelling as you type. You can still, however, check the spelling of all the text in one pass, after you have finished typing.

● If you wish to stop Word from checking the grammar, click once in the **Check grammar as you type** tick box. The tick disappears and the grammar checker is turned off.

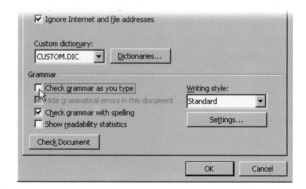

2 CHECKING THE DOCUMENT

● Drop down the **Tools** menu from the menu bar.

● Click on **Spelling and Grammar** from the **Tools** menu. Word will work through your document with the **Spelling and Grammar** dialog box, prompting you at every error that is found.

● If you want to accept a suggested spelling, click on the correct one from the **Suggestions** box and click on the **Change** button.

● If you want to correct the error yourself, click inside the **Not in Dictionary** box and position the insertion point over the error. Make the text correction yourself by using the keyboard and click on the **Change** button.

● If you don't think that there is an error, click on the Ignore button.

● Word moves on to the next error in your text until it can find no more and the information box appears telling you that the check is complete. Click on **OK**.

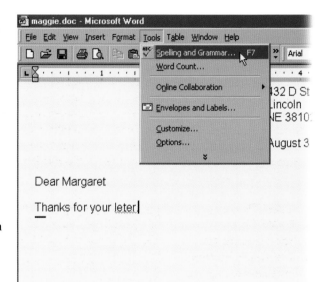

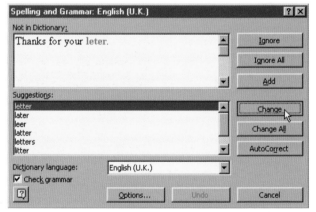

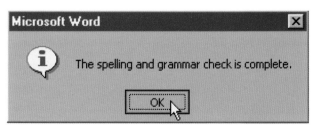

TEMPLATES

Usually when you come to create a new file, either you work from the blank file that Word creates when it is launched, or you create a new blank file by choosing the Blank Document option from the **New** dialog box. This time, you can save yourself some of the work involved in laying out a document by creating a preformatted letter and filling in the blanks. As an example of this, follow the steps below to create a letter using the **Elegant Letter** template.

1 CREATE A NEW FILE

● Drop down the **File** menu and click on **New**.
● In the **New** dialog box click on the **Letters & Faxes** tab and click on the icon labeled **Elegant Letter**.
● Click on **OK**.

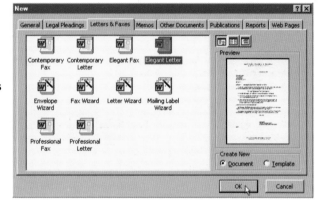

2 FILLING IN THE BLANKS

● Your new file will now be open on the screen.
● Click on the box at the top of the letter marked **Click here and type in company name**. The box itself is not printed out - it's only to show you the boundaries of where you can type.

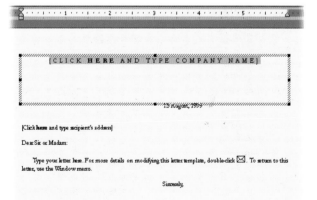

● Click on the line of text that reads **Click here and type recipient's address.** You can begin typing the recipient's address – the line of text vanishes when you begin typing.

13 Augu

[Click **here** and type recipient's address] ⁏

Dear Sir or Madam:

Type your letter here. For more details on modifying this letter letter, use the Window menu.

Sincerely,

● Using the insertion point or the mouse pointer, select the text of the paragraph that is already in place and begin typing. The old text disappears as you begin to start typing.

13 Augu

[Click **here** and type recipient's address]

Dear Sir or Madam:

Type your letter here. For more details on modifying this letter letter, use the Window menu.

Sincerely,

● Add your name and job title over the lines of text at the end of the letter. Just click in these lines to select them, and start typing.

Sincerely,

[Click **here** and type your name] ⁏
[Click **here** and type job title]

● Your address goes at the foot of the Elegant Letter. Scroll down the page and add your address into the address box.

● You have now created a letter using the Elegant Letter template.

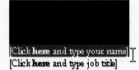

|STREET ADDRESS| · |CITY/STATE| · |ZIP/POSTAL CODE|
PHONE· |PHONE NUMBER| · FAX· |FAX NUMBER|

WIZARDS

Wizards are a simple way of producing formatted letters quickly. There is no need to type names and addresses directly into the letter – Word uses dialog boxes for you to supply the information and then adds this to the letter. You can create the same letter using the Letter Wizard that you did using the template.

1 STARTING THE WIZARD

● Drop down the **File** menu and click on **New** as usual.

● Click the **Letters & Faxes** tab and click on the icon marked **Letter Wizard**.

● Click on the **OK** button.

● A small dialog box appears along with the office assistant.

● Click on **Send one letter**.

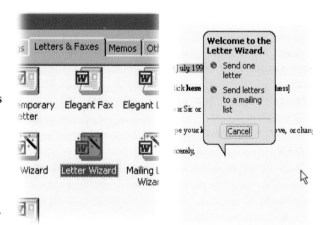

2 LETTER FORMAT

● The **Letter Wizard** dialog box opens. There are four steps in the Letter Wizard – the first is **Letter Format**.

● Drop down the **Choose a page design** menu and choose the one you want. You will notice that **Elegant Letter**, the template we used earlier in this section, is one of the designs.

● Drop down the **Choose a letter style** menu and choose from **Full Block** (no indents), **Modified Block** (some indenting), or **Semi-Block** (full, with stylish first line indents).

● Click on the **Next** button to go to the next section.

3 RECIPIENT'S INFORMATION

● The **Letter Wizard** dialog box now shows the **Recipient Info** step.

● Enter the recipient's name and address in the relevant text boxes.

● Choose a salutation from the drop-down menu under **Salutation**, or type in your own.

● Click on the **Next** button.

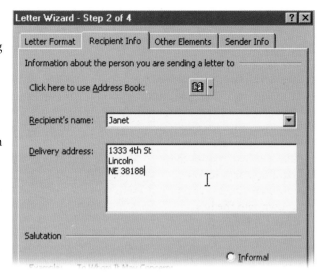

4 OTHER ELEMENTS

● The **Letter Wizard** dialog box now shows the **Other Elements** step.

● If you want to include a reference line, click on the check box to the left of **Reference line**. A check will appear in the box. You can now drop down the **Reference line** menu and use the available options.

● Do the same for any other features you want: **Mailing instructions, Attention, Subject**.

● If you wish to send a courtesy copy, insert the details into the boxes at the foot of the dialog box.

● Click on the **Next** button.

5 SENDER INFORMATION

- The last step of the **Letter Wizard** dialog box is the **Sender Info** step.
- Type your name into the Sender's name box.
- Type your address into the **Return address** box.
- Select a closing from the **Complimentary closing** drop-down menu – or type your own into the box.
- Click on **Finish** to allow the Letter Wizard to create your document.

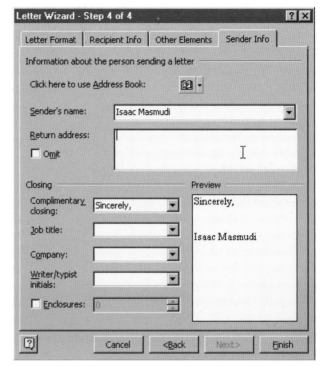

6 START TYPING

- The **Letter Wizard** dialog box vanishes. The office assistant appears and asks you if you want to do any more to your letter.
- Make a selection or click on **Cancel**.
- Your letter is ready. Everything is in place except the paragraphs of main text.
- Start typing as with the Elegant Letter template.

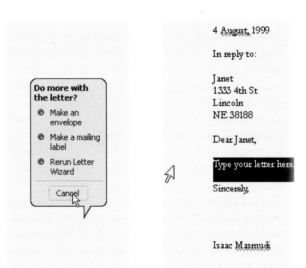

MAIL MERGE

Mail merge is a way of sending personalized letters to a number of people. Although more often used by business, mail merge is useful for telling people about the large events in our lives.

MAIN DOCUMENTS AND DATA SOURCES

So far you have only been working with letters to individual recipients. You may however wish to create a letter to be sent to a number of people – for instance, to notify all your friends that you have moved. You could produce a letter addressed to one person, print it out, change the recipient's name and address, print out the new letter to the next person, and so on. This would however be a very tedious and time-consuming process. To save you this trouble you can use a feature called Mail Merge. This allows you to create a standard letter and a list of names and addresses. The letter and the list are then merged to create personalized letters to everyone in the list. The standard letter is called a Main Document – the list is called a Data Source. Let's start by creating a Main Document from scratch.

1 CREATE A MAIN DOCUMENT
● Drop down the **Tools** menu and click on the **Mail Merge** option.

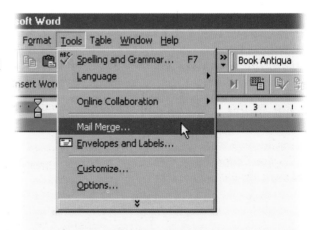

- The **Mail Merge Helper** dialog box opens.
- Click on the **Create** button under **Main document**.
- A menu drops down. Click on **Form Letters** at the top of the menu.
- A dialog box opens. Click on **New Main Document**.
- A blank document will appear under the **Mail Merge Helper** dialog box. This is your Main Document.

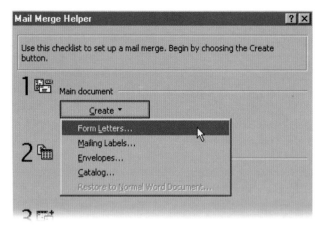

2 CREATE A DATA SOURCE

- Before working on your new Master Document, you need to create a structure for your data. You need a Data Source to do this.
- Click on the **Get Data** button under **Data Source** in the **Mail Merge Helper** dialog box.
- Click on **Create Data Source** in the menu.

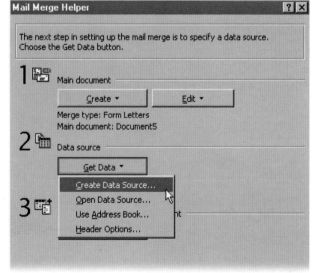

- The **Create Data Source** dialog box opens.
- The list shows the fields (see Fields and Records below) that are going to make up the Data Source.
- You won't need all the fields. You can remove the fields with the **Remove Field Name** button. Add new ones by typing a new field name into the **Field name** box and clicking on **Add Field Name**.
- Remove all the fields except **Address1**, **Address2**, **City**, and **PostalCode**.
- Now type **Name** into the **Field name** box. Click on the **Add Field Name** button. You have created a new field called **Name**.
- Your list of fields should appear as shown at right.
- Now click on **OK**.

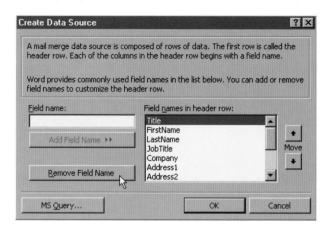

FIELDS AND RECORDS

Each kind of data in the Master Document that is attached to the Data Source (such as the recipient's names, or each line of their addresses) is called a field. Fields are what link the Master Document to the Data Source. The actual data in the fields – such as in the Name field, James, Mr. Doncaster, Mom & Dad – are called records.

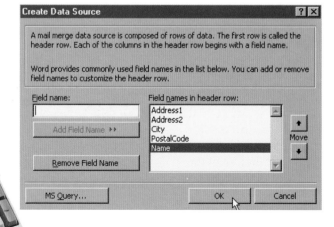

- The **Save As** dialog box opens. Type **List** in the **File Name** box and click the **Save** button.
- You have now created a Data Source.
- A dialog box will appear. Click on **Edit Data Source**.

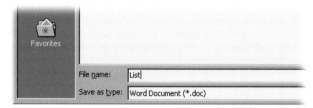

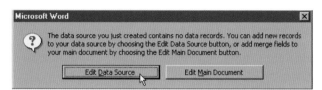

3 ENTER RECORDS

- The **Data Form** dialog box opens and you can edit the Data Source.
- Type the name and address of your first recipient into the boxes in the dialog box.
- When you have finished with the first recipient, move to a fresh record by clicking the **Add New** button. The field boxes empty and you are ready to type in a new record.
- Add as many records as you want. You can go back to your old records and correct them with the buttons at the foot of the dialog box.
- When you have finished entering all the records that you wish to include, click on **OK**.

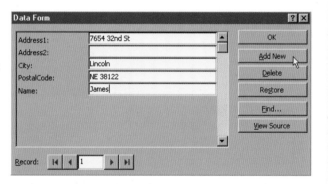

4 INSERT MERGE FIELDS

- The **Data Form** dialog box closes. You will now see the Main Document.
- Type in your own address and the date.
- Instead of typing the first line of the recipient's address, click on the **Insert Merge Field** button on the Mail Merge toolbar at the top of the screen.
- A menu drops down. Click on Address1.
- The field will appear in the letter as <<**Address1**>>. Don't worry, it won't print out like this – it is a way of showing you the structure of your Main Document before it is merged with the Data Source.
- Add the remainder of the address by entering one line in each field.
- Type **Dear**, leave a space, and add the Name field from the **Insert Merge Field** drop-down menu.
- Finish your letter in the normal way.

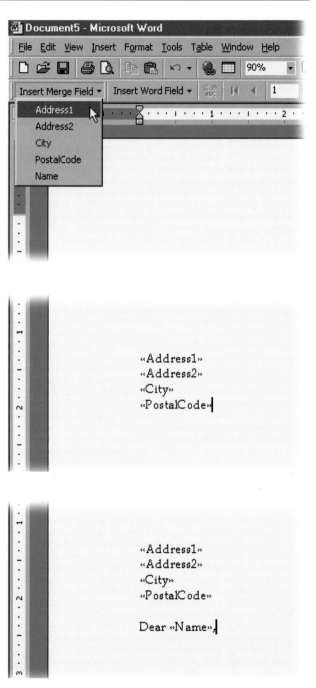

5 READY TO MERGE

● Check your Main Document. It should look something like the document shown at right.

● To make sure you are ready to print your mail merge, click on the **View Merged Data** button on the Mail Merge toolbar at the top of the screen.

● This shows your letter as it will go out to each person. The arrow buttons on the Mail Merge toolbar allow you to move through different records.

«Address1»
«Address2»
«City»
«PostalCode»

Dear «Name»,

Just a quick note to let you kno
the launch of Masmudi Enterp

We would love to see you ther
come.

Many thanks

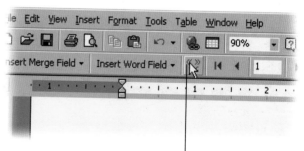

View merged data button ●

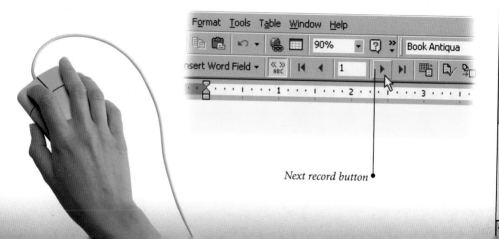

Next record button ●

6 CHECK YOUR MAIL MERGE

● With the **View Merged Data** button down (it will stay down until you click it again – don't try to hold it down with the mouse), you will be able to see the different versions of the same letter that are going out to different recipients.

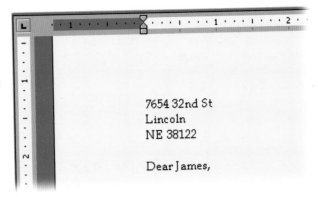

7654 32nd St
Lincoln
NE 38122

Dear James,

● Each letter displays the same basic text, but the details of the individual recipient's are different.

3129 4th Avenue
Manhattan
New York
NY 56178

Dear Mr Doncaster,

● When you have finished viewing, click on the **View Merged Data** button again to return to normal view of the Main Document.

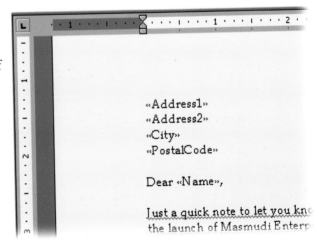

«Address1»
«Address2»
«City»
«PostalCode»

Dear «Name»,

Just a quick note to let you kno
the launch of Masmudi Enterp

7 PRINT MERGE

- You are now ready to print out your mail merge.
- Drop down the **Tools** menu and click on **Mail Merge** to bring up the **Mail Merge Helper** dialog box.
- Click the **Merge** button in the **Mail Merge Helper** dialog box. The **Merge** dialog box opens.
- Drop down the **Merge to** menu with the small down arrow box at the side of the **Merge to** box.
- Click on **Printer**.
- The **Merge to** box now contains the word **Printer**.
- Click on **Merge**. The **Print** dialog box opens.
- Click on **OK**.
- All copies of the letter, each personalized for the individual recipient, will now be printed.

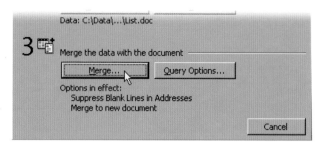

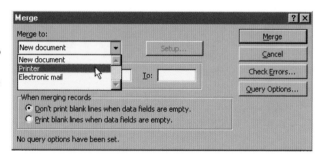

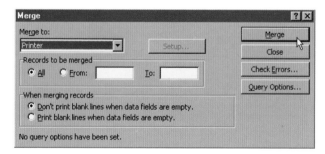

8 SAVING THE FILES

- Once you have finished with your mail merge, close down the file as normal (click on **Close** from the **File** menu). You will be prompted with a dialog box asking you if you want to save the changes to your Data Source. Click on **Yes**

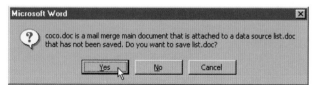

to save your current data. Then, if you have made any changes to the Main Document, you will be asked if you want to save the changes, as normal. Click on **Yes** if you want to keep the changes.

DESIGNING DOCUMENTS

THIS SECTION CONCENTRATES ON THE facilities that Word offers to help you design more interesting and professional documents than those produced by simply using the default settings that Word provides. These facilities include font selection, customizing and manipulating paragraphs, adding colored borders and backgrounds, using tabs, columns, and lists, and creating your own style sheets.

WORKING WITH FONTS

There are several different levels of formatting and styling available in Word. This chapter looks at changing the font, resizing it, and changing the spacing and color of the letters.

CHANGING THE FONT

The default font in Microsoft Word is Times New Roman, which is one of the most popular fonts. There are many other fonts available and, while you can use as many fonts as you wish in a document, it is better to use no more than three in any one section. Increasing the number of fonts can have the effect of fragmenting the text and making it look messy, and certain fonts do not look good together.

THE CHOSEN VIEW

Throughout this book it is recommended that you work in Print Layout view, as many of the effects used are only displayed in this view of a document. To do this, click on **View** in the Menu bar and select **Print Layout**, or click on the **Page Layout View** button at the bottom of the screen.

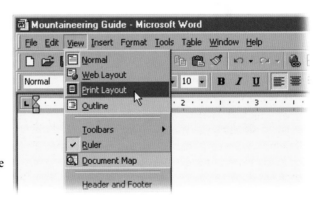

A VARIETY OF FONTS

In the examples of styling and formatting text that are used throughout this book, the text is displayed in a variety of fonts. While Microsoft Word includes a range of the most commonly used fonts, you may not have all the fonts shown here. This will not affect your ability to work your way through the examples, but you will need to choose alternative fonts. An almost limitless number of fonts can be bought from stores or over the internet.

❷❶ Page Layout View

1 CREATING THE TEXT

● In the example used here, we are writing a document for a mountaineering company that offers guided expeditions and more.

● Begin by typing their contact details in a new document, and press ⏎Enter⎯ at the end of each line with an extra ⏎Enter⎯ after the zip code.

● You'll see that when the email address is typed in, Word recognizes it for what it is and automatically shows it in blue.

Email address ●

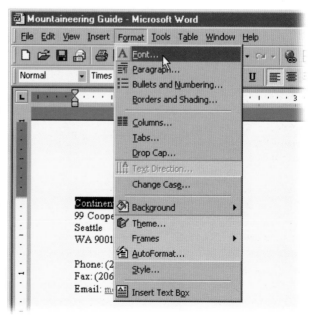

2 SELECTING A NEW FONT

● Although this text is perfectly clear, it lacks any impact. The first change that you can make is to use different fonts to emphasize the different parts of the company's details.

● Highlight the company name, click on **Format** in the Menu bar, and click on **Font** at the top of the drop-down menu.

● The Font dialog box now opens. In the Font: selection menu, use the scroll bar to move to another font (we have chosen Charlesworth, which has only upper-case letters). The Preview panel at the foot of the dialog box shows how the text will appear in your document. Click on OK.

● For the rest of the contact details, except for the email address, we are going to use another font. Highlight the text to be selected, open the Font dialog box again, and choose another font (we selected BankGothic Md BT). Now click on OK.

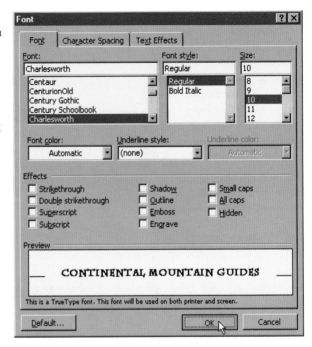

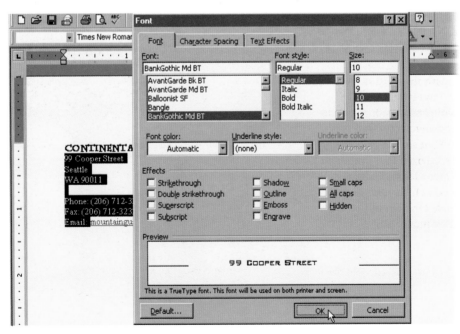

● The fonts have now been changed, and the company name, company address, and email address are each in a different font, which distinguishes the various elements from each other.

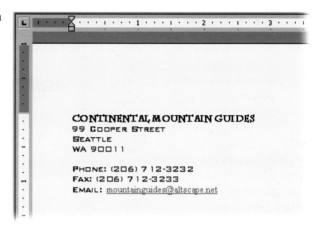

CHANGING THE FONT SIZE

Word's default font size of 10 points (a point is one seventy-second of an inch) is fine for the bulk of the text that you are likely to produce, but different parts of your document, such as headings, can benefit from being in a larger font size.

USING THE FONT SIZE SELECTOR BOX

● With the text that you wish to resize already highlighted (in this case the company name), click on the Font size selector box 🖹 in the Formatting toolbar, scroll to **16** (meaning 16 point), and click on it. The lettering of the selected text is now larger.

Selected font size ●

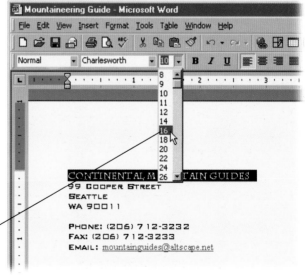

15 ㉖ **Font size selector**

● Highlight the next three lines of the address and follow the same sequence to change the font size to 14 pt, and then do the same to change the final three lines to 12 pt. Your text should now appear as shown in this example.

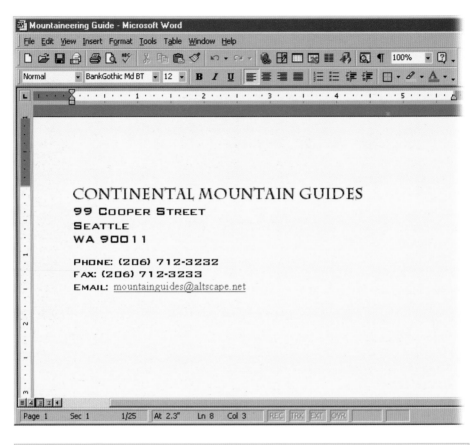

FONT STYLES

You will see that, as well as offering a choice of fonts, the **Font** dialog box also has a **Font style:** panel. Choosing different options in this panel will enable you to turn the font from its normal, or regular, form to italic, bold, or italic bold type, providing that all these variations are available in the particular font that you are using. These options can be used to emphasize parts of your text.

Alternative font styles

CHANGING THE FONT EFFECT

As well as bold, italic, and underline, there are a number of effects available in Word that you can use to change the appearance of your text. For example, shadowed, outlined, embossed, and engraved effects can all be used. Once you have followed this example, try out the other effects, some of which can be very useful.

EMBOSSING TEXT

● Begin by highlighting the company name in the address and open the **Font** dialog box, and click on the **Font** tab at the top of the dialog box.

● In the center of the **Effects** section of the **Font** dialog box, you'll see check boxes for **Shadow**, **Outline**, **Emboss**, and **Engrave** effects. Click in the check box next to **Emboss** and then click on OK.

● Click anywhere on your page to remove the highlighting, and the embossed effect on the lettering becomes visible.

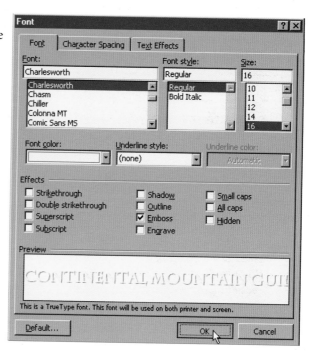

CONTINENTAL MOUNTAIN GUIDES
99 COOPER STREET
SEATTLE
WA 90011

PHONE: (206) 712-3232
FAX: (206) 712-3233
EMAIL: mountainguides@altscape.net

77 **Selecting a new font**

CHANGING THE LETTER SPACING

Changing the amount of space between individual letters can also be used to emphasize important parts of the text.

In this example, we will space out the letters of the company name to give it greater weight on the page.

INCREASING THE LETTER SPACING

● Highlight the company name again, open the **Font** dialog box 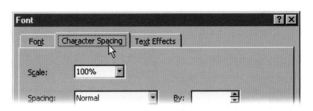, and click on the **Character Spacing** tab.

● In the **Spacing:** box, click on the arrow next to **Normal** and select **Expanded**. In the **By:** box, enter the figure **3**, meaning 3 pt, and click on **OK**.

● Click on the company name again to see how the name now extends across the page.

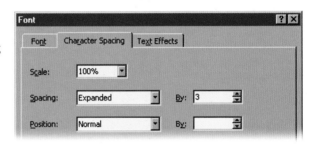

┌──┐
│77│ **Selecting**
└──┘ **a new font**

CHANGING THE FONT COLOR

With the increasing availability, and falling cost, of color printers, using some of the color options in Word offers a simple and effective way of making selected text stand out. Bear in mind that it's best not to combine too wide a range of colors.

1 SELECTING THE COLOR PALETTE

- Although the snowy-whiteness of the embossed text is appropriate for the company's business, it's a little pale. To change the font color, highlight the company name and then open the **Font** dialog box.
- Click the arrow to the right of the **Font color:** selection box and the color palette will appear.

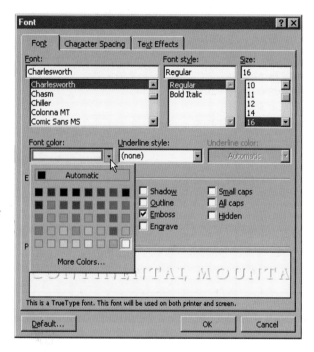

2 CHOOSING THE COLOR

- Move the mouse cursor down to **Blue** and click once. This color has now been selected for the text.

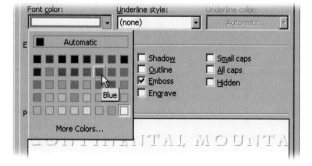

● The text in the **Preview** window now shows you the effect of the color change. If you are happy with this color, click on **OK**.

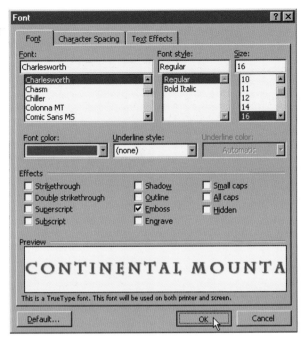

● Click anywhere on your page to remove the highlighting and reveal the text in the new color.

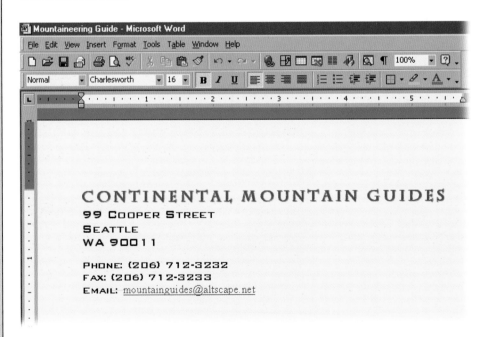

3 CHOOSING FURTHER COLORS

● As Word automatically colors the email address in blue, the contact details above the email address can also have their own colors. Try changing the **Phone:** details to orange and the **Fax:** line to sea green to achieve the effect shown in the example here.

Lines of text stand out from each other ●

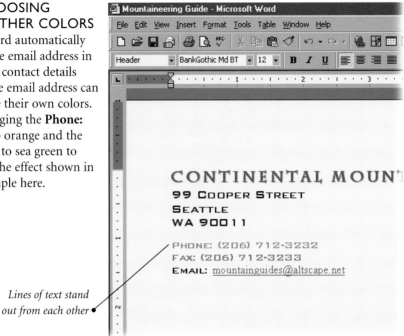

Bold, Italic, and Underline

The quickest way to change your text by using these effects is to highlight the text that you want to change and then click on one of these three buttons ⬒ in the Formatting toolbar. You're not limited to just one of these effects for a piece of text. You can have text that is bold and italic, as well as being underlined, if that's what you want.

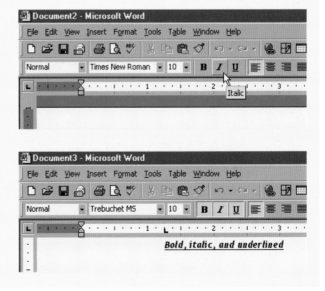

15 ❷⓿ Bold, ❷⓿ Italic, ❷⓿ Underline

STYLING PARAGRAPHS

As far as Word is concerned, a paragraph is any piece of text that ends with a paragraph mark, so the styling shown here can be applied to a single letter or to several pages of text.

ALIGNING PARAGRAPHS

There are four possible ways to align paragraphs in Word: left-aligned, centered, right-aligned, and justified. Left-alignment is the default paragraph alignment in Word. Each line of a paragraph starts against the left margin, and the line endings are "ragged" in the way a typewriter would produce them. Centered alignment has the effect of centering each line of a paragraph on the midpoint between the margins. Right-alignment has the effect of aligning the right-hand end of each line up against the right-hand margin leaving the start of each line ragged, and justified alignment produces a straight edge at both the beginning and the end of each line by adding spaces to make every line of text the same length.

1 SELECTING THE TEXT

● The company's details are going to be the heading of the guide, and a heading frequently benefits from having its own alignment, in order to distinguish it from the text on the rest of the page. Begin by highlighting all of the company's details.

CONTINENTAL MOUNTAIN GUIDES
99 COOPER STREET
SEATTLE
WA 90011

PHONE: (206) 712-3232
FAX: (206) 712-3233
EMAIL: mountainguides@altscape.net

2 ALIGNING TEXT TO THE RIGHT

● First we'll see how right-aligning affects the appearance, so click on the **Align Right** button ◻ in the Formatting toolbar.

● Click off the highlighted text to see the effect.

● Although the shorter lines are obviously right-aligned, the company name has hardly moved because it almost fills the width of the page, and it sticks out way beyond the other lines.

CONTINENTAL MOUNTAIN GUIDES
99 COOPER STREET
SEATTLE
WA 90011

PHONE: (206) 712-3232
FAX: (206) 712-3233
EMAIL: mountainguides@altscape.net

3 CENTERING THE TEXT

● The start of the company name looks as if it's out on a limb, so the whole heading would look better if it were centered.

● Highlight the company details again and click on the **Center** button ◻ in the Formatting toolbar.

● Click off the highlighted text to see how the separate lines of the company's details now all appear to be part of a single unit.

CONTINENTAL MOUNTAIN GUIDES
99 COOPER STREET
SEATTLE
WA 90011

PHONE: (206) 712-3232
FAX: (206) 712-3233
EMAIL: mountainguides@altscape.net

15 | ㉜ **Right-aligned Text**

15 | ㉛ **Centered Text**

INSERTING A DROPPED CAPITAL

First paragraphs can be made more noticeable by starting them with a large initial capital letter that drops down more than one line. This dropped capital letter is familiarly known as a "drop cap," and it is easily achieved in Word.

WHAT WE DO

Continental Mountain Guides has built up a fine reputation that now extends beyond the climbing community following two heavily publicized rescues that we were fortunate enough to be called to carry out. The expeditions we lead are always safe and successful, and one enthusiastic climber suggested out motto should be: "We ain't lost one yet." But as we never intend to, the suggestion was put to one side. We offer many climbing opportunities for the absolute beginner and to the climbing professional who might need our specialized knowledge of specific mountaineering regions. Guides join our staff when they have at least ten year's of climbing. And they have to demonstrate to us that they are dedicated to climbing and to sharing that passion.

1 SELECTING THE DROP CAP BOX

● The Mountaineering Guide has an introductory section with a heading that has been formatted in BankGothic Md BT 16 pt, and a paragraph formatted in Trebuchet MS 10 pt. This paragraph would be more interesting if it began with a drop cap.

● Place the cursor over the paragraph and click to position the insertion point within it. Go to **Format** in the Menu bar and select **Drop Cap**. The **Drop Cap** dialog box opens.

● Click on **Dropped** in the **Position** options.

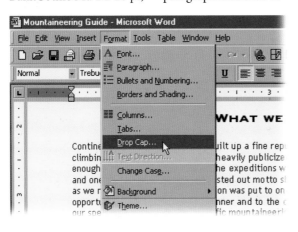

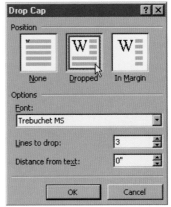

2 CHOOSING THE SIZE

● The **Lines to drop:** box shows the default number of lines for the capital letter to drop is 3. This is too large a drop cap for a short paragraph, so change the figure to 2 and click on **OK**.

● The drop cap is shown surrounded by a frame.

● Click elsewhere on the document and the altered paragraph, with its new dropped capital, appears as it will on the printed page.

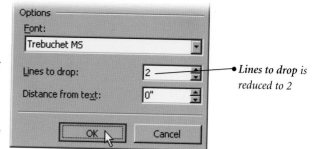

● Lines to drop is reduced to 2

3 CREATING JUSTIFIED TEXT

● Finally, this paragraph would sit better with the company details above it if it were justified.

● Highlight the text and click on the **Justify** button in the Formatting toolbar.

● Both the beginnings and endings of the lines of the paragraph now align, and the start of the document is beginning to look neater.

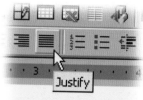

Justify

OUNTAI

PER STREET

WHAT WE DO

Continental Mountain Guides has built up a fine reputation that now extends beyond the climbing community following two heavily publicized rescues that we were fortunate enough to be called to carry out. The expeditions we lead are always safe and successful, and one enthusiastic climber suggested out motto should be: "We ain't lost one yet." But as we never intend to, the suggestion was put to one side. We offer many climbing opportunities for the absolute beginner and to the climbing professional who might need our specialized knowledge of specific mountaineering regions. Guides join our staff when they have at least ten year's of climbing. And they have to demonstrate to us that they are dedicated to climbing and to sharing that passion.

15 **❸ Justified Text**

ADDING SPACE BETWEEN PARAGRAPHS

Creating space between paragraphs can improve the look of your document. This can be done by simply inserting a number of paragraph returns ([Enter ←]). However, there is a better way of choosing precisely the amount of space you wish to insert.

1 SELECTING THE PARAGRAPH

● In a section of the Mountaineering Guide on seminars and expeditions, paragraphs are separated by paragraph marks (you can make these visible using the Standard toolbar ⎚).

● A better method of separating paragraphs, particularly when a large amount of space is required between them, is to select manually how much space there should be.

Extra paragraph returns add a fixed amount of space ●

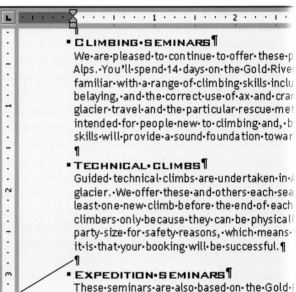

● First delete the paragraph marks separating the paragraphs, and highlight the first paragraph. Then click on **Format** in the Menu bar and choose **Paragraph** from the menu.

2 DEFINING THE SPACE

● The **Paragraph** dialog box opens. In the **Spacing** section, click on the up arrow in the **After:** panel. The entry now reads **6 pt** and the **Preview** panel shows the increased space following the paragraph. Click on **OK**.

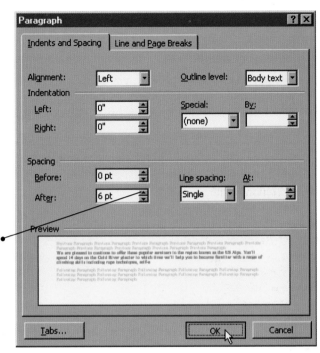

Up arrow increases the spacing after paragraph ●

● The paragraph is now separated from the following paragraph by a 6 pt space without an extra Enter ↵ being inserted.

*Using the **Paragraph** formatting menu, this space can be made exactly the size you want it* ●

CLIMBING·SEMINARS¶
We·are·pleased·to·con tinue·to·offer·these·p
Alps.·You'll·spend·14·days·on·the·Gold·Rive
familiar·with·a·range·of·climbing·skills·inclu
belaying,·and·the·correct·use·of·ax·and·cra
glacier·travel·and·the·particular·rescue·me†
intended·for·people·new·to·climbing·and,·b
skills·will·provide·a·sound·foundation·towar

TECHNICAL·CLIMBS¶
Guided·technical·climbs·are·undertaken·in·
glacier.·We·offer·these·and·others·each·sea
least·one·new·climb·before·the·end·of·each
climbers·only·because·they·can·be·physica ll
party-size·for·safety·reasons,·which·means·
it·is·that·your·booking·will·be·successful.¶

EXPEDITION·SEMINARS¶
These·seminars·are·also·based·on·the·Gold·
and·concentrate·on·the·different·demands·

CHANGING THE INDENT

In printing terms, a "displayed" paragraph is one where the beginning and ends of the lines are indented compared to the paragraphs before and after it, producing a narrower column of text. This has the effect of emphasizing the paragraph.

1 SETTING THE LEFT INDENT

● Highlight the first paragraph, about climbing seminars, and place the mouse cursor over the **Left Indent** box on the ruler.

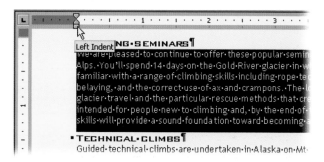

● Holding the mouse button down, drag the cursor to the right until the left indent box and the two indent arrows are over the quarter-inch mark, and release the mouse button. The left-hand edge of the paragraph is now indented.

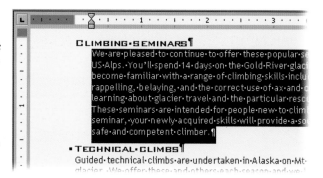

2 SETTING THE RIGHT INDENT

● Now place the mouse cursor over the right-hand indent arrow, hold down the mouse button, and drag the mouse cursor to the 5.5-inch position on the ruler and release the mouse button to set the indent.

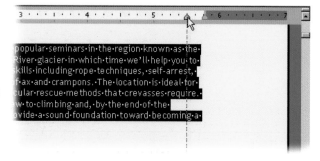

- The right-hand line endings of the paragraph are now indented.

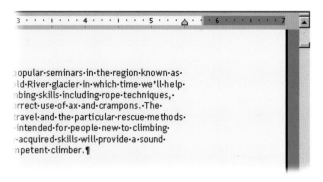

```
opular·seminars·in·the·region·known·as·
ld·River·glacier·in·which·time·we'll·help·
nbing·skills·including·rope·techniques,·
orrect·use·of·ax·and·crampons.·The·
travel·and·the·particular·rescue·methods·
intended·for·people·new·to·climbing·
acquired·skills·will·provide·a·sound·
npetent·climber.¶
```

ADDING A BORDER

Word allows you to emphasize a selected paragraph by adding a border in a range of styles and colors. We are going to create a border around the outside of the selected text, but there are other options available in the **Outside Border** menu.

1 OPENING THE BORDER MENU

- Highlight the paragraph and click on the **Outside Border** button in the Formatting toolbar.

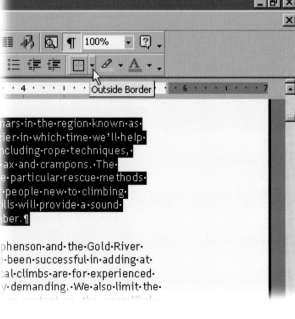

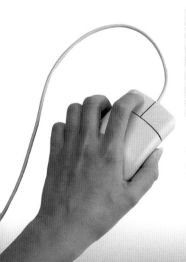

2 SELECTING OUTSIDE BORDER

- A menu of border selections appears. Click on the **Outside Border** option.

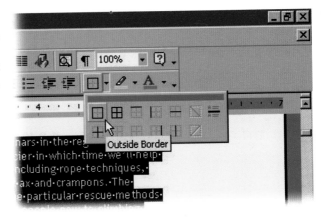

- The paragraph is now enclosed within a border.

CLIMBING·SEMINARS¶
We·are·pleased·to·continue·to·offer·these·popular·seminars·in·the·region·known·as·
the·US·Alps.·You'll·spend·14·days·on·the·Gold·River·glacier·in·which·time·we'll·help·
you·to·become·familiar·with·a·range·of·climbing·skills·including·rope·techniques,·
self-arrest,·rappelling,·belaying,·and·the·correct·use·of·ax·and·crampons.·The·
location·is·ideal·for·learning·about·glacier·travel·and·the·particular·rescue·methods·
that·crevasses·require.·These·seminars·are·intended·for·people·new·to·climbing·
and,·by·the·end·of·the·seminar,·your·newly·acquired·skills·will·provide·a·sound·
foundation·toward·becoming·a·safe·and·competent·climber.¶

TECHNICAL·CLIMBS¶

3 CHANGING THE BORDER STYLE

- With the text within the border highlighted, go to the **Format** menu and click on **Borders and Shading**.

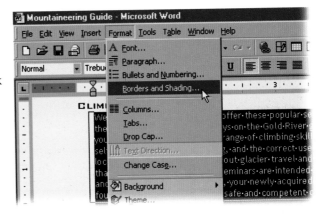

● The **Borders and Shading** dialog box opens. Click on the **Borders** tab if it is not already at the front. In the **Style:** panel, click on the down arrow and select one of the selection of borders by clicking on it. Click on **OK**.

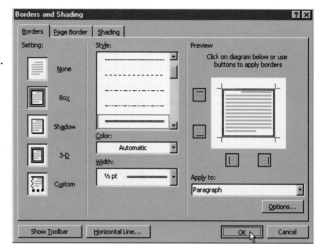

● The border around the paragraph changes to the selected style.

CLIMBING·SEMINARS¶

We·are·pleased·to·continue·to·offer·these·popular·seminars·in·the·region·known·as· the·US·Alps.·You'll·spend·14·days·on·the·Gold·River·glacier·in·which·time·we'll·help· you·to·become·familiar·with·a·range·of·climbing·skills·including·rope·techniques,· self-arrest,·rappelling,·belaying,·and·the·correct·use·of·ax·and·crampons.·The· location·is·ideal·for·learning·about·glacier·travel·and·the·particular·rescue·methods· that·crevasses·require.·These·seminars·are·intended·for·people·new·to·climbing· and,·by·the·end·of·the·seminar,·your·newly·acquired·skills·will·provide·a·sound· foundation·toward·becoming·a·safe·and·competent·climber.¶

TECHNICAL·CLIMBS¶
Guided·technical·climbs·are·undertaken·in·Alaska·on·Mt·Stephenson·and·the·Gold·River· glacier.·We·offer·these·and·others·each·season·and·we·have·been·successful·in·adding·at·

RESIZING BORDERS MANUALLY

There are two ways in which you can change the distance between the text and the border that encloses it. If you open the **Borders and Shading** dialog box you will see an **Options** button that allows the precise adjustment of the distance between the text and the border. An alternative method is simply to place the cursor against one of the sides of the border, hold down the mouse button, and drag the edge of the border to a new position.

4 ADDING COLOR TO THE BORDER

- With the text within the border highlighted, go to the Format menu and click on **Borders and Shading**. Click in the **Color:** box to display the color palette.

- Move the mouse cursor down and click on **Tan**.

- Click on **OK** and the border is now colored.

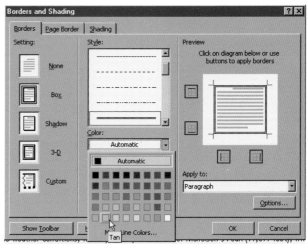

ill tell you whether expedition climbing is really for you.

CLIMBING·SEMINARS¶

We·are·pleased·to·continue·to·offer·these·popular·seminars·in·the·region·known·as· the·US·Alps.·You'll·spend·14·days·on·the·Gold·River·glacier·in·which·time·we'll·help· you·to·become·familiar·with·a·range·of·climbing·skills·including·rope·techniques,· self-arrest,·rappelling,·belaying,·and·the·correct·use·of·ax·and·crampons.·The· location·is·ideal·for·learning·about·glacier·travel·and·the·particular·rescue·methods· that·crevasses·require.·These·seminars·are·intended·for·people·new·to·climbing· and,·by·the·end·of·the·seminar,·your·newly·acquired·skills·will·provide·a·sound· foundation·toward·becoming·a·safe·and·competent·climber.¶

TECHNICAL·CLIMBS¶

5 REMOVING A BORDER

- With the text within the border highlighted, click on the **Outside Border** button in the Formatting toolbar. The menu of border selections appears.
- Move the mouse cursor over the **No Border** option and click to remove the border.

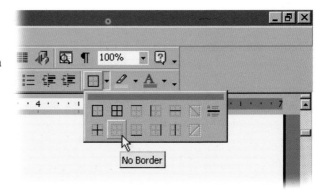

SHADING A PARAGRAPH

Whether or not a paragraph has been given a border, the text can be made to stand out by shading or coloring the background. Even if you don't have a color printer, this method can be used to choose a shade of gray, which can be effective.

1 SELECTING THE DIALOG BOX
● Highlight the paragraph, go to the Format menu in the toolbar and click on **Borders and Shading**. Now click on the **Shading** tab in the **Borders and Shading** dialog box to bring it to the foreground.

2 CHOOSING A COLOR
● Click on **Light Green** on the bottom row of the color palette, and the preview panel shows what this will look like.

● Click on **OK**, and the paragraph is now colored.

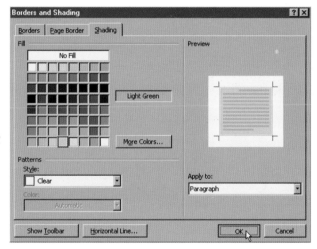

CLIMBING·SEMINARS¶
We·are·pleased·to·continue·to·offer·these·popular·seminars·in·the·region·known·as· the·US·Alps.·You'll·spend·14·days·on·the·Gold·River·glacier·in·which·time·we'll·help· you·to·become·familiar·with·a·range·of·climbing·skills·including·rope·techniques,· self-arrest,·rappelling,·belaying,·and·the·correct·use·of·ax·and·crampons.·The· location·is·ideal·for·learning·about·glacier·travel·and·the·particular·rescue·methods· that·crevasses·require.·These·seminars·are·intended·for·people·new·to·climbing· and,·by·the·end·of·the·seminar,·your·newly·acquired·skills·will·provide·a·sound· foundation·toward·becoming·a·safe·and·competent·climber.¶

TECHNICAL·CLIMBS¶
Guided·technical·climbs·are·undertaken·in·Alaska·on·Mt·Stephenson·and·the·Gold·River· glacier.·We·offer·these·and·others·each·season·and·we·have·been·successful·in·adding·at·

REMOVING SHADING FROM A PARAGRAPH

If you wish to remove shading that you have already created, follow these steps. With the paragraph highlighted, open the **Borders and Shading** dialog box via the Format menu, and choose **Shading**. Now click in the **No Fill** box above the color palette, click **OK**, and the shading is removed.

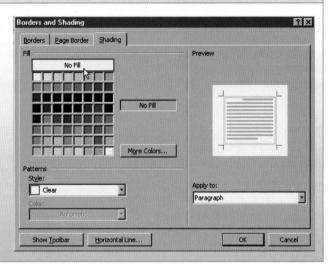

3 ALIGNING THE TEXT

● When text is within a rectangular border, it can look better being justified ⌐. Highlight the paragraph and click on the **Justify** button in the Formatting toolbar. The text now fits neatly within the border.

CLIMBING·SEMINARS¶

We·are·pleased·to·continue·to·offer·these·popular·seminars·in·the·region·known·as·the·US·Alps.·You'll·spend·14·days·on·the·Gold·River·glacier·in·which·time·we'll·help·you·to·become·familiar·with·a·range·of·climbing·skills·including·rope·techniques,·self-arrest,·rappelling,·belaying,·and·the·correct·use·of·ax·and·crampons.·The·location·is·ideal·for·learning·about·glacier·travel·and·the·particular·rescue·methods·that·crevasses·require.·These·seminars·are·intended·for·people·new·to·climbing·and,·by·the·end·of·the·seminar,·your·newly·acquired·skills·will·provide·a·sound·foundation·toward·becoming·a·safe·and·competent·climber.¶

TECHNICAL·CLIMBS¶

Aligning Paragraphs

USING FORMAT PAINTER

Once you've decided on a paragraph format that you want to apply to other paragraphs, you can apply the style by using a feature of Word known as **Format Painter**, rather than going through each individual step again for each paragraph.

1 SELECTING THE FORMAT TO COPY
● Select the paragraph whose format you wish to apply to another paragraph. Make sure that the paragraph mark is also selected. Click on the **Format Painter** button on the Standard toolbar.

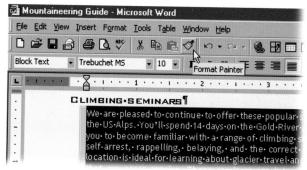

2 SELECTING THE NEW PARAGRAPH
● The cursor changes to a paintbrush icon. Move to the paragraph that is to be formatted in the same way as the selected paragraph.
● Click on the paragraph.

● All the formatting that has been done, including adding space, indenting the paragraph, adding a colored border and shading, and justifying the text, will be applied instantly to the chosen paragraph.

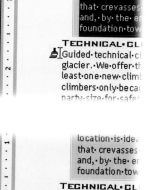

MULTIPLE PAINTING

If you want to apply the same format to more than one paragraph by using **Format Painter**, double-click on the **Format Painter** button when you select it. You can then format as many paragraphs with the chosen format as you want by clicking in each one. When you've finished applying the format, either click on the **Format Painter** button to deselect or press the [Esc] key.

14 ⓫ **Format Painter**

LISTS AND COLUMNS

Some data looks neater and more readable when presented as a list or in a column. In this chapter we look at the list and column options available in Word, and how to use them.

NUMBERED LISTS

Displaying items line by line, each new entry starting with a number, is probably the most common form of list. Text that has already been typed in can be turned into a list, and Word also has the facility to create a list automatically as you type.

1 SELECT BULLETS AND NUMBERING
● Type in a list of items, starting a new line each time. Now highlight the list, go to the **Format** menu in the toolbar, and select **Bullets and Numbering**.

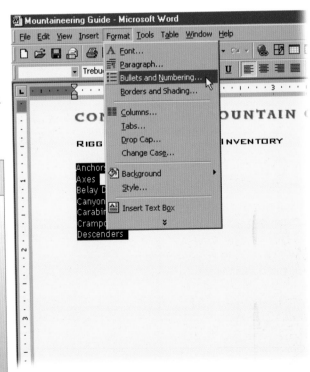

AUTOMATIC NUMBERING

Word detects when you are manually creating a numbered list. If you type a line of text that begins with a **1** followed by a space, when you press the [Enter ↵] key, Word automatically begins the new line with a **2** and inserts a tab.

2 CHOOSING THE OPTION

● The **Bullets and Numbering** dialog box opens. Click on the **Numbered** tab to view the numbering options.

● Select the numbering style immediately to the right of the **None** box by clicking on that box. The chosen box is highlighted by a blue rectangle. Now click on **OK**.

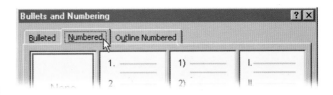

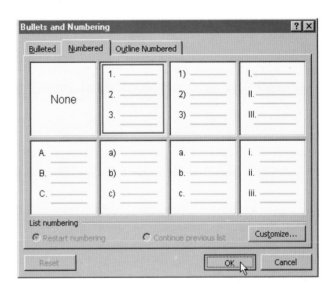

● The list of items is now numbered.

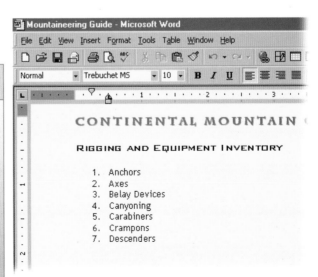

CHANGING THE INDENTS

As you have seen on the previous page, when you turn a list into a numbered list, Word automatically indents it. To remove the indent, or indent the list further, follow these steps. This method also works for other kinds of lists and for normal text.

1 SELECTING THE LIST

● If the list is not already highlighted, begin by doing so. Don't worry if the numbers themselves aren't highlighted. This is because Word treats them differently from regular text.

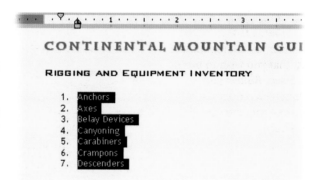

2 CHANGING THE INDENT

● Move the cursor up to the Formatting toolbar and click on the **Decrease Indent** button.

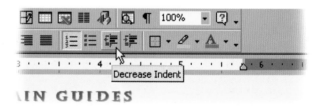

● The whole list moves to the left, aligning with the text above it.
● If you want to increase, rather than decrease, the indent, click on the **Increase Indent** button, which is to the right of the **Decrease Indent** button.

36 Decrease Indent

15

37 Increase Indent

15

BULLETED LISTS

Even when the lines in a list do not need to be numbered, you may still wish to emphasize the entries. Word offers a range of bulleted lists suited to different purposes. For example, you might use check marks for a list of completed tasks.

1 SELECTING THE LIST

● Begin by highlighting the list that you wish to bullet.
● Select **Bullets and Numbering** from the **Format** menu in the toolbar ◻.

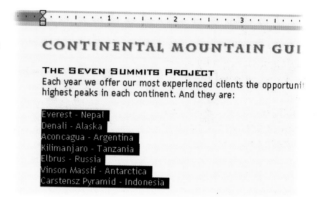

2 SELECTING THE BULLETED TAB

● In the **Bullets and Numbering** menu, click on the **Bulleted** tab to bring it to the front.

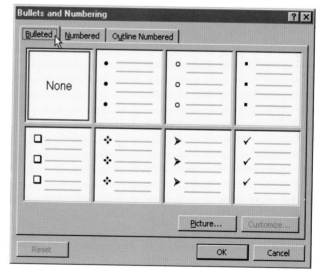

100 **Select Bullets and Numbering**

3 SELECTING THE BULLET STYLE

● There are several bullet styles that you can use, but in this example we are selecting the option next to **None**. Now click on **OK**.

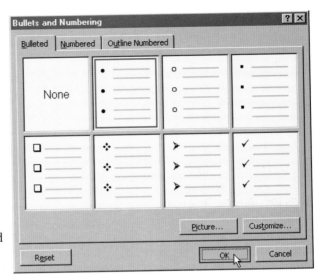

● The list now has a bullet at the start of each line, and you can change the indent, if you want to, as before.

PICTURE BULLETS

Word offers a very wide range of picture bullets. Click on **Picture** in the **Bulleted** tab of the **Bullets and Numbering** dialog box. A palette menu opens, and you can select a particular combination of shape and color from the variety available.

CONTINENTAL MOUNTAIN GUI

THE SEVEN SUMMITS PROJECT
Each year we offer our most experienced clients the opportuni
highest peaks in each continent. And they are:

- Everest - Nepal
- Denali - Alaska
- Aconcagua - Argentina
- Kilimanjaro - Tanzania
- Elbrus - Russia
- Vinson Massif - Antarctica
- Carstensz Pyramid - Indonesia

QUICK LISTS

If you are happy with the default style of numbering or bullet size, there is a quick way to produce a numbered or bulleted list. Once you have typed in the list of items, highlight the list, and then click on either the Numbering button 📄 or the Bullets button 📄 in the Formatting toolbar.

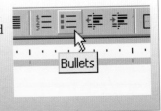

34 Numbered List 15

35 Bulleted List 15

CREATING A TABBED LIST

Microsoft® Word includes the facility to set out text or figures in neat tables (see *Tables, Charts & Graphs* section), but for small amounts of information it can often be easier to create columns by turning the entries into a tabbed list.

1 INSERTING TABS BETWEEN ITEMS

● Type a list of items and press the [Tab⇄] key between each item on each line. With the Formatting Marks turned on, the tab mark (the right-pointing arrow) shows where each tab has been inserted.

Tab marks indicate where a tab has been inserted

2 BRINGING UP THE TABS DIALOG BOX

● Take a look at the list and decide which is the longest left-hand entry. In this case it is the Mexican entry, at just over 1.5 inches wide.
● Ignoring the line of headings for the moment, highlight the rest of the list.
● Click on **Format** in the Menu bar, and choose **Tabs**.

3 SETTING A TAB STOP POSITION

● The **Tabs** dialog box opens. Given the length of the Mexico destination, we are going to set the first column at 2 inches, so in the **Tab stop position:** box type **2**. Now click on **Set**, and then click on **OK**.

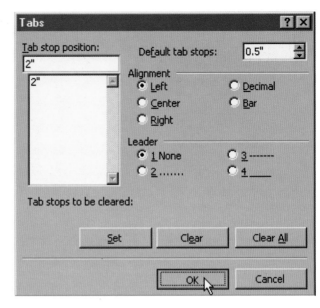

● A tab stop appears in the ruler at the 2-inch position, and the months are now lined up in a column.

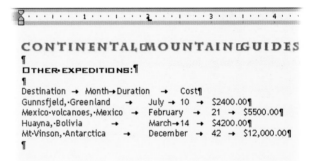

4 SETTING THE NEXT TAB STOP

● With the list still highlighted, follow the same steps to set another tab at 3 inches. The numbers of the duration are now lined up.

5 SETTING A DECIMAL TAB

● So far we've only used a left tab, that is, the items are lined up down their left-hand side. The cost figures would look better lined up down their right-hand side, so we will use a decimal tab.

● With the list highlighted, open the **Tabs** dialog box again. Set a tab at 4 inches and click on the **Decimal** radio button.

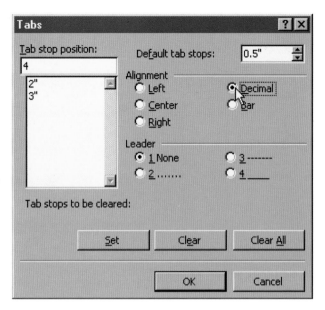

● Click on **Set** and then on **OK**. A decimal tab stop appears on the ruler, and the prices are now aligned down the decimal point at the 4-inch position.

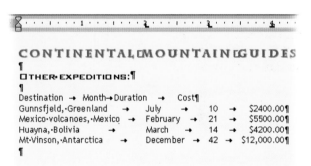

REMOVING A TAB SETTING FROM THE RULER

A quick way to remove a tab setting is first to highlight the text that contains the tab. Place the mouse cursor on the ruler tab setting that you want to remove, and hold the mouse button down. The vertical alignment line appears, but all you need to do is to drag the tab symbol down off the ruler and release the mouse button. The tab disappears.

SETTING TABS BY THE RULER

As is the case with many of the functions in Microsoft® Word, there is more than one way of setting tabs. Using the ruler provides a more visual method than the **Tabs** dialog box, and allows you to make quick adjustments until you are satisfied.

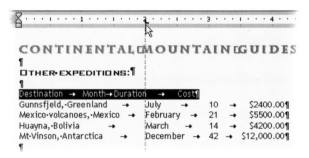

1 SETTING THE FIRST TAB IN THE RULER

● The headings above the list still need aligning over their respective columns. Highlight that line and click on the ruler at the 2-inch mark. A left tab appears on the ruler.

● The **Destination** heading remains aligned to the left, but the **Month** heading now lines up with the months below it.

2 SELECTING A CENTER TAB

● With the line of headings still highlighted, click on the **Left Tab** symbol at the left-hand end of the ruler. The symbol for a **Center Tab** appears. This tab has the effect of centering text on the tab.

3 SETTING THE CENTER TAB

● Click on the ruler at the 3-inch mark. A center tab is set and the word **Duration** is almost centered above the list of days.

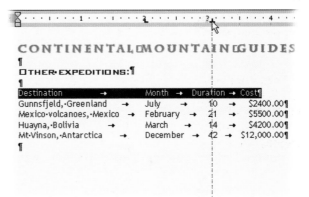

CONTINENTAL⬛MOUNTAIN⬛GUIDES ¶
¶
☐THER·EXPEDITIONS:¶
¶

Destination →	Month →	Duration →	Cost¶
Gunnsfjeld,·Greenland →	July →	10 →	$2400.00¶
Mexico·volcanoes,·Mexico →	February →	21 →	$5500.00¶
Huayna,·Bolivia →	March →	14 →	$4200.00¶
Mt·Vinson,·Antarctica →	December →	42 →	$12,000.00¶

¶

4 FINE TUNING THE SETTING

● The word **Duration** is slightly to the left of center, so move the cursor up to the ruler, place it over the center tab, and hold down the mouse button. A dotted vertical alignment line now appears down the screen. Move the cursor slightly to the right until this line falls exactly between the digits.

● Release the mouse button, and the heading is now precisely centered over the column of numbers.

CONTINENTAL⬛MOUNTAIN⬛GUIDES ¶
¶
☐THER·EXPEDITIONS:¶
¶

Destination →	Month →	Duration →	Cost¶
Gunnsfjeld,·Greenland →	July →	10 →	$2400.00¶
Mexico·volcanoes,·Mexico →	February →	21 →	$5500.00¶
Huayna,·Bolivia →	March →	14 →	$4200.00¶
Mt·Vinson,·Antarctica →	December →	42 →	$12,000.00¶

¶

CONTINENTAL⬛MOUNTAIN⬛GUIDES ¶
¶
☐THER·EXPEDITIONS:¶
¶

Destination →	Month →	Duration →	Cost¶
Gunnsfjeld,·Greenland →	July →	10 →	$2400.00¶
Mexico·volcanoes,·Mexico →	February →	21 →	$5500.00¶
Huayna,·Bolivia →	March →	14 →	$4200.00¶
Mt·Vinson,·Antarctica →	December →	42 →	$12,000.00¶

¶

5 SELECTING A RIGHT TAB

- Finally, click through the options of the tab button at the left-hand end of the ruler until the **Right Tab** symbol appears.

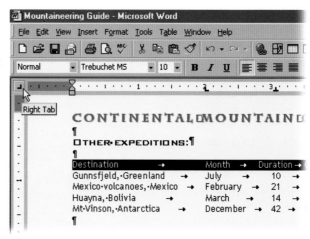

6 SETTING THE RIGHT TAB

- Click on the ruler at about the 4.2-inch mark. The end of the word **Cost** is now aligned with the trailing zeroes of the amounts in the column.

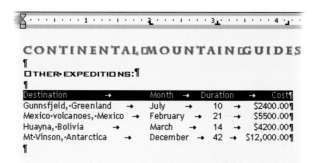

7 CHECKING THE EFFECT

- The right tab lines up the right-hand end of the text. To see the effect, change **Cost** to **Cost/person**. The words move to the left as you type, and the end of "person" is aligned with the zeroes. The effect is clearer with the formatting marks turned off.

CONTINENTAL MOUNTAIN GUIDES

OTHER EXPEDITIONS:

Destination	Month	Duration	Cost/person
Gunnsfjeld, Greenland	July	10	$2400.00
Mexico volcanoes, Mexico	February	21	$5500.00
Huayna, Bolivia	March	14	$4200.00
Mt Vinson, Antarctica	December	42	$12,000.00

90 | **Selecting the Paragraph**

8 ADDING LEADERS BETWEEN ITEMS

- One way of making it easier to read across tabbed columns is to add a leader between each one.
- Highlight the list of destinations and click on **Tabs** in the **Format** menu. The **Tabs** dialog box opens. Click on the radio button next to **2.......**, and then click on **Set**.

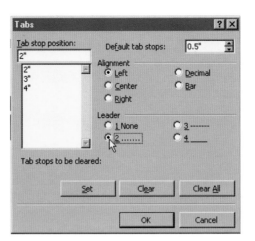

- Now highlight 3" in the **Tab stop position:** list of tabs, click on the radio button next to **2.......** again, and then click on **Set**.

- Repeat this process for the 4" tab position and click on **OK**. The list of expeditions now has rows of leaders to make the list more readable.

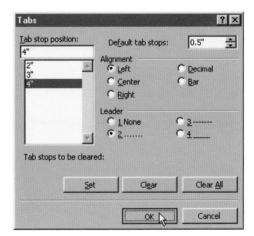

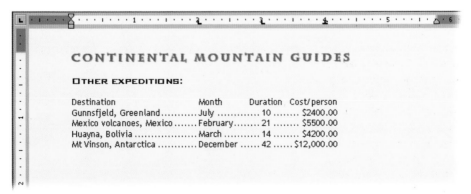

CONTINENTAL MOUNTAIN GUIDES

OTHER EXPEDITIONS:

Destination	Month	Duration	Cost/person
Gunnsfjeld, Greenland	July	10	$2400.00
Mexico volcanoes, Mexico	February	21	$5500.00
Huayna, Bolivia	March	14	$4200.00
Mt Vinson, Antarctica	December	42	$12,000.00

USING MULTIPLE COLUMNS

We have looked at ways of turning lists into columns, but there are times when continuous text benefits from being set in columns, too. This can give the page a newspaper-like appearance, and can be useful in newsletters and pamphlets.

1 CHOOSING THE COLUMNS OPTION

● In this example, the Mountain Guides brochure includes a section on rented accommodation, which we are going to set in columns.

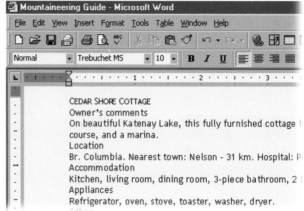

● Begin by highlighting the text that you want to be laid out in columns.
● Then click on **Format** in the Menu bar and choose **Columns** from the drop-down menu.

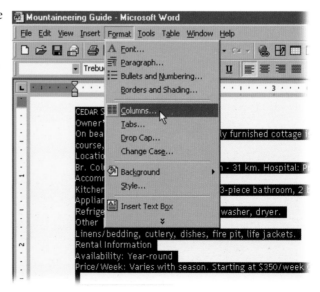

2 SET THE NUMBER OF COLUMNS

● The **Columns** dialog box opens. Click on box **Three** in the **Presets** section of the dialog box to select three columns, and click on **OK**.
● The preview panel shows how the text will look.

● Click on **OK**, and the selected text is now set out in three columns, with the default space of 0.5 inches between them.

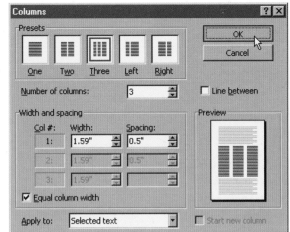

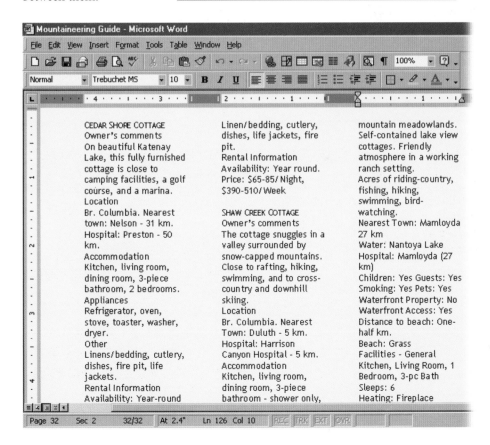

CEDAR SHORE COTTAGE
Owner's comments
On beautiful Katenay Lake, this fully furnished cottage is close to camping facilities, a golf course, and a marina.
Location
Br. Columbia. Nearest town: Nelson - 31 km. Hospital: Preston - 50 km.
Accommodation
Kitchen, living room, dining room, 3-piece bathroom, 2 bedrooms.
Appliances
Refrigerator, oven, stove, toaster, washer, dryer.
Other
Linens/bedding, cutlery, dishes, fire pit, life jackets.
Rental Information
Availability: Year-round

Linen/bedding, cutlery, dishes, life jackets, fire pit.
Rental Information
Availability: Year round.
Price: $65-85/Night, $390-510/Week

SHAW CREEK COTTAGE
Owner's comments
The cottage snuggles in a valley surrounded by snow-capped mountains. Close to rafting, hiking, swimming, and to cross-country and downhill skiing.
Location
Br. Columbia. Nearest Town: Duluth - 5 km. Hospital: Harrison Canyon Hospital - 5 km.
Accommodation
Kitchen, living room, dining room, 3-piece bathroom - shower only,

mountain meadowlands. Self-contained lake view cottages. Friendly atmosphere in a working ranch setting. Acres of riding-country, fishing, hiking, swimming, bird-watching.
Nearest Town: Mamloyda 27 km
Water: Nantoya Lake
Hospital: Mamloyda (27 km)
Children: Yes Guests: Yes
Smoking: Yes Pets: Yes
Waterfront Property: No
Waterfront Access: Yes
Distance to beach: One-half km.
Beach: Grass
Facilities - General
Kitchen, Living Room, 1 Bedroom, 3-pc Bath
Sleeps: 6
Heating: Fireplace

3 INSERTING COLUMN BREAKS

● The information would be clearer if each column began with a new entry. This can be done by using column breaks.

● Place the cursor at the point in the text where you would like to start a new column, click on **Insert** in the **Menu** bar, and choose **Break** from the menu.

● The **Break** dialog box opens. Click on the radio button next to **Column break** and click on **OK**.

● By using this method, each column can begin with a new entry.

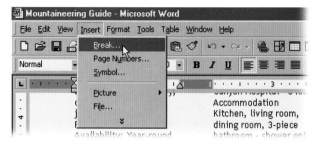

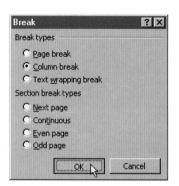

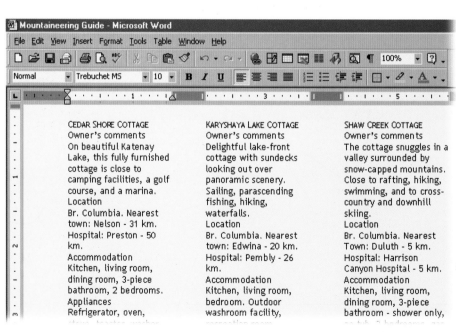

4 INSERTING VERTICAL LINES

● Rather than having blank spaces between columns, you can insert a vertical line between them. Place the cursor anywhere in the columns, open the **Columns** dialog box 🔲, and click in the **Line between** check box.

● Click on **OK** and the columns are now separated by a vertical line, which helps lead the eye in the same way that we saw earlier with tab leaders 🔲.

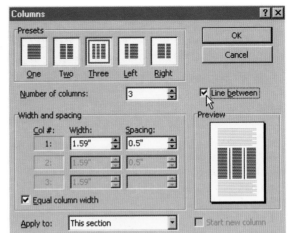

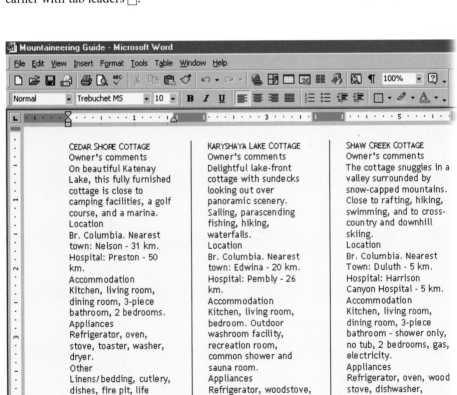

| 112 | **Choosing the Columns Option** |
| 111 | **Adding Leaders Between Items** |

USING STYLE SHEETS

This chapter deals with style sheets, a feature of Word that enables you to define many aspects of the style of each kind of text and apply the defined styles throughout your document.

THE POWER OF THE STYLE SHEET

Style sheets are one of the most powerful – and least understood – features of Word. Each style sheet is a list of formatting instructions, or styles, that can be applied to text. Every document is based on a style sheet. When you open a new document by clicking on the **New Blank Document** button in the Standard toolbar, Word automatically bases it on the normal style sheet, which is why the word **Normal** appears in the **Style** box at the end of the Formatting toolbar.

DEFINING FEATURES
A style sheet can define many features of a section of text. These include the font, and its size, color, and effects; the shape of a paragraph as determined by indents, spacing, and how page breaks are controlled; the position and alignment of tabs; what borders and shading are used, if any; and how bullets and numbering are styled. The smallest unit to which a style sheet can be applied is a paragraph, which need only be one line that ends with a paragraph mark.

CHOOSING ELEMENTS
To apply styles sensibly to a document, first identify the various parts of the text that play different roles. For example, in a book, the title, the table of contents, main text, captions, and index all play different roles, and can all be styled differently. The styles can be set in separate style sheets and applied.

SAVING TIME
Once a style sheet has been created, any changes that you make to that sheet are automatically applied to all parts of your document that are based on that style.

CEDAR SHORE COTTAGE

Owner's comments
On beautiful Katenay Lake, this fully furnished cottage is close to camping facilities, a golf course, and a marina.

Location
Br. Columbia. Nearest town: Nelson - 31 km. Hospital: Preston - 50 km.

Accommodation
Kitchen, living room, dining room, 3-piece

Styled text •

Using a style sheet, a defined font, type size, and indent has been applied to every instance of this kind of text each time it appears in the document.

CREATING A NEW STYLE SHEET

Style Sheets come into their own when applied to a document in which the information falls into various categories, and in which these categories are used repeatedly. In the example below, each entry in the directory contains the same categories of information, such as **Owner's comments**, **Location**, and **Accommodation**.

1 SELECTING THE TEXT

● The list of cabins and their details has all been formatted in Trebuchet 10 pt. Now, new styles are going to be designed for each part of the details of the properties, starting with the name of the property.
● Highlight the name of the first property and click on **Format** in the **Menu** bar. Now click on **Style** in the drop-down menu.

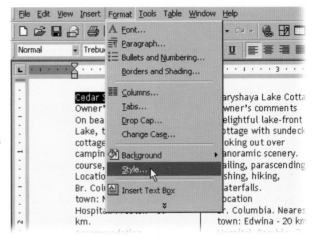

2 OPENING A NEW STYLE OPTION

● The **Style** dialog box opens. Click on **New** to create a new style for the property name. The text that you have highlighted can be seen in the preview box, and this will show the effects of any changes that you make to its style.

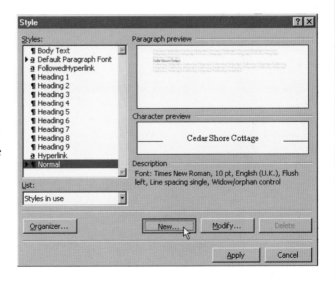

3 NAMING THE STYLE

● The **New Style** dialog box now opens. The first task is to give a name to the new style that we are creating, so type **Property Name** in the **Name:** box. A descriptive name like this will help you to know which style to choose when you are styling text at a later date.

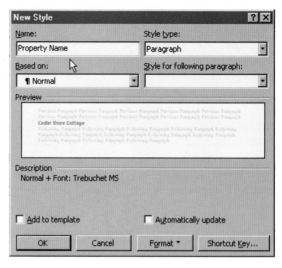

4 CHOOSING THE FONT

● Now click on **Format** at the bottom of the **New Style** dialog box, and click on **Font** in the pop-up menu.

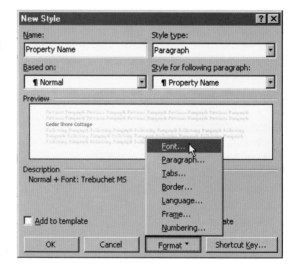

● The **Font** dialog box opens. This box offers you a range of possibilities for changing the appearance of the font, including the font itself, its style (Italic etc.), and its size.

● In the **Font:** selection box choose **BankGothic Md BT**, and you will see that the text is now shown in this font in the preview panel.

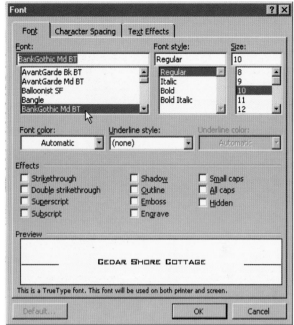

5 CHANGING THE FONT SIZE

● In the **Size:** selection box choose **14**. Again, the text in the preview panel now reflects this change.

- BankGothic Md BT is an uppercase only font, that is, it does not use lowercase letters. However, if you are using a font that is upper- and lowercase, click the **Small caps** check box of the **Effects** section. This has the effect of turning all the lowercase letters into small capital letters.
- Click on **OK**.

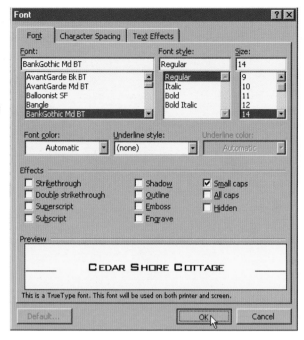

6 INTRODUCING SPACE AFTER

- The appearance of the text on the page would be improved if there were a small space between the name and the text that follows it.
- Click on **Format** in the **New Style** dialog box and then click on **Paragraph** in the pop-up menu.

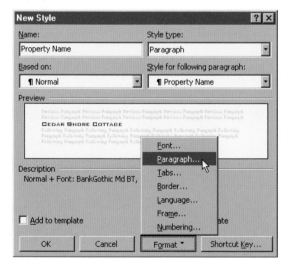

● The **Paragraph** dialog box opens. In the **Spacing** section, click once on the up arrow to the right of the **After:** box. The figure of **6 pt** appears in the panel, meaning that a 6 point space will be inserted after the property name.

● Click on **OK** to close the **Paragraph** dialog box.

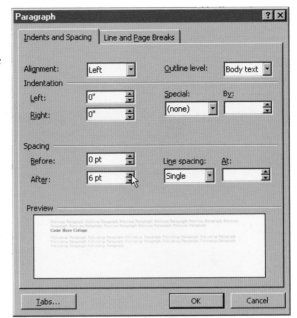

● The **New Style** dialog box now reappears. In the **Description** box, the new formatting that has been chosen is shown.

● Click on **OK** to close the **New Style** dialog box and save this new style.

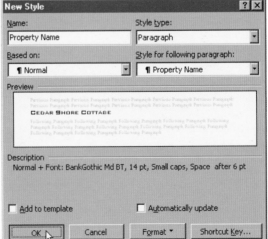

7 APPLYING THE NEW STYLE

● Click on **Apply** in the **Style** box, which is now visible again.

● The new style is now applied to the name of the property.

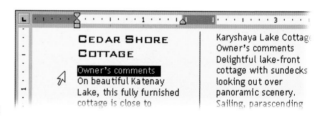

8 CREATING ANOTHER STYLE

● The details of each property are divided into sections, and a style is needed for the section heads. Highlight the words **Owner's comments**. Choose **Style** from the **Format** menu and click on **New** to open the **New Style** dialog box. Call this style **Section Head**.

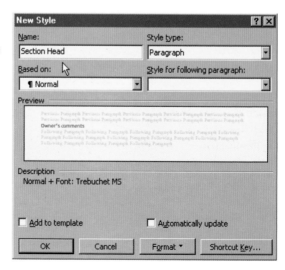

● Click on **Format** and again click on **Font** to open the **Font:** dialog box.
● Choose **Californian FB** as the font and choose **Bold** in the **Font style:** box. Click on **OK**.

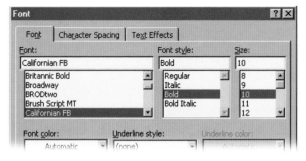

● The **New Style** dialog box reappears. Click on **Format**, select **Paragraph** to open the **Paragraph** dialog box, and in the **Spacing After:** box type **2**. This will introduce a small space after the heading. Click on **OK** to close the **Paragraph** dialog box.

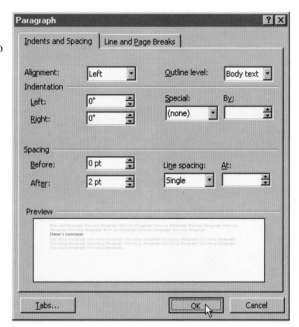

● Click on **OK** in the **New Style** dialog box and click on **Apply** in the **Style** dialog box. The section heading now has the required style.

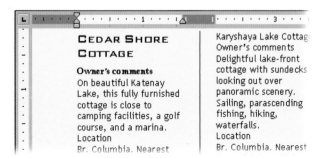

9 STYLING THE MAIN TEXT

● The text of each section needs its own style. Click in the paragraph below the newly styled **Owner's comments**, select **Style** from the **Format** menu, click on **New** to open the **New Style** dialog box, and call this style **Section Details**.

● Click on **Format** and select **Font** to open the **Font** dialog box. This time choose **Trebuchet MS** and make it 9 pt. Click on **OK** to return to the **New Style** box.

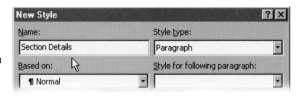

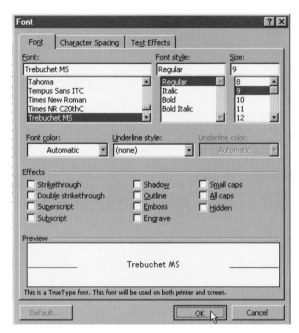

10 INDENTING THE TEXT

● The text will stand out more if it is indented. From the **Format** pop-up menu choose **Paragraph** and in the **Indentation** section of the **Paragraph** dialog box click on the up arrow of the **Left:** box. The figure of **0.1"** appears. Click on **OK**.

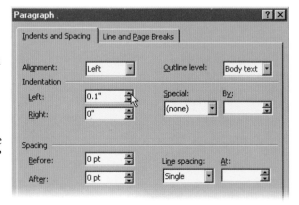

● Click **OK** again in the **New Style** box, click on **Apply**, and the text that appears, in the chosen font, is indented.

11 APPLYING YOUR STYLE SHEETS

● Highlight the name of the second property at the top of the second column.

● Click on the down arrow to the right of the **Style** selection box and move the cursor down to **Property Name**. (The other styles in the **Style** menu shown here may not be identical to the list in your **Style** menu.)

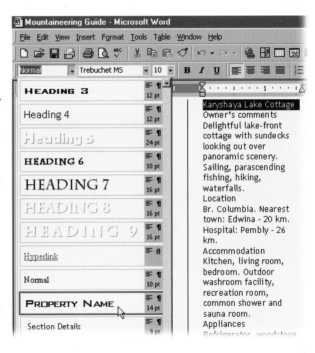

● Click on **Property Name** and that style is applied to the second property name.

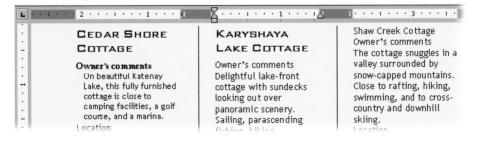

● Highlight **Owner's comments** beneath it and select the **Section Head** style.

● Click on **Section Head** and the style is applied to the heading.

Text now changes to Section Head style ●

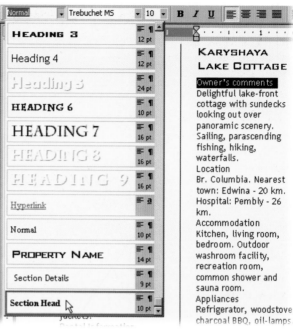

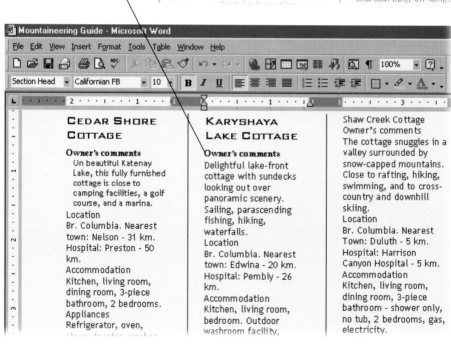

● Highlight the text beneath that heading and from the style list select **Section Details**. Click on **Section Details** and the style is applied to the highlighted text.

● Follow these steps to apply the style sheets to all the text throughout your document.

Text now changes to Section Details style ●

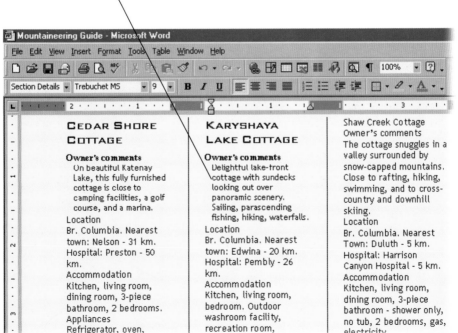

USING FORMAT PAINTER TO APPLY STYLES

We have seen how to create style sheets and apply them to all the text throughout a document, but this last process can be laborious if the text is extensive. Luckily, Word offers a solution – Format Painter enables you to do the job much faster.

1 STYLING THE PROPERTY NAME

● Highlight the property name at the top of the second column and make sure that you include the paragraph mark because this contains all the style details for the paragraph. (You can turn on the Formatting Marks to ensure that the paragraph mark is highlighted ⬚.)

● Click on the **Format Painter** icon in the Standard toolbar ⬚.

● Your cursor now has a paintbrush icon next to it. Go to the property name at the top of the third column and highlight it.

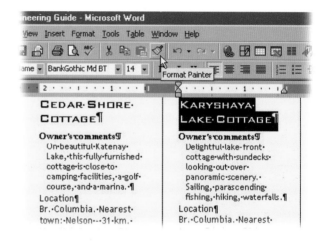

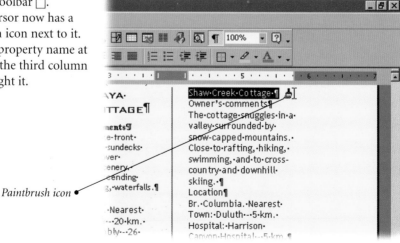

Paintbrush icon ●

● Release the mouse button, and the text is now styled in the selected style.

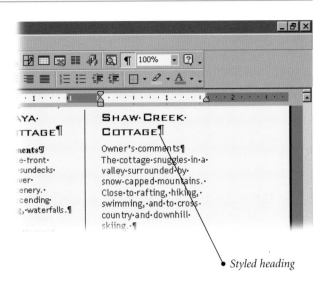

Styled heading

2 STYLING THE SECTION HEAD

● Select **Owner's comments** near the top of the first paragraph and double-click on the **Format Painter** button. You can now "paint" all the section heads in the text with the **Section Head** style. Press the [Esc] key, or click on the **Format Painter** button again when you have produced this result.

Styled Section Head

Multiple Painting

99

3 STYLING THE SECTION DETAILS

● Finally, highlight the first paragraph in the first column that has been formatted with the **Section Details** style, double-click on the **Format Painter** button, and apply the style to all the remaining unstyled paragraphs.

● The document should now look like the one below, with all text in the chosen styles.

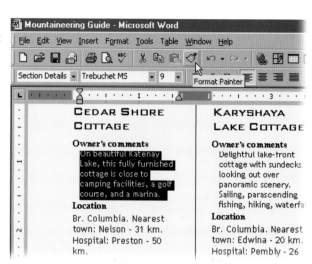

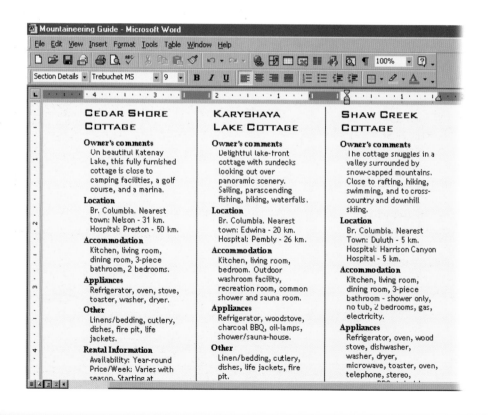

MAKING ONE STYLE FOLLOW ANOTHER

Once you have decided that one style is always to be followed by a second particular style, you can instruct Word always to follow the first style with the second. Begin by clicking on **Format** in the **Menu** bar and selecting **Style** to open the **Style** dialog box.

1 SELECTING THE FIRST STYLE

● In the **Style** dialog box, select the first of the two styles, in this case **Section Head**, and click on **Modify**.

Chosen style

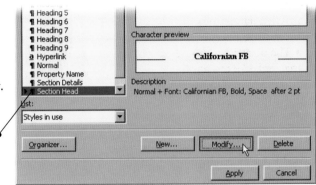

2 SELECTING THE SECOND STYLE

● The **Modify Style** dialog box opens. The first style, **Section Head**, appears in the **Name:** box. Click on the down arrow to the right of the **Style for following paragraph:** box to drop down the list of styles.
● Click on the style that is to follow the first style, in this case **Section Details**.

Modify Style

Name:
Section Head

Style type:
Paragraph

Based on:
¶ Normal

Style for following paragraph:
¶ Section Head
  ¶ Note Heading
  ¶ Plain Text
  ¶ Property Name
  ¶ Salutation
  ¶ Section Details
  ¶ Section Head

Preview

Previous Paragraph Previous Paragraph Previous Paragraph Previous Paragraph Previous Paragraph
Accommodation
Following Paragraph Following Paragraph Following Paragraph Following Paragraph Following Paragraph Following Paragraph Following Paragraph

Description
Normal + Font: Californian FB, Bold, Space after 2 pt

☐ Add to template   ☐ Automatically update

OK   Cancel   Format ▾   Shortcut Key...

3 SAVING THE CHANGES

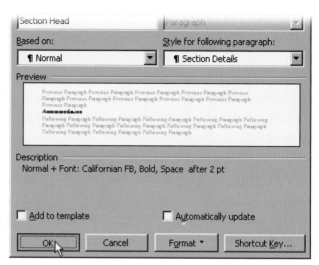

● **Section Details** appears in the **Style for following paragraph:** box.

● Click on **OK**, and the **Modify Style** dialog box closes. Now click on **Close** in the **Style** dialog box to complete the changes.

● On each occasion now when **Section Head** is used as a style and the Enter↵ key is pressed, the following text will be formatted with the **Section Details** style.

STYLING FROM A TEXT SELECTION

So far we have created styles by choosing each of the features for the style through the **Style** dialog box. An alternative method is to begin by formatting a paragraph with all the style features that you want to be in a style sheet.

1 FORMATTING THE TEXT

● In this example, the following formatting has been applied to the text:
Font: *Gill Sans Ultra Bold*
Font size: *16 pt*
Font color: *Red*
Space after: *12 pt*
Border setting: *Shadow*
Border style: *Thin-thick*
Border color: *Tan*
Shading: *Light Yellow*
Text: *Centered*
Right indent: *3.77 inches*

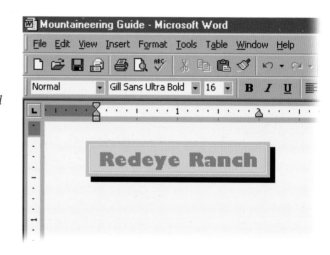

2 FROM A FORMAT TO A STYLE

● Highlight the text that you have formatted, click on **Format** in the **Menu** bar, select **Style** to open the **Style** box, and click on **New** near the foot of the dialog box to open the **New Style** dialog box. Word has picked up the formatting specifications of the selected text and almost all of them are shown in the **Description** section of this dialog box. Certain elements are not shown only because the **Description** box is too small to contain them all. Enter a name for the new style (here the name **Redeye** has been chosen). Click on **OK** to close the **New Style** dialog box.

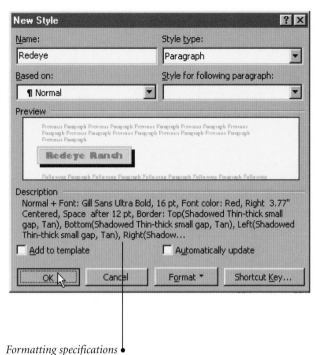

Formatting specifications •

3 MAKING THE STYLE AVAILABLE

● The **Style** dialog box reappears with the new style listed in the **Style** menu to the left. To close the dialog box, just click on **Apply** even though the text already contains the required formatting. This style is now available to be applied quickly to any chosen text.

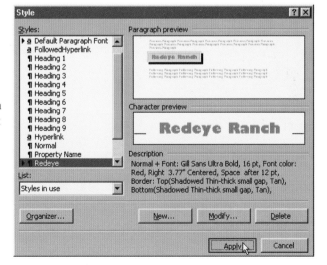

TABLES, CHARTS, AND GRAPHS

I N THIS SECTION OF THE BOOK we will use Word to produce professional-looking graphical presentations of data. Word's fully featured range of commands and controls to create tables, charts, and graphs are clearly and simply described. If you are uncertain of how to use the more basic functions in Word, you may need to refer back to the first part of the book, since this section is designed for users of Word who know how to open documents, enter text, and save the results.

CREATING A TABLE

Using Microsoft Word, you can set up, edit, design, and format a simple table easily. This chapter takes you through the steps involved in creating and completing your first table.

INSERTING YOUR FIRST TABLE

Before you begin to create your first table, click on **View** on the Menu bar and choose **Print Layout** from the drop-down menu. This view allows easy selection, resizing of tables, and other options that are not always available in Normal view.

1 INSERT TABLE

● Click on Table in the Menu bar, move down to Insert, and select Table from the submenu.

CHOICE OF FONT

Although the default font in Microsoft Word 2000 is Times New Roman 10 pt, in the examples of tables used in this section of the book, the font used is Arial 12 pt. This font produces very readable text both on-screen and on the page. If your font is not currently Arial, open a new document before you begin to insert a table. Toward the left-hand end of the Formatting toolbar is the Font selection box. Click on the down arrow to the right of the Font selection box, and choose **Arial** from the drop-down menu. Click on the down arrow to the right of the Font size selection box and click on **12 pt** from the list of font sizes. Your first table will now mirror the examples in this book.

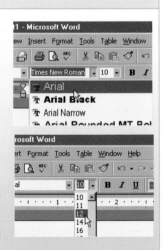

2 ROWS AND COLUMNS

● The **Insert Table** dialog box opens. In the **Table size** section of the box, enter the figure **6** in the **Number of columns** box, and enter the figure **5** in the **Number of rows** box.

● Click on **OK**. The table with the specified layout is inserted into the document.

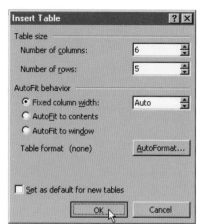

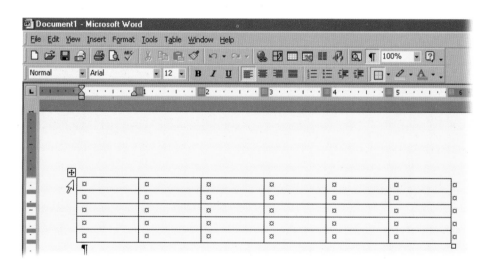

TABLE INSERT BUTTON

The Standard toolbar contains an **Insert Table** button. When you click on this button, a grid drops down representing columns and rows. The number of columns and rows is selected by holding down the mouse button and dragging the cursor over the grid until the required table size is shown. Release the mouse button to insert the table.

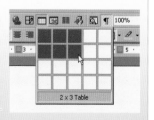

HOW TO WORK WITH TABLES

Before working with your table, a few terms and operations need to be explained. The parts of a table are explained here, as well as viewing a large table, selecting a whole table, row, or column, and moving around a table.

1 PARTS OF THE TABLE

● All tables consist of:
Cells – which contain data.
Rows – horizontal lines of cells.
Columns – vertical lines of cells.

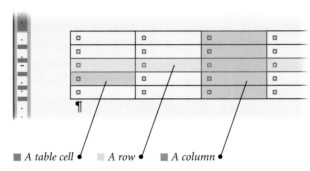

■ *A table cell* ●   *A row* ●   ■ *A column* ●

2 VIEWING THE TABLE

● If your table is larger than the screen, the table above or below the visible area can be viewed by clicking and dragging the vertical scroll bar. Use the horizontal scroll bar to view wide tables.

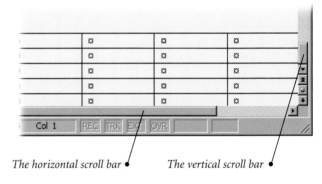

The horizontal scroll bar ●   *The vertical scroll bar* ●

3 SELECTING A WHOLE TABLE

● Position the cursor over the top left corner and the Table Move handle appears.
● Place the cursor over it and the cursor changes to a four-way arrow. Click once to select the whole table.

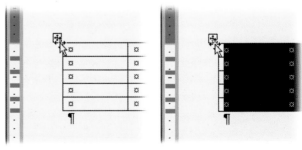

4 SELECTING TABLE ROWS

● Position the cursor to the left of the required row and click once to select the row.
● To select more than one row, click to the left of the first row, hold down the mouse button, and drag over the required rows. Release the mouse button.

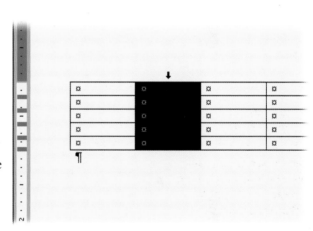

5 SELECTING TABLE COLUMNS

● Place the cursor just above the column until it becomes a black arrow.
● Click once and the column is selected.
● Select more than one column by holding down the mouse button when the black arrow appears and drag it across the columns.

Moving around

To move from one cell to the cell to the right in a row press the [Tab⇆] key. The [←] and [→] keys move the cursor horizontally across cells, while the [↑] and [↓] keys move the cursor vertically. The Table Move handle, as its name suggests, is used to move a table anywhere within a document. It can also be used to select a whole table. The Table Resize handle at the bottom-right corner is clicked on and dragged to make a table larger or smaller.

INPUTTING TEXT

Having set up the basic table and understanding how to move around and make selections, the next step is to input the data. This section deals with column headings, manipulating them, entering data, and controlling how it's printed.

1 COLUMN HEADINGS

● If the insertion point is not in the first cell of the table, click in that cell.
● Enter the heading for the first column.
● Use the Tab key to move from cell to cell, or move the mouse cursor to the next cell, click with the left mouse button, and enter the column heading.

2 REPEATED HEADINGS

● When a table extends over two or more pages, you may want your table headings to be repeated at the top of each new page.
● Select the headings row and click on **Table** on the Menu bar.
● Click on **Heading Rows Repeat** in the drop-down menu. Your table headings are now repeated at the top of each new page.

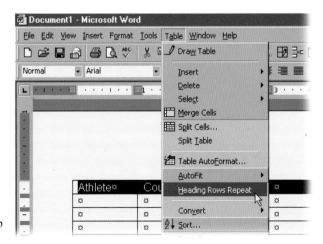

3 ENTERING DATA

● Now you can begin to enter the data.
● If the data does not fit on one line, Word increases the size of the row.

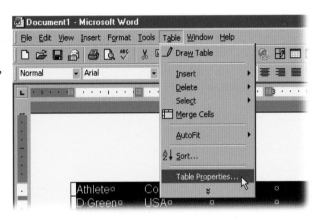

4 KEEPING DATA TOGETHER

● When the data in a table occupies two or more rows, the data may split across two pages when printing. To prevent this, select the whole table ⬦, click on **Table** in the Menu bar, and select **Table Properties**.
● The **Table Properties** dialog box opens; click on the **Row** tab. If there is a checkmark in the **Allow row to break across pages** checkbox, click on that box to clear it.
● Click on **OK** and all the data in the rows of the table will be kept together.

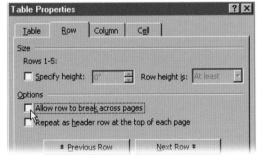

The completed decathlon table

Athlete	Country	100 m	Shot put	High jump	Total
D Green	USA	799	854	888	2541
S Belossovski	Estonia	767	771	944	2482
W Harris	UK	852	728	887	2467
L Reyaud	France	856	648	803	2307

138 Selecting a Whole Table

SORTING DATA

Tables are most frequently used for organizing data, and you may have information in a table that needs to be sorted into alphabetical order. This is a simple task using the **Sort Ascending** or **Sort Descending** functions in Word.

1 SORTING ALPHABETICALLY

- Select the whole table to be sorted ⌐.
- Click on **Table** on the Menu bar and then on the A-Z **Sort** option.
- The **Sort** dialog box opens. In the **Sort by** section, pull down the menu and click on **Country**, which will be the basis for the sort.
- Click the **Ascending** radio button to create a list in alphabetical order.
- To prevent the row of headings from being included in the sort, click the **Header row** radio button to tell Word to exclude it from the sort.

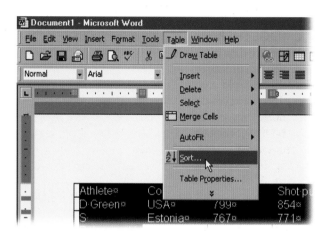

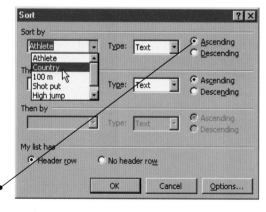

Ascending sort radio button

● Click on **OK** and the rows of the table are sorted into order according to the second column in the table, which lists the athletes' countries of origin.

● Click anywhere on the text area outside the table to deselect the table.

Athlete	Country	100·m	Shot·put	High·jump	Total	
S· Belossovski	Estonia	767	771	944	2482	
L·Reyaud	France	856	648	803	2307	
W·Harris	UK	852	728	887	2467	
D·Green	USA	799	854	888	2541	

¶

2 SORTING NUMERICALLY

● This table is ideal for sorting the results of a contest. Begin by selecting the Total column .

● Open the **Sort** dialog box (opposite), select **Total** in the **Sort by** box, and click the **Descending** radio button to produce a list with the highest number at the top.

● Click on **OK** and the entries are sorted in order of the points achieved.

100·m	Shot·put	High·jump	Total	
767	771	944	2482	
856	648	803	2307	
852	728	887	2467	
799	854	888	2541	

Athlete	Country	100·m	Shot·put	High·jump	Total	
D·Green	USA	799	854	888	2541	
S· Belossovski	Estonia	767	771	944	2482	
W·Harris	UK	852	728	887	2467	
L·Reyaud	France	856	648	803	2307	

¶

139 Selecting Table Columns

DESIGNING THE TABLE

Now you have set up your basic table, you can make changes to the appearance and layout. This chapter deals with options such as adding rows and columns, and changing the size of the table.

ADJUSTING COLUMNS AND ROWS

The number of columns and rows usually needs to be adjusted in any table. Columns may need to be added or deleted. Columns and rows may need to be of equal size, or they can be made only as wide or deep as the data requires.

1 ADDING COLUMNS

● To add another column to a table, select the column in the table next to where you want to add a column ⬆. In the example, the Country column has been selected because an extra column is to be added to the right to contain the details of another event.

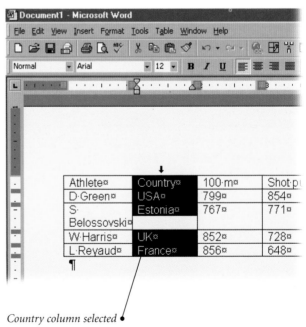

Country column selected ●

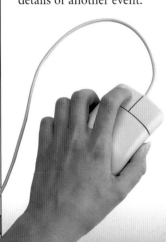

139 **Selecting Table Columns**

● Click on **Table** on the Menu bar and click on **Insert** in the drop-down menu. In the submenu, click on the **Columns to the Right** option.

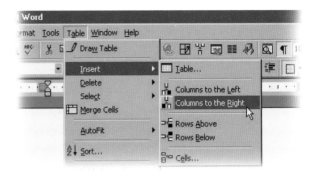

● An extra, blank, column is added to the table into which data can be inserted.

Quick rows

To add a row at the bottom of the table, click in the last cell and press the [Tab⇆] key. Alternatively, click outside to the right of the last cell of the table and press [Enter ←].

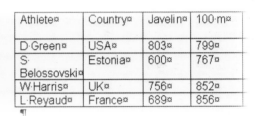

2 ADDING ROWS

● To add more rows to a table, select the row in the table next to where you wish to add an additional row ⬚. In the example, the last row in the table has been selected.

Athlete¤	Country¤	Javelin¤	100·m¤
D·Green¤	USA¤	803¤	799¤
S· Belossovski¤	Estonia¤	600¤	767¤
W·Harris¤	UK¤	756¤	852¤
L·Reyaud¤	France¤	689¤	856¤

139 Selecting Table Rows

● Click on the **Table** menu, followed by **Insert,** and then click on **Rows Below**.
● A new row is added to the foot of the table, which can be completed in the usual way.

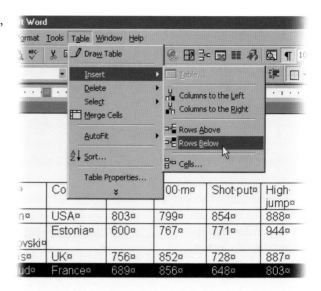

Athlete	Country	Javelin	100·m	Shot·put	High·jump	Total	
D·Green	USA	803	799	854	888	3344	
S·Belossovski	Estonia	600	767	771	944	3082	
W·Harris	UK	756	852	728	887	3223	
L·Reyaud	France	689	856	648	803	2996	

Athlete	Country	Javelin	100·m	Shot·put	High·jump	Total	
D·Green	USA	803	799	854	888	3344	
S·Belossovski	Estonia	600	767	771	944	3082	
W·Harris	UK	756	852	728	887	3223	
L·Reyaud	France	689	856	648	803	2996	
O·Ngecki	Zambia	699	823	659	803	2984	

3 MAKING CELLS THE SAME SIZE

● The cells' sizes in the table may be different as a result of the different amounts of data contained in each cell.

● To make all the cells the same size, the width of the columns needs to be identical, as does the depth of the rows. Begin by selecting the whole table ⌐.

● Click on **Table** in the Menu bar and click on **AutoFit** in the drop-down menu. In the submenu that appears, select **Distribute Rows Evenly**.

● Click on **Table** in the Menu bar again, select **Autofit**, and this time click on **Distribute Columns Evenly** in the submenu.

● The table cells are now all identical in size.

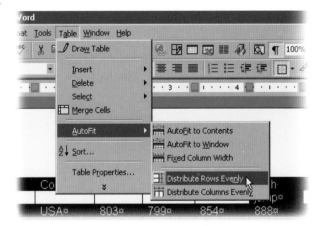

Athlete¤	Country¤	Javelin¤	100·m¤	Shot·put¤	High· jump¤	Total¤	¤
D·Green¤	USA¤	803¤	799¤	854¤	888¤	3344¤	¤
S· Belossovski¤	Estonia¤	600¤	767¤	771¤	944¤	3082¤	¤
W·Harris¤	UK¤	756¤	852¤	728¤	887¤	3223¤	¤
L·Reyaud¤	France¤	689¤	856¤	648¤	803¤	2996¤	¤
O·Ngecki¤	Zambia¤	699¤	823¤	659¤	803¤	2984¤	¤

¶

4 CHANGING THE COLUMN WIDTH

● You might wish to have columns in a table that have different widths. Word can do this automatically or you can do it manually.

● To have Word decide the column widths, begin by selecting the whole table 🖰.

● Click on the **Table** menu, followed by **AutoFit,** and then click on **AutoFit to Contents**. The table columns' widths are automatically adjusted.

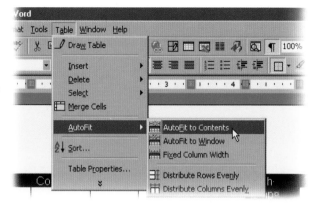

5 CHANGE WIDTH MANUALLY

● Decide on the column divider to be moved and place the insertion point over it. The point changes to a vertical double line with two arrows pointing right and left.

● Hold down the mouse button and a dotted line appears down the screen.

● Drag to the right or left and release the mouse button when the column is the required width.

t·put	High·jump	Total	
	888	3344	
	944	3082	

t·put	High·jump	Total	
	888	3344	
	944	3082	

Country	Javelin	100·m	Shot·put	High·jump	Total	
USA	803	799	854	888	3344	
Estonia	600	767	771	944	3082	

138 Selecting a Whole Table

6 RESIZING USING THE RULER

● Place the cursor over the small square grids on the ruler, known as *markers*. The cursor turns into a two-way arrow, and the **Move Table Column** ScreenTip is displayed beneath it.

● Hold down the mouse button and a dotted line appears down the screen.

● You can now increase or decrease the width by dragging with the mouse. Release the mouse button when the column is the required width.

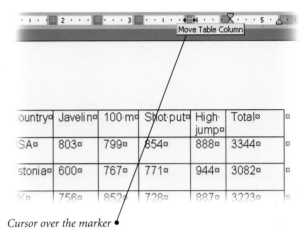

Country¤	Javelin¤	100·m¤	Shot·put¤	High· jump¤	Total¤	¤
USA¤	803¤	799¤	854¤	888¤	3344¤	¤
Estonia¤	600¤	767¤	771¤	944¤	3082¤	¤
UK¤	756¤	852¤	728¤	887¤	3223¤	¤

Cursor over the marker ●

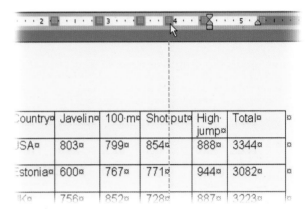

Country¤	Javelin¤	100·m¤	Shot·put¤	High· jump¤	Total¤	¤
USA¤	803¤	799¤	854¤	888¤	3344¤	¤
Estonia¤	600¤	767¤	771¤	944¤	3082¤	¤
UK¤	756¤	852¤	728¤	887¤	3223¤	¤

Displaying the width

To display the width of a column in units of measurement, hold down the Alt key as you click and drag the marker and the units are shown on the ruler.

Country¤	Javelin¤	100·m¤	Shot· put¤	High· jump¤	Total¤	¤
USA¤	803¤	799¤	854¤	888¤	3344¤	¤
Estonia¤	600¤	767¤	771¤	944¤	3082¤	¤
UK¤	756¤	852¤	728¤	887¤	3223¤	¤

7 CHANGING THE ROW HEIGHT

● Select the row line that you wish to change, and position the insertion point over it. The point changes to a horizontal double line with two vertical arrows.

| L·Reyaud¤ | France¤ | 689¤ | 856¤ | 648 |
| O·Ngecki¤ | Zambia¤ | 699¤ | 823¤ | 659 |

● Hold down the mouse button and a horizontal dotted line appears across the screen.
● Move the mouse up or down, and the dotted line follows the cursor.

| L·Reyaud¤ | France¤ | 689¤ | 856¤ | 648 |
| O·Ngecki¤ | Zambia¤ | 699¤ | 823¤ | 659 |

● When the row is the correct height, release the mouse button.

W·Harris¤	UK¤	756¤	852¤	72
L·Reyaud¤	France¤	689¤	856¤	648
O·Ngecki¤	Zambia¤	699¤	823¤	659

8 DELETING ROWS

● To delete a row, begin by selecting it.
● Now click on **Table** in the menu bar followed by **Delete** and select **Rows**.

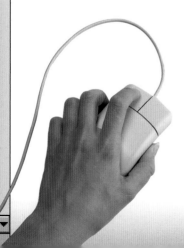

ent1 - Microsoft Word

View Insert Format Tools Table Window Help

Arial

	Insert	▶
	Delete	▶	Table
	Select	▶	Columns
	Merge Cells		Rows
			Cells...
	AutoFit	▶
	Sort...	
	Table Properties...	

Athlete¤	C	00·m¤	Shot· put¤	High jump
D·Green¤	USA¤	803¤	799¤	854¤	888
S·Belossovski¤	Estonia¤	600¤	767¤	771¤	944
W·Harris¤	UK¤	756¤	852¤	728¤	887
L·Reyaud¤	France¤	689¤	856¤	648¤	803

- The row is deleted and those above and below are closed up to fill the space.

Athlete	Country	Javelin	100·m	Shot put
D·Green	USA	803	799	854
S·Belossovski	Estonia	600	767	771
W·Harris	UK	756	852	728
O·Ngecki	Zambia	699	823	659

9 RE-SORTING THE TABLE

- Adding the Javelin points means the table needs re-sorting. Select the **Total** column and open the **Sort** dialog box 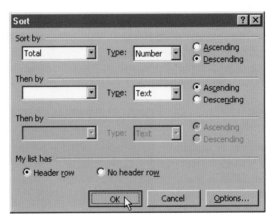.
- Click the **Header row** radio button and **Total** appears in the **Sort by** box.
- Click the Sort by **Descending** radio button and click on **OK**.
- The table is re-sorted in the order of points gained.

Athlete	Country	Javelin	100·m	Shot put	High jump	Total	
D·Green	USA	803	799	854	888	3344	
W·Harris	UK	756	852	728	887	3223	
S·Belossovski	Estonia	600	767	771	944	3082	
O·Ngecki	Zambia	699	823	659	803	2984	

FORMATTING THE TABLE

Once you have entered and organized the data in your table, the table itself can be formatted to emphasize different parts of the data and to improve the appearance of the table.

AUTOMATIC FORMATTING

Using Word's automatic formatting feature makes it easy to change the appearance of your table. Automatic formatting also helps you avoid "over-designing" the table, which can conceal data rather than making it more readable.

1 TABLE AUTOFORMAT
● Click anywhere in the table you wish to format.
● Click on **Table** in the Menu bar and select **Table AutoFormat** from the drop-down menu.

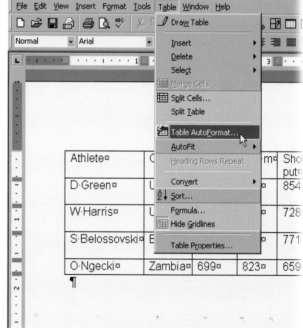

● The **Table AutoFormat** dialog box opens. The format selected by default is called **Simple 1**, and its appearance is shown in the **Preview** panel.

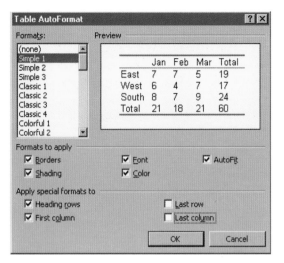

● There are a number of different styles of format, which you can scroll through and view to decide which style best suits your type of table.
● Click on the **Colorful 1** style of formatting and your table appears in that format.

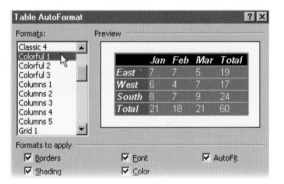

Athlete¤	Country¤	Javelin¤	100·m¤	Shot· put¤	High· jump¤	Total¤
D·Green¤	USA¤	803¤	799¤	854¤	888¤	3344¤
W·Harris¤	UK¤	756¤	852¤	728¤	887¤	3223¤
S·Belossovski¤	Estonia¤	600¤	767¤	771¤	944¤	3082¤
O·Ngecki¤	Zambia¤	699¤	823¤	659¤	803¤	2984¤

¶

2 AUTOFORMAT OPTIONS

● The predesigned formats can be used either as they are presented or they can be customized. There are two sections of the **Table AutoFormat** dialog box in which customized settings can be selected or excluded by clearing the relevant checkbox. In the **Formats to apply** section there are checkboxes for various effects to be applied or cancelled. In the **Apply special formats to** section, different parts of the table can be either included or excluded from the formatting of the table.

● In the sample table shown, the borders have been excluded.

● If you decide not to use AutoFormat, open the **Table AutoFormat** dialog box and in the **Formats** menu click on (**none**) and then click on **OK**. Your table is returned to its original format.

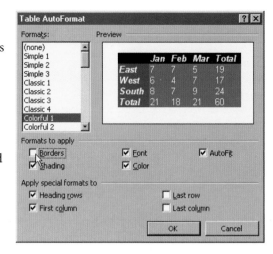

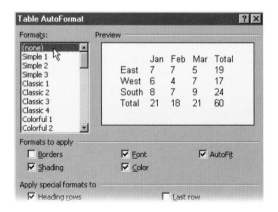

BORDERS AND LINES

To improve the appearance of a simple table, you may wish to give it a border, or gridlines, within the table, or to shade the whole table with a combination of colors. These options can easily be applied by using the **Borders and Shading** feature.

1 CHOOSING THE LINES TO CHANGE

● Click within the table and click on **Format** in the Menu bar.

● Click on **Borders and Shading** in the menu to open the **Borders and Shading** dialog box.

● Click on the **Borders** tab if that part of the dialog box is not displayed. The **Settings** section at the left of the box shows the border options. When you click on an option, the **Preview** panel shows how the setting affects the text.

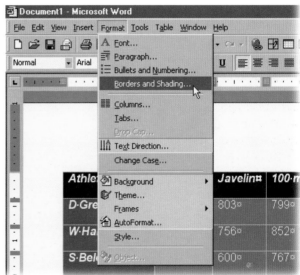

Box – *Only the outside of the table is given a border*

All – *The table and each cell has a border applied to it*

Grid – *The outside has the chosen border style and the cell borders are made bold*

Custom – *This option allows you to decide where you wish to have borders. This is the option we are going to use, so click on* **Custom**

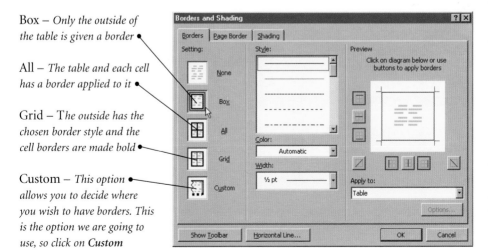

2 CHOOSING THE STYLE

● Click on the type of line you require by scrolling through the **Style** box.

● Click on the down arrow to the right of the **Color** text box, and a palette of colors drops down.

● Select one of the colors. Plum has been selected in the example, and it appears in the **Color** preview bar.

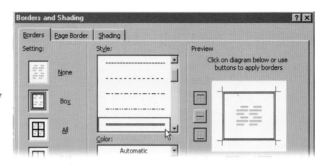

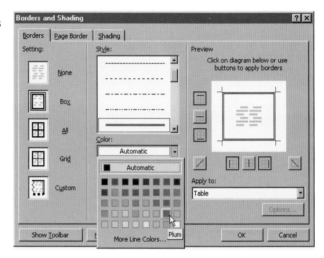

3 CHOOSING THE WIDTH

● Now choose the width of your line. (Note that not all lines are available in all widths. For example, the double wavy line is only available in the three-quarter point size.)

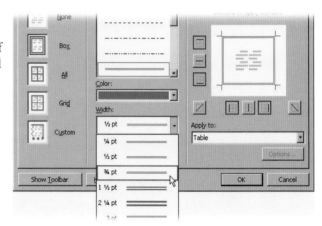

● By clicking on the boxes around the **Preview** panel (or on the diagram itself) you can decide where the lines are to appear.

● When you have selected a particular line for one part of the table, the same process can be used to select other lines for other areas of the table.

● When you have finished, click on **OK** and the lines are automatically applied to your table.

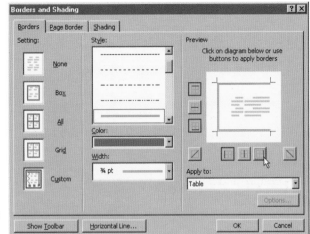

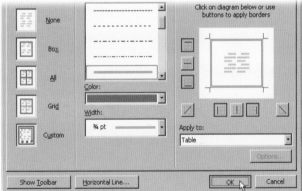

Athlete¤	Country¤	Javelin¤	100·m¤	Shot· put¤	High· jump¤	Total¤
D·Green¤	USA¤	803¤	799¤	854¤	888¤	3344¤
W·Harris¤	UK¤	756¤	852¤	728¤	887¤	3223¤
S·Belossovski¤	Estonia¤	600¤	767¤	771¤	944¤	3082¤
O·Ngecki¤	Zambia¤	699¤	823¤	659¤	803¤	2984¤

CHARTS AND GRAPHS

Another way of presenting data visually is by using a chart or graph. Word enables you to choose from a wide range of charts, or you can create and save your own chart designs.

BASIC CHART TERMS

This chapter takes you through creating, editing, and formatting simple charts and graphs. Before we create our first chart, a few chart terms need to be explained. The most important terms are Datasheet, Axis, Plot Area, and Data Series.

BASIC TERMINOLOGY

DATASHEET

The datasheet is just like a table of information, but it is linked directly to a chart or graph. Using the datasheet you can input your chart data and see it automatically appear on your chart. Every chart and graph has an associated datasheet, which is displayed each time you double-click on your chart.

AXIS

An axis is a line that borders one side of a chart and provides a means to compare different values and categories. In our "Student Classes" example, which is used later in this chapter, the vertical axis, otherwise called the Value (Y) axis, shows the numbers of students. The horizontal axis of the graph, known as the Category (X) axis, shows the types of students, that is, girls, boys, women, and men.

PLOT AREA

As the name suggests, this is the area of the chart where the actual data is plotted; the location of the plot area depends on the type of chart chosen. The examples in this chapter show plot areas where columns and tubes illustrate the graphs.

DATA SERIES

This is a group of related points in a chart that originates from the rows and columns held on the datasheet. It is easy to see a data series because each one has a unique color or pattern on the chart or graph. In our Student Classes example, we have four data series – one for each category of girls, boys, women, and men.

A CHART FROM A WORD TABLE

Here we convert the data held in the earlier table into a chart. Microsoft Graph 2000 only converts tables to charts where there is one heading row and only the first column is text. All of the other rows and columns must contain numbers.

1 CONVERTING THE TABLE

● Open the document containing the table you wish to convert to a chart.
● As only the first column can contain text, delete the Country column by selecting it, selecting **Delete** from the **Table** menu, and selecting **Columns** from the submenu.
● Now select the whole table ⬚.
● Click on the **Insert** menu and then select **Object**.

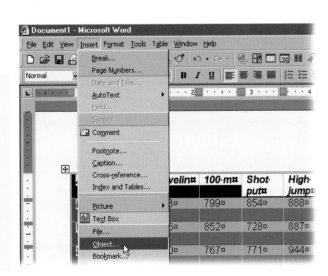

Athlete¤	Javelin¤	100-m¤	Shot put¤	High jump¤
D·Green¤	803¤	799¤	854¤	888¤
W·Harris¤	756¤	852¤	728¤	887¤
S·Belossovski¤	600¤	767¤	771¤	944¤
O·Ngecki¤	699¤	823¤	659¤	803¤

Existing data
Word 2000 allows you to convert existing data, held in tables, to a chart or graph; or you can set up a chart from scratch in just a few simple steps. You can also import data from other programs such as Microsoft Excel.

● The **Object** dialog box opens. If necessary, click on the **Create New** tab at the top of the dialog box to view its options.

● Scroll down through the options, click on **Microsoft Graph 2000 Chart**, and click on **OK**.

● Now there are two new panels on the screen – a datasheet and a column graph, both containing the data held in the table.

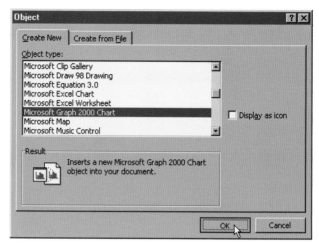

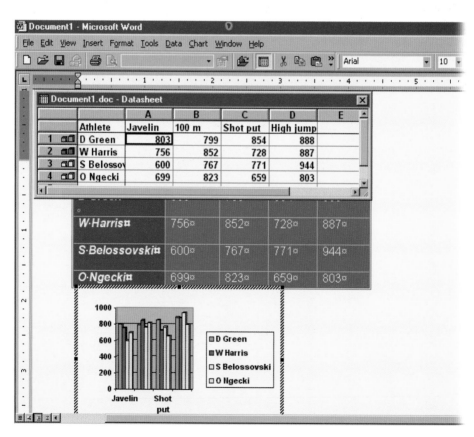

2 POSITIONING THE CHART

● The datasheet and the table occupy most of the visible area, making it difficult to move the chart anywhere. Remove them by first clicking on the **View Datasheet** icon on the Standard toolbar (or on **x** at the top right-hand corner of the datasheet window) to remove the datasheet from the screen.

● Now select the whole table and delete it by clicking on the **Table** menu followed by **Delete** and then **Table**.

● The chart automatically moves to the position occupied by the table.

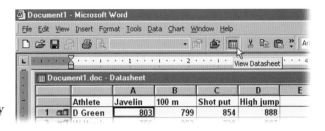

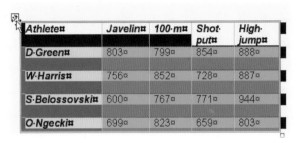

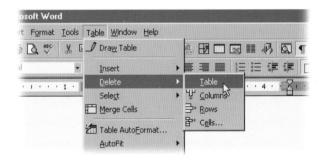

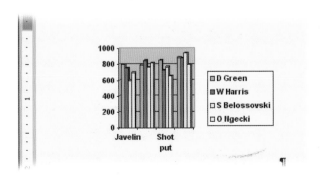

3 MOVING THE CHART

● If you wish to move the chart within the existing text on the page (which need only be paragraph marks), first click on the chart to select it.
● Hold down the mouse button and a small copy box appears below the mouse cursor.
● Drag the cursor to the new location and release the mouse button.
● To move the chart across the page to the right, press the [Tab⇄] key.
● To relocate the chart back across the page to the left, hold down the [⇧ Shift] key and press the [Tab⇄] key.

Cut and paste charts

If you wish to move a chart across several pages in a document, cut and paste is quicker than manually dragging the chart. Click on the chart to select it, click on **Edit** in the Menu bar and select **Cut** from the drop-down menu; the chart is placed on the clipboard. Move the insertion point to the new position for the chart and click on **Paste** in the **Edit** menu.

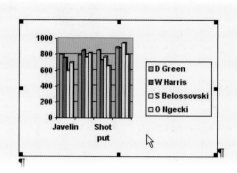

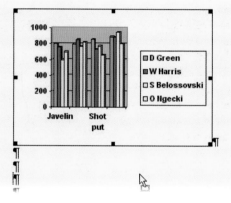

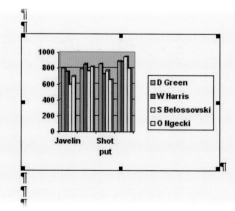

4 DIFFERENT CHARTS

The standard columns chart does not show the data in the table very clearly, and a different chart can be selected.

- Double-click on the chart. The word **Chart** appears on the Menu bar and the datasheet reappears. The chart now has a thicker border showing that it can now be edited and is not simply selected as before.

- As it's not necessary to display the datasheet for selecting a chart type, close it by clicking on the **View Datasheet** icon on the Standard toolbar or click on the **x** button on the datasheet.

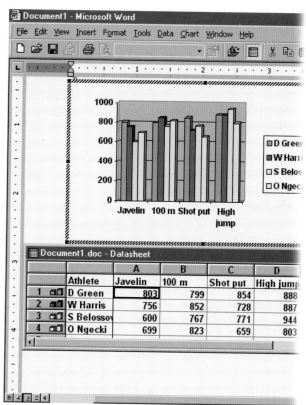

	Athlete	Javelin	100 m	Shot put	High jump
1	D Green	803	799	854	888
2	W Harris	756	852	728	887
3	S Belossov	600	767	771	944
4	O Ngecki	699	823	659	803

Click to close the datasheet

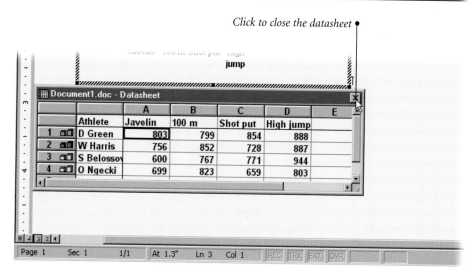

	Athlete	Javelin	100 m	Shot put	High jump	E
1	D Green	803	799	854	888	
2	W Harris	756	852	728	887	
3	S Belossov	600	767	771	944	
4	O Ngecki	699	823	659	803	

● Click on **Chart** on the
Menu bar, followed by
Chart Type.

● The **Chart Type** dialog
box opens. If necessary,
click on the **Standard Types**
tab at the top of the dialog
box. **Column** is highlighted
in the **Chart Type** menu
because it is the default
chart type, which is why
the table was first converted
into a chart with columns.

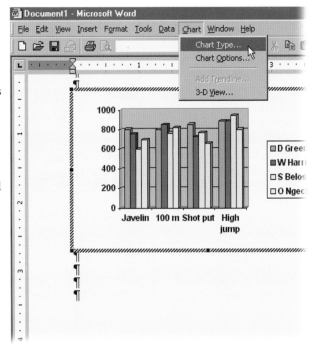

*Column selected as
the default chart type*

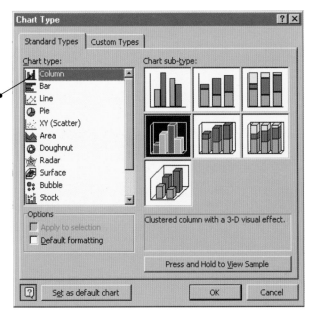

● Click on the **Cone** chart option on the left and select one of the subtypes on the right.

● Click on the **Press and Hold to View Sample** button at the foot of the window and hold down the mouse button. The data is shown in the chart format that you have selected.

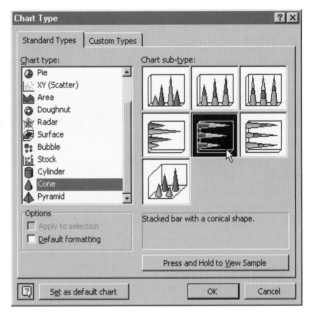

Tip
If the chart seems to be missing some text or data, it could be because it needs to be enlarged ◁.

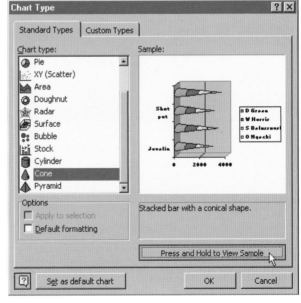

◁ 170 **Resizing the Chart**

5 CUSTOM CHARTS

● If none of the **Standard Types** of charts seems to display the data as you require, you can investigate the **Custom Types** on the next tab in the dialog box.

● Click on the **Custom Types** tab at the top of the dialog box.

● Scroll through the options available on the left of the dialog box. With these charts, the table data is automatically displayed in the **Sample** panel.

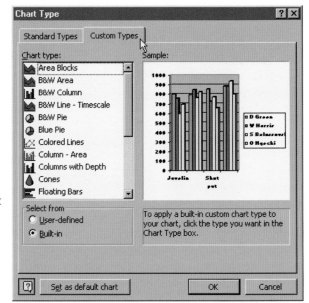

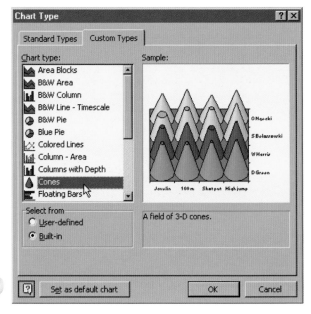

- The **Columns with Depth** option appears to show the table data more clearly, and this is the one that is to be used.
- Click on **Columns with Depth** and then **OK**. The chart is now showing the data in this type.

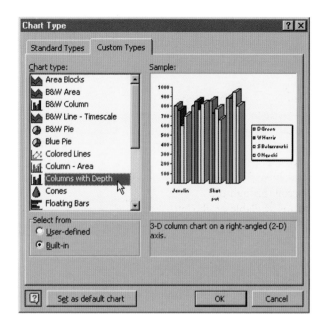

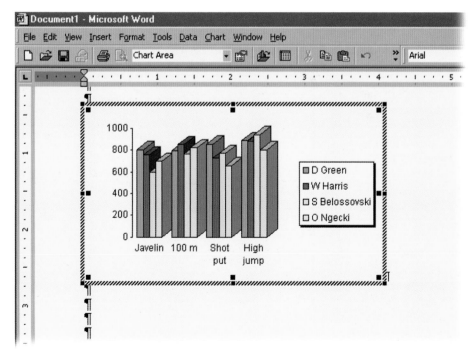

CREATING A CHART FROM SCRATCH

If you want to create a chart from scratch and enter data not held anywhere in the computer, you can do this by using the **Microsoft Graph 2000 Chart**. The program provides a sample chart and datasheet containing dummy information to help show you where you can enter your own column headings, rows, and data. This part of the book also covers some of the basic editing that you can do.

1 GETTING THE SAMPLE CHART

● Click in the document where you wish to position your chart.
● Click on the **Insert** menu and then on **Object**.

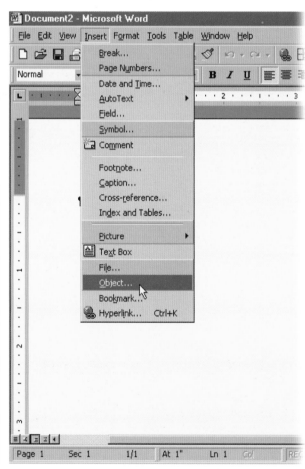

Choosing the view

If you want to be able to switch between the chart and datasheet without hiding the datasheet, just click on the chart or datasheet and both remain visible. If the datasheet is not visible, just click on the **View Datasheet** icon on the Standard toolbar. You can also click this icon to remove the datasheet from the screen when necessary.

● The **Object** dialog box opens. If necessary, click on the **Create New** tab.

● Scroll down the **Object type** menu and click on **Microsoft Graph 2000 Chart** and click on **OK**.

● Two new windows open on-screen – a datasheet and a column graph, both containing sample data.

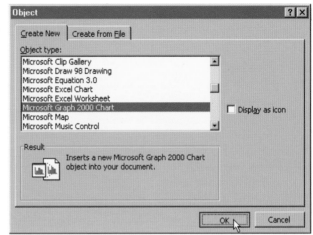

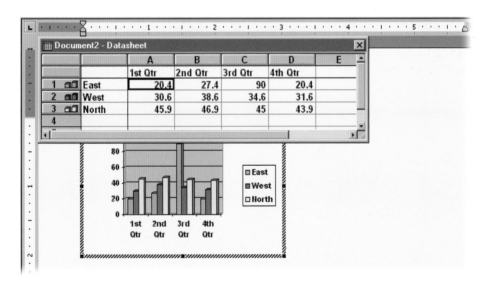

2 ENTERING DATA

● On the datasheet, click on the first column heading and enter the heading.

● Continue to add the information into the cells of the datasheet.

		A	B	C	D
		Girls	Boys	Women	Men
1	Yoga	20	39	45	23
2	Fencing	12	45	38	29
3	Painting	27	19	47	50
4	Driving	21	29	20	49
5					

Document1 - Datasheet

3 RESIZING THE CHART

● Currently the chart is too small to see all the data.

● Close the datasheet by clicking on the **View Datasheet** button.

● Place the mouse cursor over the right handle, hold down the mouse button, and drag the edge of the chart to the right.

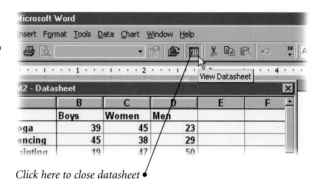

Microsoft Word

Insert Format Tools Data Chart Window Help

View Datasheet

t2 - Datasheet

	B	C	D	E	F
	Boys	Women	Men		
oga	39	45	23		
encing	45	38	29		
ainting	19	47	50		

Click here to close datasheet ●

Document2 - Microsoft Word

File Edit View Insert Format Tools Data Chart Window Help

Walls

□ Yoga
■ Fencing
□ Painting
□ Driving

Girls   Women

● When the chart is large enough to display all the information, release the mouse button and click off the chart to see the effect.

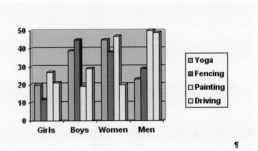

4 A DIFFERENT CHART TYPE

● To select a different chart type, first double-click on the chart and close the datasheet in the usual way if it appears.

● Click on **Chart** in the Menu bar and from the list select **Chart Type**.

● The **Chart Type** dialog box opens. Click on the **Custom Types** tab.

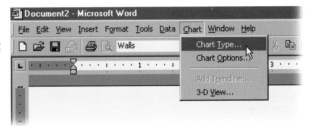

*The **Custom Types** tab*

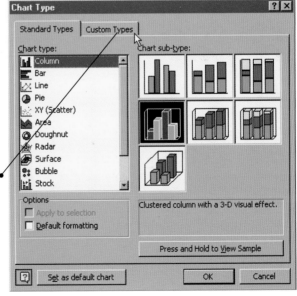

5 SELECTING A CHART TYPE

● Select the chart type that best suits your data ⬆. The chart chosen here is **Tubes** from the menu.

● Click on **OK** when you are satisfied with the type of chart chosen.

*Choosing **Tubes** from the list of chart types* ●

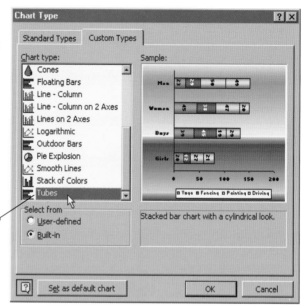

Moving the datasheet

Sometimes you might want to move the datasheet out of the way so that you can see the chart and the datasheet at the same time. Place the mouse cursor over the Title bar of the datasheet – the blue band at the top – and hold down the mouse button. Drag the datasheet to its new location and release the mouse button.

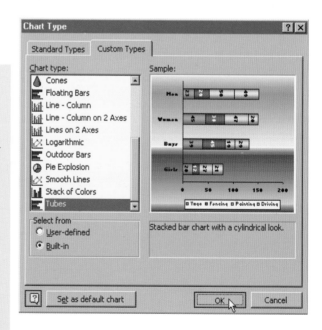

166 **Custom Charts**

● Your chart is automatically displayed in the new format.

● If you want to change the data in your graph, double-click on the graph, click on the **View Datasheet** button if the datasheet does not appear, and amend the data as described above.

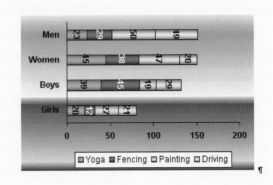

6 CHOOSING CHART OPTIONS

● Now that you have set up the basic chart or graph, you may wish to add a title to the chart and have text against each of the axes. The Microsoft Graph 2000 Chart program contains standard options that allow you to add further details to your chart or graph.

● If **Chart** is not already displayed on the Menu bar, double-click on the chart.

● Click on **Chart** on the Menu bar followed by **Chart Options**.

● The **Chart Options** dialog box opens.

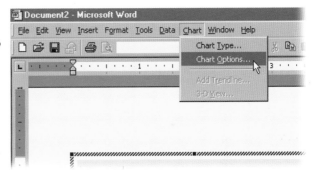

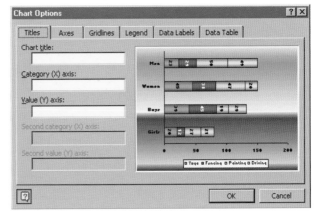

7 ENTERING TITLES

● Click on the **Titles** tab if it is not displayed, and in the first text box named **Chart title** enter a title for the chart, for example, **Student Classes**.

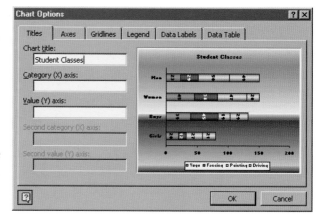

● Click in the next box, **Category (X) axis**. The title **Student Classes** appears at the top of the graph image at right.

● Enter the text for the **Category (X) axis**, for example **Student Type**.

● The X-axis is always along the *logical* bottom of the graph – in this case on the left side of the graph at the end of the tubes.

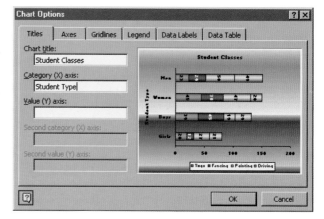

● Click on the **Value (Y) axis** text box and enter **Numbers of Students**.

Y-axis label ●——

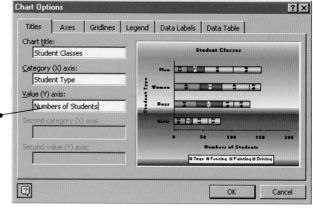

● If you wish to make any changes to the text, just highlight the text in the box and key in the new text. Let's change the X-axis text to **Type of Student**.

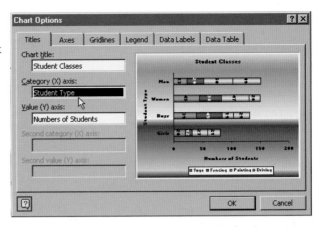

Tip
If at any time you press the [Enter ←] key by mistake before completing all of the options, don't worry. Just double-click on the chart and continue as described above.

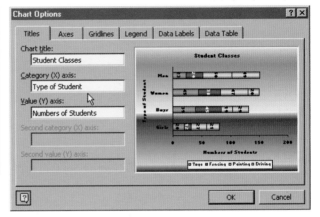

8 CUSTOMIZING THE AXES

● There are a number of options available with which you can manipulate the axes.
● Begin by clicking on the **Axes** tab.

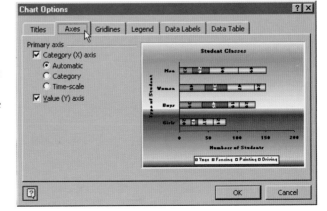

● The **Primary Axis, Category (X) axis** is normally checked. In the example, it details the categories of Girls, Boys, Women, and Men. If you click the **Category (X)** box off, the categories do not appear on your graph.

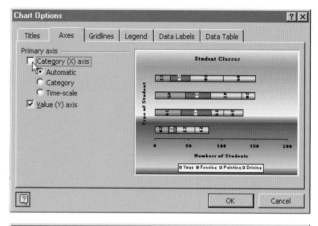

● Similarly, the **Value (Y) axis** may also be clicked off. In our example, it is showing the total number of students by type.

Rules of axes

When designing a chart, the conventions that are usually followed are that the Y-axis is the value axis along which data values are shown, and the X-axis shows the categories to which the data values apply.

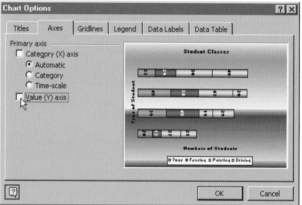

9 ADDING GRIDLINES

● Gridlines can make your chart more readable. To access them, click on the **Gridlines** tab.

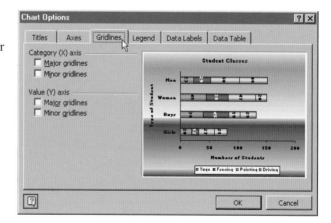

● There are **Major** and **Minor gridlines** available for both the Category (X) axis and Value (Y) axis.

● On this occasion, let's just leave on the **Major gridlines** on the Value (Y) axis.

● Click on **OK** to close the **Chart Options** box and click off the chart to see the effects of the gridlines.

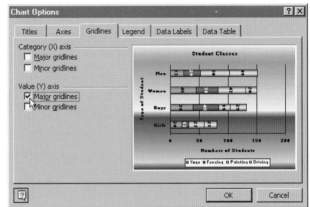

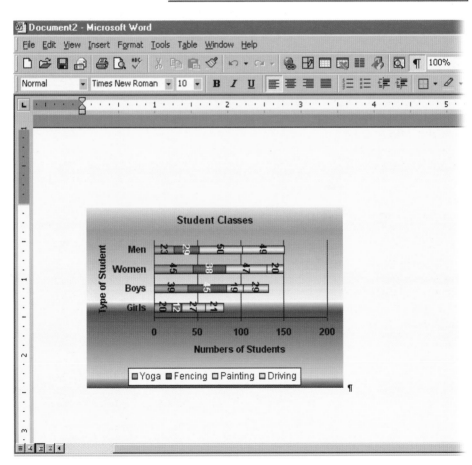

EDITING THE CHART

This chapter covers manipulating data in the datasheet which is then reflected in the chart. You can also add and delete columns and rows of data, as well as editing text on the chart.

ADDING ROWS

1 LOCATION OF THE NEW ROW

● If you need to add data to a chart, you might need to add rows for new data.

● Double-click on the chart if the **Chart** menu options are not already available in the Menu bar.

● Click on the **View Datasheet** icon on the Menu bar if the datasheet is not on the screen.

● Hold the mouse arrow over the row heading until it turns into a white cross.

● Click on the row heading below where you wish the new row to be inserted.

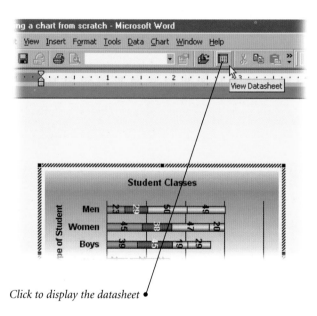

Click to display the datasheet ●

2 ADDING DATA TO THE NEW ROW

● Click on **Insert** on the Menu bar, and then **Cells**.
● A new row is inserted into the datasheet and you can now fill the row with your additional data. The data is immediately shown on the chart.

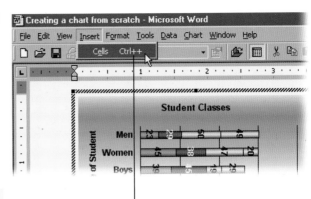

This option adds new cells ●

Adding columns

You can add columns to the datasheet by clicking on the column heading to the right of where you want a new column. Click on **Insert** in the Menu bar and then on **Cells**. The new column appears in the datasheet.

		A	B	C	D
		Girls	Boys	Women	Men
1	Yoga	20	39	45	23
2	Fencing	12	45	38	29
3	Aquafit	26	10	34	24
4	Painting	27	19	47	50
5	Driving	21	29	20	49
6					

Creating a chart from scra... - Datasheet

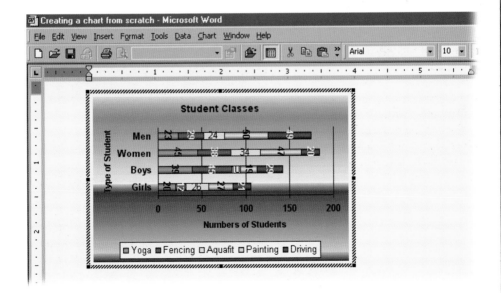

EDITING THE CHART AND TEXT

You might want to alter parts of the chart, such as the title, or the Value Y and Category X axis labels, without having to use the Microsoft Graph 2000 Chart program. It is possible to do this by working directly on the chart itself.

1 SELECT THE TEXT TO BE CHANGED

● Double-click on the chart to select it. If the datasheet appears, close it in the usual way.

● Hold the mouse cursor over the title of the chart and the words **Chart Title** are displayed.

● Click on the chart title, which will now be enclosed inside a text box.

● Enter the new title.

● Press the [Esc] key twice.

● The chart now shows the new title.

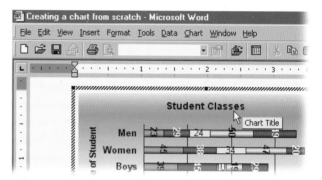

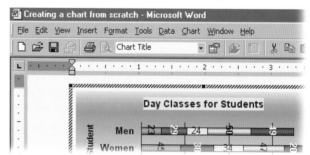

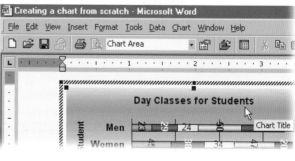

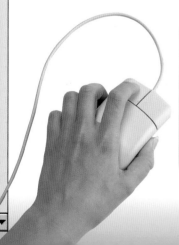

2 SELECTING OTHER CHART ITEMS

● You can select any part of the chart by using the **Chart Objects** box below the Menu bar at the top of the screen. Let's just look at the Plot Area – the background of the chart – and change the Chart Type.

● Double-click on the chart and the chart menu bar is displayed.

● Click on the black arrow to the right of the **Chart Objects** box and the list of chart objects is displayed.

● Click on the item you wish to see on the chart. Let's choose the **Plot Area** of the chart.

● Note that the Plot Area now has a border around it.

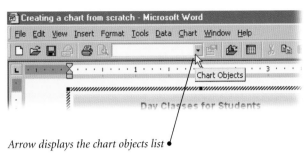

Arrow displays the chart objects list

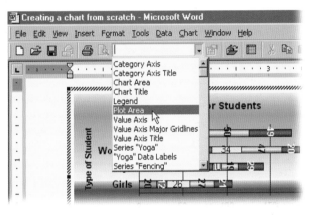

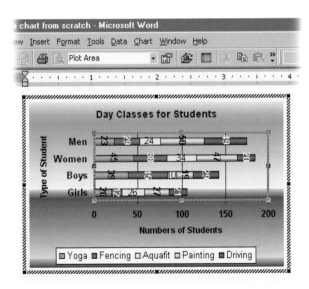

Tip
To revert to an original chart type, click on **Edit** on the Menu bar and select **Undo Chart Type** from the list of actions.

3 CHANGING THE CHART TYPE

● Double-click on the chart and click on **Chart** on the Menu bar.

● Select **Chart Type** to open the **Chart** dialog box.

● Scroll through the **Chart Type** menu and select a different style of chart. **Column - Area** is the type of chart selected here.

● Click on **OK** and the data is now plotted in a different chart type.

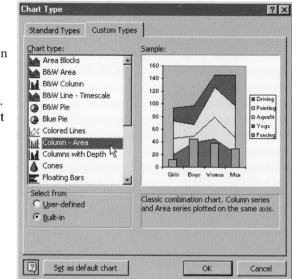

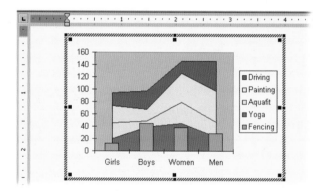

4 SAVING FOR FUTURE USE

● Later in the book (page 186), we customize the appearance of a chart using this chart type from the **Columns** options. If you wish, you can change your chart to this type and save it for later use.

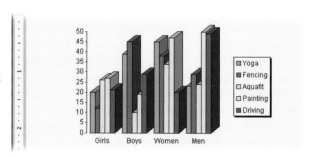

Deleting Data and Deleting Charts

Your chart may contain data that is no longer relevant. A quick way to delete data from a chart is to delete it from the datasheet. This section shows you how to delete data by using this method, and finally shows you how to delete a chart.

1 DELETING DATA

● Double-click on the chart if the **Chart** option is not displayed on the Menu bar.

● Click on the **View Datasheet** icon on the Standard toolbar so that the datasheet is again shown on-screen below the chart.

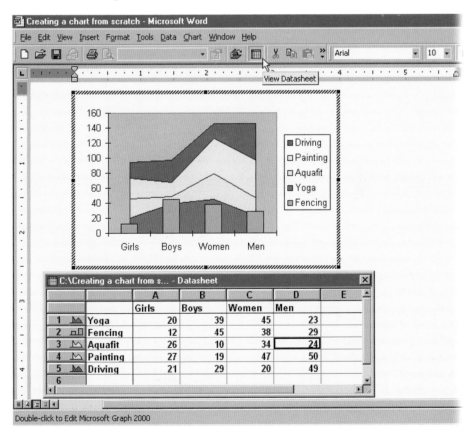

2 SELECTING AND DELETING DATA

● Position the cursor over a lettered column heading until the cursor turns into a white cross.

● Hold down the mouse button and drag the mouse to the left (or right) to highlight the columns to be deleted and release the mouse button.

● Click on **Edit** on the Menu bar and select **Delete**.

● The highlighted columns are now deleted from the datasheet, and the chart is redrawn accordingly.

● Similarly, you can click on row headings and carry out the same steps to delete rows of data from a datasheet and the chart.

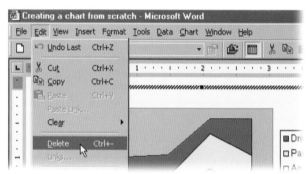

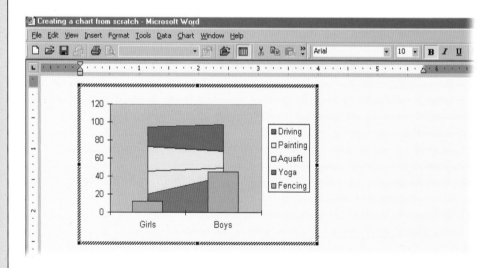

3 DELETING A CHART

● If you need to delete a chart from your document, you can easily do this. User-defined charts can also be deleted easily.

● Click once on the chart to be deleted, so that there is a thin black line surrounding it.

● Click on the **Cut** icon on the Standard toolbar and your chart is deleted.

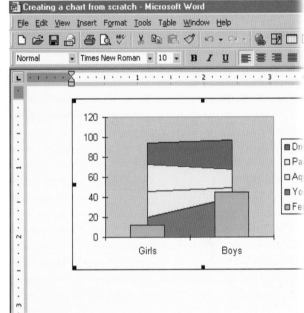

● Now go to the **Edit** menu in the toolbar and select **Cut** from the pull-down menu. The chart is now deleted from the document.

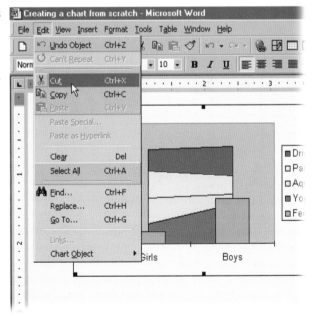

FORMATTING CHARTS

Using the formatting features of Word 2000, you can make any chart or graph look professional and give maximum visual impact to your data.

COLORS, BORDERS, AND BACKGROUNDS

This section of the book covers some of the main formatting features including customizing the border, adding colors, patterns, and backgrounds to charts, selecting gradients of color, and customizing the shading and texture.

1 SELECTING THE PLOT AREA

● If you saved the chart from page 182, open it to follow these steps. We'll alter the look of the chart by changing the Plot Area.

● Double-click on the chart and, if necessary, remove the datasheet from the screen.

● Move the mouse arrow over the main area of the chart until the **Plot Area** ScreenTip is displayed.

● Click once and the Plot Area is surrounded by a gray border showing that it has been selected.

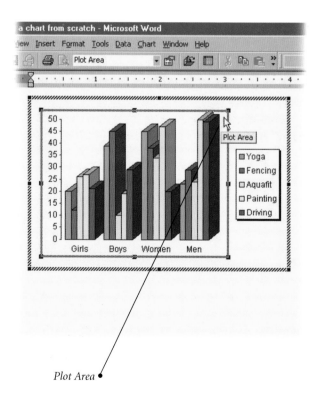

Plot Area ●

2 THE PLOT AREA DIALOG BOX

● Click on **Format** in the Menu bar and choose **Selected Plot Area** as the area to be formatted.
● The **Format Plot Area** dialog box opens with the **Patterns** tab at the top.

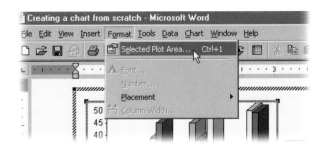

3 CUSTOMIZING THE BORDER

● To design your own border, begin by clicking on the **Custom** radio button.
● The first element of the border that can be decided on is the **Style**. Click on the down arrow to the right of the **Style** box to view a drop-down menu of the different styles of borders that are available. Select one by clicking on it.
● The **Sample** panel at the foot of the dialog box displays your selection.

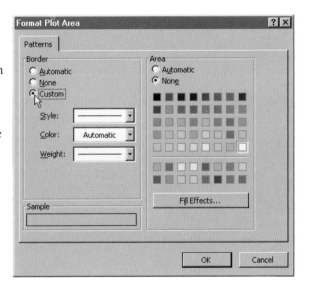

4 SELECTING THE COLOR

● The border can be given a color by first clicking on the arrow to the right of the **Color** box. A color palette drops down.

● A color is selected by clicking on it. Your choice appears in the **Color** box and as a border in the **Sample** box.

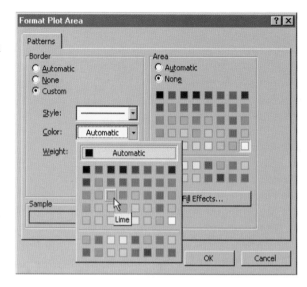

5 SELECTING THE WEIGHT

● The thickness of a border is known as its weight. Click on the down arrow to the right of the **Weight** box and select one of the options, which again is shown in the **Sample** box.

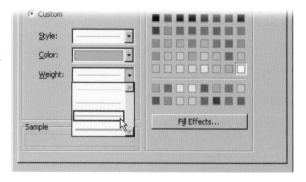

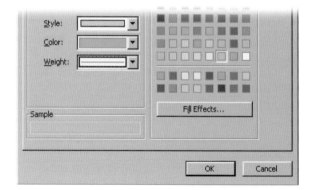

6 SELECTING A FILL AND AN EFFECT

- You can choose a solid-color fill by clicking on a color in the **Area** palette. Here we have selected one of the yellows.

- There also different background effects to choose from. Click on the **Fill Effects** button bar.

- The **Fill Effects** dialog box opens with four tabs along the top, each of which offers a selection of different effects. The **Gradient** tab is selected when you first open the dialog box.

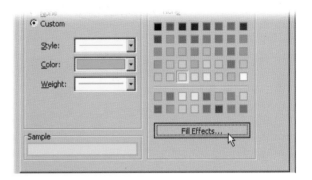

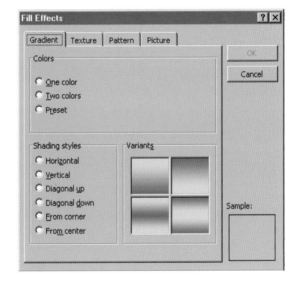

LAST CALL

It should be noted that it is always the last format choice that is applied to your chart. If you have made selections under the **Gradient** tab and then made further choices under the **Shading Style** tab, the **Shading Style** choices supersede the **Gradient** once you have clicked on OK. This is also true for any choices made under **Textures**, **Patterns**, or **Pictures**. You must have your chosen color format showing on the screen when you click on OK.

7 CUSTOMIZING THE GRADIENT

● If you click on **One Color**, and you have chosen a color previously, that color is displayed in the **Color 1** box.

● To change the color, click on the down arrow to the right of the **Color 1** box and the standard colors are displayed. You can choose a different color from here.

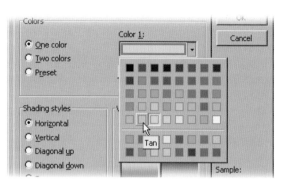

● To make the colors darker or lighter, drag the **Dark/Light** scroll bar to the right or left, or click on the **Dark** or **Light** arrows.

● If you click on **Two Colors**, you can choose a second color that will be combined with **Color 1**.

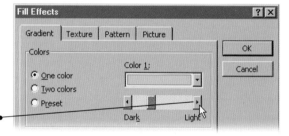

Lighten the color selection ●

Choices recorded

If you choose a **Preset** design, and then click on the **One** or **Two Color** buttons, the choice you made under **Preset** is still available.

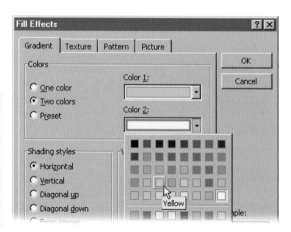

- If you click on **Preset**, you are given a large number of predesigned color combinations that you may choose from for your chart. The Preset colors **Daybreak** are shown in the example.

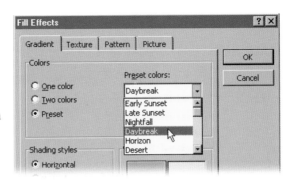

SELECTING A SHADING STYLE

- Click on each shading style in turn and the **Variants** preview panel displays your selection.
- As each one is chosen, it is displayed in the **Sample** box in the bottom right-hand corner of the window. In our example, we have chosen **From center**.

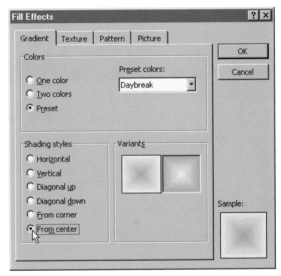

8 SELECTING A TEXTURE

- Click on the **Texture** tab at the top of the dialog box.
- Scroll up and down the texture choices to see the options that are available.

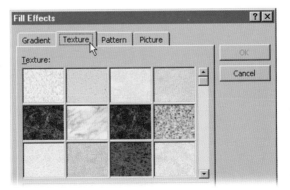

● The selection is shown in the **Sample** box at the bottom right-hand corner of the window.

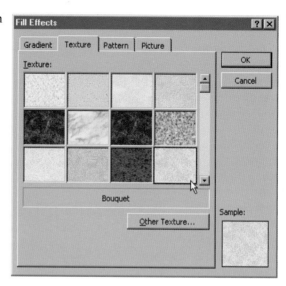

9 SELECTING A PATTERN

● Click on the **Pattern** tab at the top of the dialog box.
● Click on your preferred choice of pattern.
● The selection is again shown in the **Sample** box at the bottom right-hand corner of the dialog box.

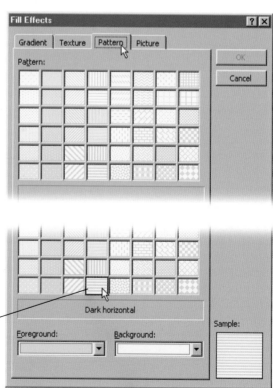

Selected pattern ●

● When you have made your final choice, click on **OK** and you are returned to the **Format Plot Area** dialog box.

● The sample shown on the bottom left-hand side of the dialog box displays your final choice of border and fill effect.

● Click on **OK** to close the dialog box.

● Click off the chart to see the results of the color combination you have chosen.

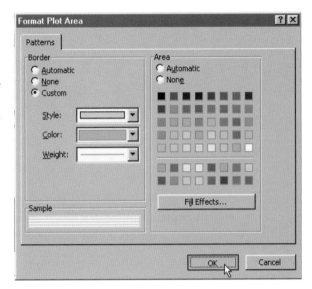

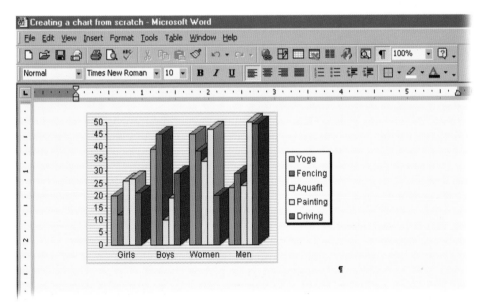

DRAWING WITH WORD

MOST PEOPLE ARE UNAWARE that, as well as being a powerful word-processing program, Word also contains a drawing capability. For various reasons, this aspect of Word is not as well understood as it deserves to be. This section attempts to redress that deficiency. To get the very best from this part of the book, some knowledge of the program will be useful. Even if you are new to Word, you will still be able to work through the operations shown, but you might find it useful first to read the first two sections of this book, which deal with the program's more basic features.

THE DRAWING TOOLS

The tools that are used in drawing with Word are all contained in dedicated toolbars, although some of the formatting commands are carried out by using the Formatting toolbar.

WHAT CAN I DRAW WITH WORD?

Word-processing programs once did exactly that – simply processed words. However, the features that have evolved and are now contained in Microsoft Word 2000 go far beyond the original, and limited, capabilities of early text processing. Microsoft Word does not pretend to be a cutting-edge, graphics-development tool. Instead, it contains the essential means for enhancing your documents with tools to create basic lines, curves, and freehand shapes. In addition, Word contains predesigned shapes that can be resized and layered to suit particular needs. Once the basic shapes have been created, there are several effects that can be applied to them including highly flexible 3-D effects, lighting, shadows, colors, and the integration of text and graphics.

FLEXIBLE INTEGRATION

With the integration of formattable text and extremely flexible graphics manipulation, Microsoft Word gives you the opportunity to combine images and words in ways that will suit the demands of most small-scale document production.

THE EFFECTS TOOLBARS

Two of the effects that are available when drawing with Word are the 3-D effect and the shadow effect. Both of these effects have their own toolbars containing buttons for modifying the effect. The toolbars are accessed via their respective buttons on the **Drawing** toolbar 📄, then clicking on **Settings** in the pop-up menu.

3-D SETTINGS TOOLBAR

This toolbar lets you control aspects of the 3-D effect, such as tilt, the depth and direction of the 3-D effect, how the object is illuminated, and its surface texture and color.

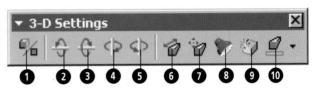

THE 3-D SETTINGS TOOLBAR

❶ 3-D On/Off	❻ Depth
❷ Tilt Down	❼ Direction
❸ Tilt Up	❽ Lighting
❹ Tilt Left	❾ Surface
❺ Tilt Right	❿ 3-D Color

SHADOW SETTINGS TOOLBAR

Applying a shadow to a drawing object is an alternative method of adding depth to the object. The toolbar provides tools to move and color the shadow effect.

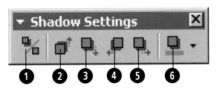

THE SHADOW SETTINGS TOOLBAR

❶ Shadow On/Off	❹ Nudge Shadow Left
❷ Nudge Shadow Up	❺ Nudge Shadow Right
❸ Nudge Shadow Down	❻ Shadow Color

199 **The Drawing Toolbar**

THE WORD TOOLBARS

The two principal toolbars that are used in drawing with Word are the **Formatting** toolbar and the **Drawing** toolbar. In the context of using Word to create drawings, the **Formatting** toolbar is mainly used to format text when it is being integrated with graphics or images. The **Drawing** toolbar contains all the tools that you are likely to need to create shapes, incorporate images, change line styles, and select a variety of effects to add to your drawings. There is no need to attempt to memorize each of these commands; the important factor is to be aware that they are available.

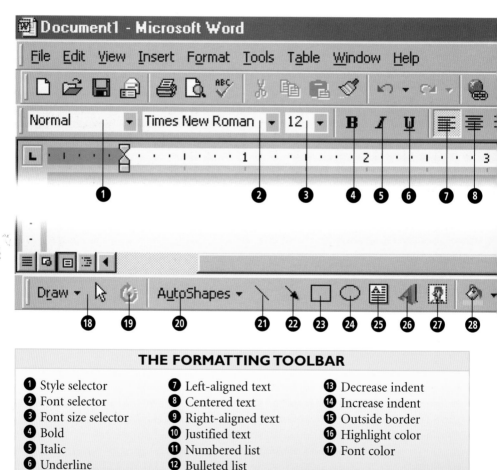

THE FORMATTING TOOLBAR

❶ Style selector
❷ Font selector
❸ Font size selector
❹ Bold
❺ Italic
❻ Underline
❼ Left-aligned text
❽ Centered text
❾ Right-aligned text
❿ Justified text
⓫ Numbered list
⓬ Bulleted list
⓭ Decrease indent
⓮ Increase indent
⓯ Outside border
⓰ Highlight color
⓱ Font color

TOOLBAR LAYOUT

For a variety of reasons that depend on settings, the toolbars and ruler in Word may adopt any one of a number of different layouts. If Word doesn't show the **Formatting** toolbar above the ruler as shown here, first place the cursor over the **Formatting** toolbar "handle" at the end of the toolbar. When the four-headed arrow appears, (right) hold down the mouse button, and drag the toolbar into position.

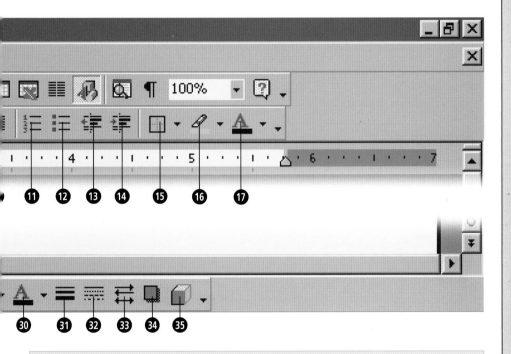

THE DRAWING TOOLBAR

18 Select objects
19 Free rotate
20 AutoShapes menu
21 Line
22 Arrow
23 Rectangle

24 Oval
25 Text box
26 Insert WordArt
27 Insert Clip Art
28 Fill color
29 Line color

30 Font color
31 Line style
32 Dash style
33 Arrow style
34 Shadow effects
35 3-D effects

LINES AND CURVES

The name that Word 2000 gives to all the marks and shapes used in drawing with Word is "drawing objects." The most common drawing objects that you will use are lines and curves.

PRINT LAYOUT VIEW AND THE DRAWING TOOLBAR

When working only with text in Word, it is usually enough to use the **Normal** view. But when drawing in Word 2000, your document needs to be displayed in **Print** **Layout View**. Select this option either from the **View** drop-down menu or from the **Print Layout View** button at the bottom-left of the document window.

THE DRAWING TOOLBAR

● The majority of the actions to be carried out in drawing with Word are selected from the Drawing toolbar. You can display this toolbar in one of several ways. The first is to click on **View** in the Menu bar, select **Toolbars**, and click on **Drawing** in the submenu.

● The **Drawing** toolbar can also be displayed by clicking on the **Drawing** button on the **Standard** toolbar.

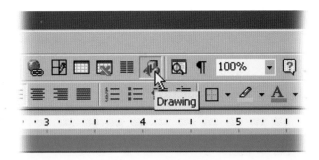

● Alternatively, right-click on an empty area of a toolbar and click on the **Drawing** option from the menu that appears.

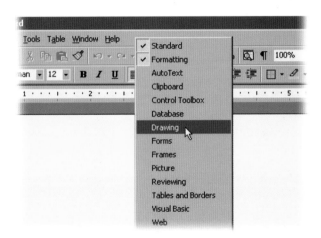

● When the toolbar appears, it may be "floating" in the document window. You might find it easier to work if the toolbar is "docked" at the foot of the window. To do this, place the cursor over the blue title bar at the top of the toolbar. Hold down the left mouse button and drag the toolbar until it locks into position below the document window.

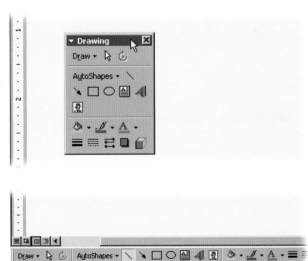

DRAWING THE LINES

The **AutoShapes** button on the **Drawing** toolbar contains most of the drawing objects that you will use. The objects range from simple lines to shapes that are tailor-made for specific uses, but lines and freeforms are where most people begin.

1 SELECTING THE LINE OPTION

- To draw a line, begin by clicking on **AutoShapes** in the **Drawing** toolbar.
- In the pop-up menu, select **Lines** and click the **Line** button in the submenu.
- The menu closes and the arrow cursor changes to a crosshair cursor.
- Move the crosshair to the position where you want the line to begin, hold down the left mouse button, drag the cursor to the point where the line is to end, and release the mouse button.
- The line appears on the page with handles at each end and an anchor icon on the left-hand edge of the page. The handles can be clicked on to resize and move the line. The anchor indicates whether the line is locked to another object or to a paragraph.

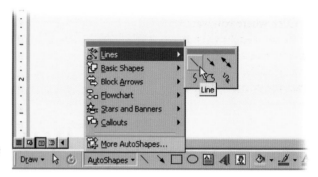

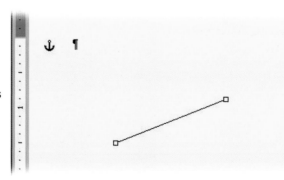

2 INSERTING A CURVE

● To draw a curve, click on **AutoShapes** on the **Drawing** toolbar, select **Lines**, and then click on the **Curve** button.

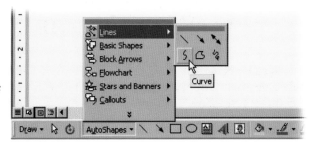

● Click where you want the curve to begin, drag the mouse to start the curve, and left-click where you want the curve to bend.

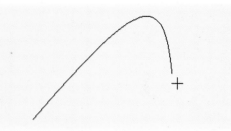

● To finish drawing the curve, double-click with the mouse. (If you want to close the shape, click near its starting point.) The curve then appears surrounded by eight handles.

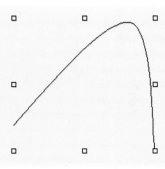

● Click off the curve to deselect it.

FREEFORM DRAWING OBJECTS

Lines and curves have their uses, but they also have their limitations as far as flexibility is concerned. Word contains a feature, called freeform, which allows you to combine both straight lines and curves in one drawing object. However, it is notoriously difficult to achieve perfect results with a freeform on the first attempt.

SELECTING FREEFORM

- On the **Drawing** toolbar, select **AutoShapes,** select **Lines,** and then select **Freeform.**
- Move the cursor to the position on the page where the freeform is to begin.

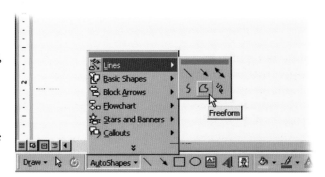

- To draw a straight line section of the freeform, left-click once, and drag the mouse.

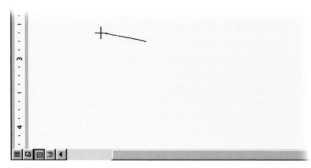

- To draw a curved section freehand, hold down the left mouse button, the cursor changes to a pencil, and drag to draw a shape.

● The freeform can be ended either as an open shape, where the ends do not meet, or as a closed shape, where they do.

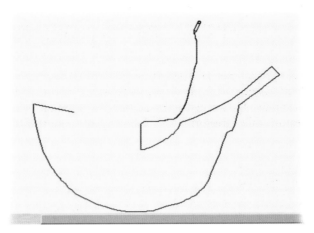

Finishing an open freeform

To finish drawing an open freeform, double-click the left mouse button. The freeform disappears briefly while Word computes its shape and then it reappears.

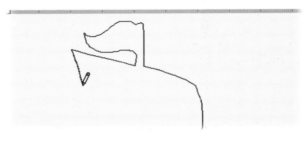

● The method of finishing a closed shape once the endpoint reaches the starting point depends on whether you are in freehand mode or are drawing a straight line.

● If you are in freehand mode with the mouse button held down, release the mouse button. If you are drawing a straight line when closing the shape, left-click once.

USING ENCLOSED SHAPES

The most commonly used shapes in drawing in Word are enclosed shapes. As well as standard circles, ovals, squares, and rectangles, there are a number of other shapes available.

OVALS AND RECTANGLES

The most basic enclosed shapes are ovals and rectangles. Word contains buttons on the **Drawing** toolbar that allow these shapes to be drawn and then resized, by using their handles, according to the requirements of your document and text.

1 ADDING OVALS

● To add an oval shape, click on the **Oval** button on the **Drawing** toolbar.

● As you move the cursor onto the document, the cursor changes into a cross-hair. Place the cursor at the approximate point where you want the oval to appear. Hold down the left mouse button and drag the mouse to draw the oval.

● Release the mouse button when the oval is the size you want. The oval appears surrounded by eight handles.

● Click off the oval to remove the handles from the display.

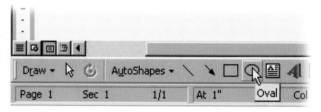

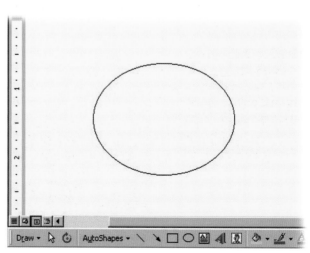

2 ADDING RECTANGLES

● To add a rectangle, click on the **Rectangle** button on the **Drawing** toolbar.

● Place the cursor where you want one of the corners of the rectangle to appear on the page. Hold down the left mouse button and drag the mouse to draw the rectangle.

● Release the mouse button when the rectangle is the size you want.

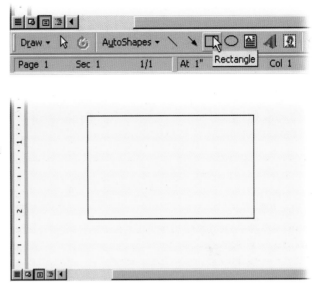

INSERTING AN AUTOSHAPE

There are a number of predesigned shapes, known as **AutoShapes**, that are available in Word. From this wide range of shapes, you can select and draw the shape, then resize and reshape it according to what you need.

AUTOSHAPE SELECTION

● Click **AutoShapes** on the **Drawing** toolbar, point to **Basic Shapes**, and from the menu that appears, select a shape by clicking on it.

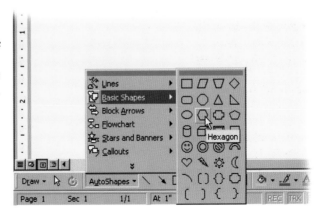

● Position the cursor in the
document window where
the shape is to appear, hold
down the left mouse button
and drag the mouse to
draw the shape.
● Release the mouse
button when you have the
required shape.

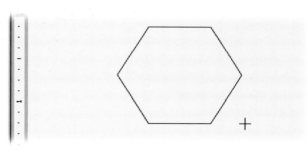

Predefined sizes
To insert an enclosed
shape with a predefined
size, select the shape
and simply left-click in
the document window.

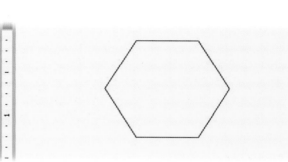

RESIZING AUTOSHAPES

AutoShapes can be resized by using one of
several methods. Precise resizing can be
done via a dialog box, where you can also
preserve the height and width ratio of the
shape. Other resizing options include
vertical, horizontal, and from the center.

1 RESIZING BY A PERCENTAGE
● Select the AutoShape
that you want to resize by
placing the cursor either
over one of its lines or
within the shape and left-
clicking.
● From the **Format** menu,
click on **AutoShape** in the
drop-down menu.

● The **Format AutoShape** dialog box opens with several tabs along the top, which contain different options. Click on the **Size** tab to the right of the **Colors and Lines** tab.

The Size tab ●

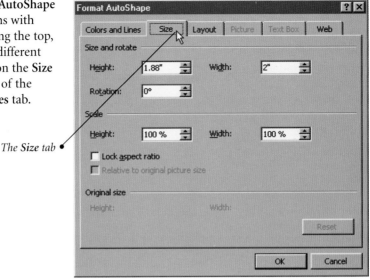

● Under **Scale**, enter the percentages that you want in the **Height** and **Width** boxes and click on **OK**.

● To retain the ratio in the AutoShape between its height and width when using this resizing method, place a checkmark in the **Lock aspect ratio** checkbox on the **Size** tab.

● The AutoShape has been resized.

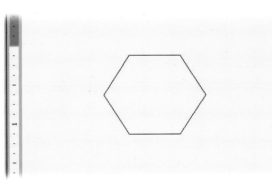

2 KEEPING OTHER PROPORTIONS

There are several combinations of keys that allow you to retain the proportion of your Auto-Shapes when resizing them.

● To maintain the ratio between the AutoShape's width and height, hold down the ⇧Shift key while you drag a corner handle. In each of these resizing methods, a dashed outline of the shape appears to show the extent of the resizing as you drag the mouse.

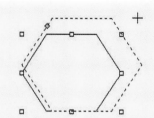

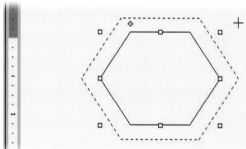

● To resize an AutoShape vertically, horizontally, or diagonally from the center outward, hold down the Ctrl key and drag one of the handles.

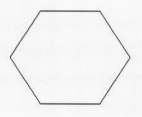

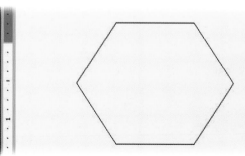

● Dragging one of the corner handles has the effect of stretching the AutoShape.

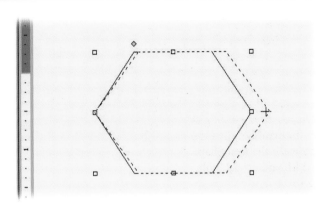

● However, if you wish to resize an AutoShape proportionally from the center outward, hold down the Ctrl and ⇧ Shift keys and drag a corner sizing handle.

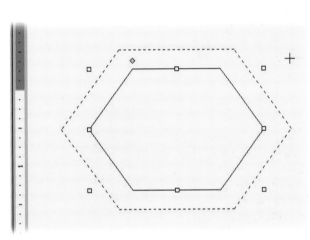

● The grab is resized without moving from its original center point.

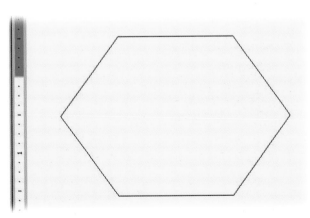

DRAWING EFFECTS

Once you have inserted a drawing object into a document, there are a number of different effects that can be applied to it. The effects include colors, gradients, shadows, line colors, and 3-D.

USING COLORS

Colors are known as "fills" in Microsoft Word since they fill an enclosed shape with the color that you select. There is a wide variety of colors from which to choose, and changing a color after using one is a very simple operation.

1 ADDING A COLOR

● Select the drawing object to which you want to add a color and click on the arrow next to the **Fill Color** button.

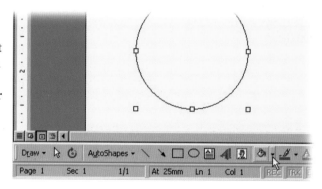

● A color palette pops up. Click on the color of your choice.

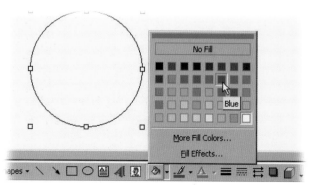

• The drawing object is filled with your selected color.

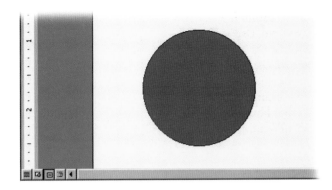

2 CHANGE A FILL COLOR

• Follow the previous steps and simply select another color from the palette. If you do not see the color you want, click on **More Fill Colors**.

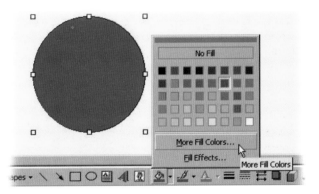

• The **Colors** dialog box opens. The **Standard** tab contains a hexagon of colors from which you can make your choice.

*The **Standard** tab* •

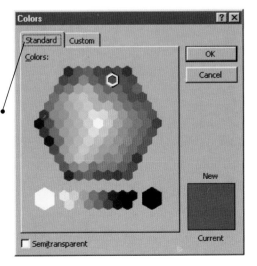

● The **Custom** tab contains a color pad. Drag the cursor across it and see the color change as you drag. Compare the new color with the current fill color in the color boxes at the bottom right.

*The **Custom** tab* ●

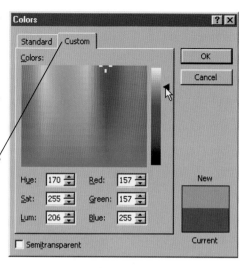

● Click on **OK** when you are satisfied with your selection.

Remove a fill from a drawing object

Select the drawing object that you want to change by clicking inside it. On the **Drawing** toolbar, click the arrow next to **Fill Color** and then click on **No Fill**. If you need to reselect an object once a fill has been removed, you'll need to click on the border of the object instead of inside it.

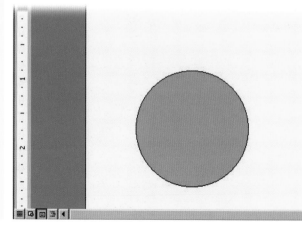

COLORS AS GRADIENTS

Gradients, or "shades," allow a more subtle use of color. Normally a gradient shades from a lighter to darker tone, or from a darker to lighter tone. However, in Word, it is possible to shade from one color to a completely different color.

1 ADD A FILL EFFECT

● Select the drawing object that you want to change. On the **Drawing** toolbar, click the arrow next to **Fill Color** and click on **Fill Effects**.

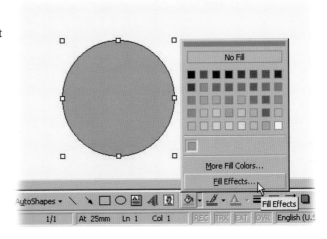

● The **Fill Effects** dialog box opens with four tabs along the top labeled **Gradient, Texture, Pattern,** and **Picture**.

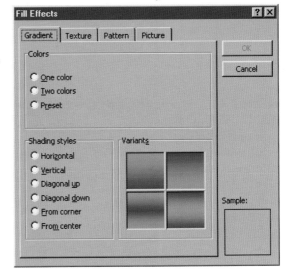

● In this example we'll use the options available under **Gradient**, also known as shade. The options on the other tabs work in a broadly similar way. In the **Shading styles** section of the **Gradient** tab, click on the **From center** radio button and click on **OK**.

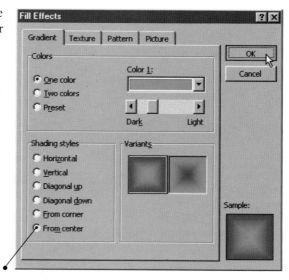

From center button ●

● The drawing object is now shaded with the lightest shade at the center and the heaviest at the perimeter.

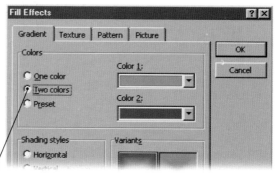

2 ADDING A SECOND COLOR

● With the drawing object still selected, display the **Gradient** tab again (as above) and click the **Two colors** radio button. A second color box, **Color 2**, appears.

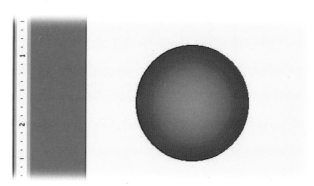

Two colors button ●

● Click on the down arrow to the right of the **Color 1** box and select a color.

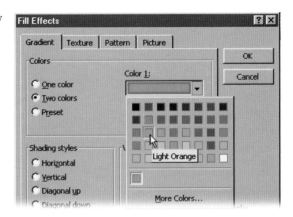

● Now click on the down arrow to the right of the **Color 2** box and select a second color.

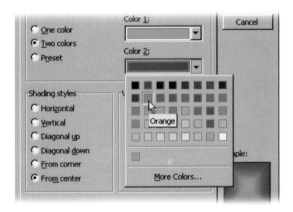

● In this example, with the gradient becoming darker toward the edges, a stronger effect is achieved if a light color is selected as the first (center) color, and a darker, but related, color is selected as the second color.

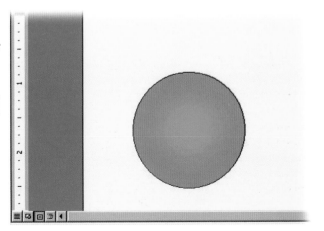

SHADOWS FOR DRAWING OBJECTS

It is possible to add depth to the objects that you create using Word by placing a shadow either in front or behind them.

The color of the shadow, the direction in which the shadow falls, and the degree of shading can all be selected and controlled.

1 ADDING A SHADOW

● Begin by selecting the drawing object and, on the **Drawing** toolbar, click **Shadow**.

Shadow colors

To see a wider range of colors, click on **More Shadow Colors** below the **Shadow Color** palette. The **Colors** dialog box opens, containing a wider selection of colors.

● A pop-up menu appears, showing several shadow options.

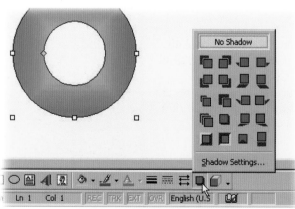

● As you place the cursor over an option, the number of the shadow style appears. Click on a shadow option to select and insert it into the document.

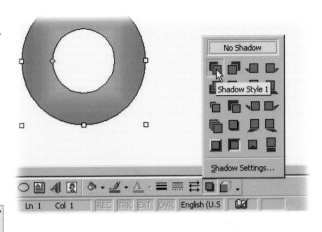

SEMITRANSPARENT SHADOWS

It is possible to change the shadow color so you can see through it. Click on **Shadow Color** on the **Shadow Settings** toolbar and then click on **Semitransparent Shadow**. This is particularly useful if you have text behind the shadow because it then becomes readable rather than hidden.

2 **CHANGING THE SHADOW COLOR**
● Select the drawing object, click **Shadow** on the **Drawing** toolbar, and click on **Shadow Settings**.

- The **Shadow Settings** toolbar appears. Click on the arrow next to **Shadow Color** and a pop-up palette appears. Click on the color you want.

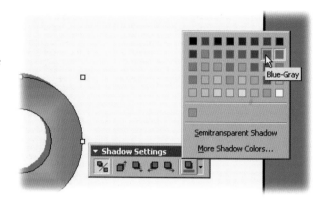

- The shadow is now colored with your selection.

3 CHANGING THE SHADOW OFFSET

- It is possible to change the position of the shadow in relation to the drawing object. This is known as the shadow offset. Follow the previous steps to display the **Shadow Settings** toolbar. The four center **Nudge Shadow** buttons on the toolbar can be used to nudge the shadow vertically or horizontally.

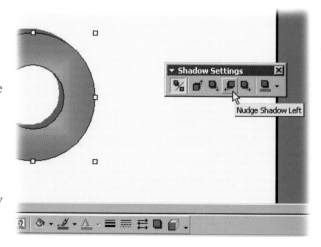

● Clicking the nudge buttons moves the shadow by 1 point (½ of an inch). To move the shadow by 6 points (½ of an inch), hold down the ⬆ Shift key while clicking the nudge buttons. Here a combination of nudging the shadow up and to the left has been used to create a larger visible area of shadow.

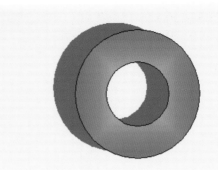

LINE COLORS AND LINE STYLES

By default, the borders of drawing objects in Word are marked by a black line. The principal controls that are available include changing the color of the line, changing the thickness of the line and, when required, removing the line.

1 ADDING A LINE COLOR

● To change the standard black line color of a drawing object, click on the object to select it. (The earlier shadow has been removed by clicking on the **No Shadow** option in the **Shadow** pop-up.) Click on the arrow next to **Line Color** and select one of the colors from the color palette that appears.

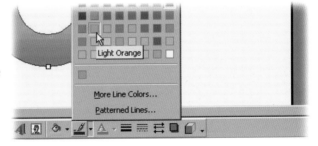

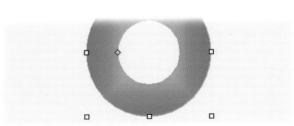

● You can also click on
More Line Colors to open
the **Colors** dialog box if
you need a wider range of
colors.

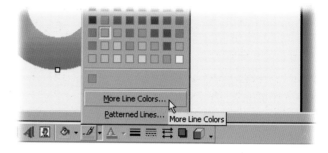

2 CHANGING THE LINE STYLE

● You can give a line a
different style, such as a
greater thickness, by
selecting the object, clicking
on **Line Style** on the
Drawing toolbar, and
selecting a style from the
pop-up menu.

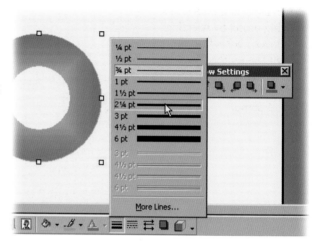

Remove a line
To remove a line from
around a drawing
object, display the **Line
Color** pop-up menu
and click on **No Line** at
the top of the menu.

USING 3-D EFFECTS

A far more dramatic method of adding depth to your drawing objects is to apply a 3-D effect to them. Word provides a range of 3-D effects that can enhance virtually any shape you use or create, and they can be customized easily.

1 ADDING A 3-D EFFECT

● A 3-D effect is added to a drawing object by selecting the object, clicking on the 3-D button on the **Drawing** toolbar, and then selecting one of the options from the pop-up menu.

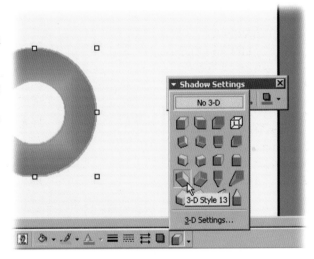

● Again, click off the object to see the effect. The 3-D effect is added to the object, which is also tilted in the direction of the chosen 3-D style.

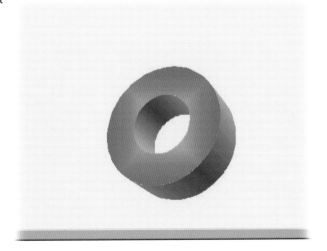

2 CHANGING A 3-D EFFECT

● Select the drawing object and click the 3-D button on the **Drawing** toolbar, then click **3-D Settings**.

● The **3-D Settings** toolbar appears; it contains several buttons with which you can alter the tilt, depth, lighting, surface appearance, and 3-D color.

● In this example, first we'll change the tilt of the object by clicking on the **Tilt Up** button repeatedly until the required tilt angle is reached.

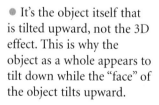

● It's the object itself that is tilted upward, not the 3D effect. This is why the object as a whole appears to tilt down while the "face" of the object tilts upward.

3 CHANGING THE LIGHTING EFFECT

● The appearance of a 3-D object can be changed dramatically by altering the way it is lit.

● Select the drawing object, click the **3-D** button on the **Drawing** toolbar, and click on **3-D Settings** on the pop-up menu to display the **3-D Settings** toolbar. Click on the **Lighting** button.

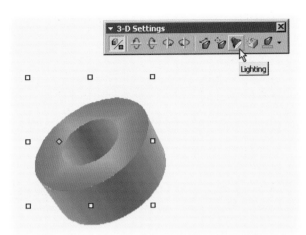

● On the drop-down menu, click on one of the buttons to select the direction from which the object is to be lit. Here, the option to light the object from below and from the left has been chosen.

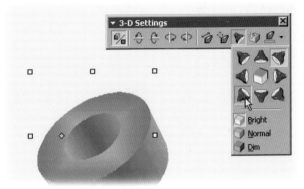

● The drop-down menu closes immediately after a selection has been made, and the drawing object now has a different light and shade effect.

● It is also interesting to experiment with the different lighting levels of **Bright**, **Normal**, and **Dim** that are available in the lighting drop-down menu.

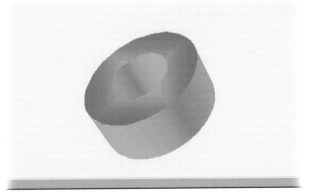

CONTROLLING OBJECTS

Once you have created drawing objects and added effects to them, there are several ways in which they can be controlled to produce the design and layout that you need.

LAYERING DRAWING OBJECTS

It's very likely that you will have more than one drawing object in your document, and it is likely that you will want to position them in a preferred order. Determining the order of objects on the page is known as layering.

1 BRING AN OBJECT TO THE FRONT

● Select the object that you want to move to the top layer (in this case, the circle) and, on the **Drawing** toolbar, click on **Draw**, choose **Order**, and then **Bring to Front**.

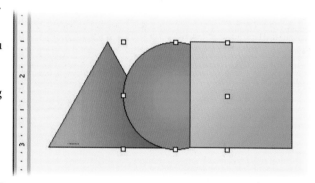

HIDDEN OBJECTS

If the object is hidden behind other objects, select one object, then press ⟨⇧ Shift⟩ + ⟨Tab⇆⟩ to select the drawing objects in the order they were created. The hidden object is eventually selected.

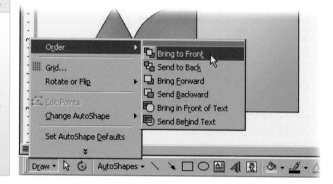

● In this case, the circle now overlays the two other objects. Click off the object to see the effect.

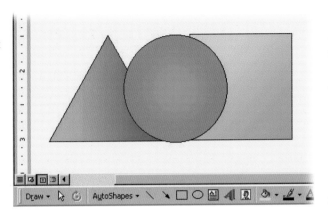

2 SEND AN OBJECT TO THE BACK

● Select the drawing object that you want to move to the lowest layer on the document page, click on **Draw** on the **Drawing** toolbar, choose **Order**, and click on **Send to Back**.

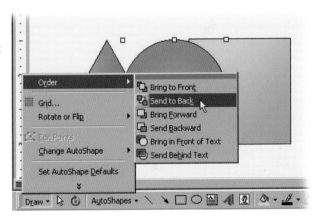

OTHER LAYERS

In the **Order** commands in the **Draw** button, there are also commands to change the object's position by only one layer – forward or backward – and for positioning an object either behind or in front of text.

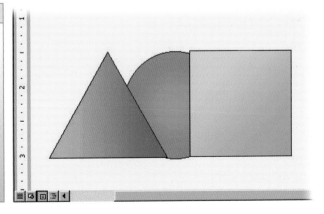

ALIGNING AND ARRANGING

In addition to arranging drawing objects in relation to one another, it is also possible to align drawing objects along any of their edges, and align them in relation to the document page. Word contains many options to arrange objects by a combination of these criteria.

1 ALIGN OBJECTS BY THEIR EDGES

● When you are handling more than one drawing object at a time, you can select several drawing objects by holding down the ⇧ Shift key as you select each one by clicking on it. Select each of the drawing objects to be aligned by their edges.

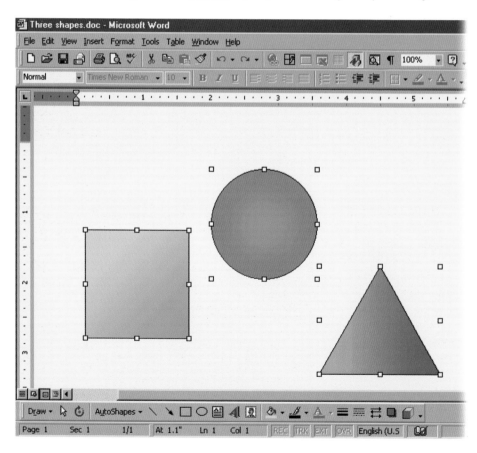

- Click on **Draw** on the **Drawing** toolbar and select **Align or Distribute**.
- In the submenu, the three center commands: **Align Top**, **Align Middle**, and **Align Bottom** move the selected objects vertically from their current positions to occupy the selected alignment. In this example, **Align Top** has been selected.

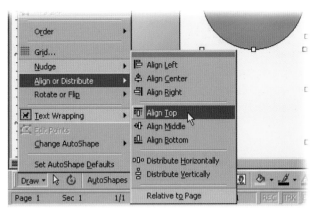

- Once **Align Top** has been selected, the objects move from their previous locations to new locations where the top parts of the objects are aligned.

2 ALIGN OBJECTS ON THE PAGE

- It is also possible to align objects relative to the edges of the page. Select the objects you want to align, click **Draw** on the **Drawing** toolbar and select the **Align or Distribute** option. In the submenu, click on **Relative to Page** to ensure that the next alignment command aligns the objects in relation to the page rather than to each other.

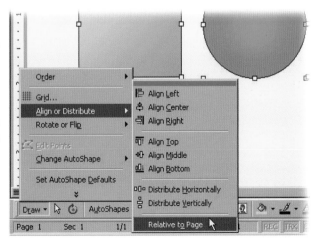

- Now on the **Drawing** toolbar, click **Draw** and then point to **Align or Distribute**. In the submenu select the page-alignment option that you want. In this example, **Align Top** is selected.
- The objects now have their tops aligned with the top of the page.

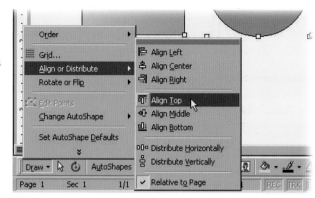

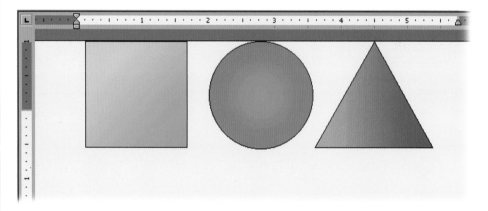

THE ALIGN OR DISTRIBUTE OPTIONS

The options available in **Align or Distribute** produce these alignments with the **Relative to Page** option checked:
Vertical alignments:
Align Left: Objects aligned down the left-hand side of the page.
Align Center: Objects aligned down the center of the page.

Align Right: Objects aligned down the right-hand side of the page.
Horizontal alignments:
Align Top: Objects aligned across the top of the page.
Align Middle: Objects aligned across the middle of the page.
Align Bottom: Objects aligned across the foot of the page.

Alignments by distribution (for three or more objects):
Distribute Horizontally: Objects are aligned across the page with equal horizontal distances between them.
Distribute Vertically: Objects aligned down the page with equal vertical distances between them.

ROTATING AND FLIPPING

An object can be rotated and/or flipped so that it adopts the orientation you want on the page. Rotation can be carried out either freehand by using the **Free Rotate** tool or precisely through 90 degrees using menu commands. The **Flip** command lets you completely reverse the orientation of an object either vertically or horizontally.

1 ROTATING TO ANY ANGLE

● Select the drawing object to be rotated and, on the **Drawing** toolbar, click on the **Free Rotate** tool.

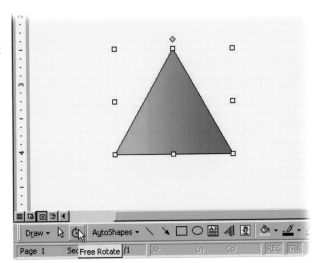

● The object now has four rotation handles around it. As you move the cursor onto the page, the object is accompanied by the rotation arrow.

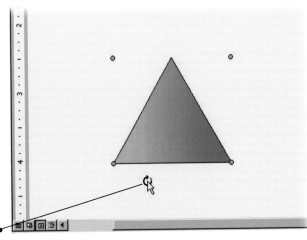

Rotation arrow ●

● Place the cursor over one of the handles of the object, hold down the left mouse button, and move the cursor in the required direction of rotation. A dotted outline appears as you rotate the object.

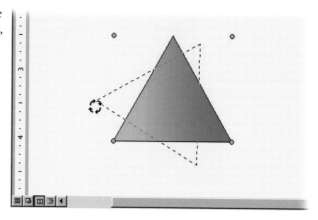

● When the amount of rotation has been reached, release the mouse button, and the object assumes its new orientation.
● You can either click on another object to rotate it, or press the [Esc] key to cancel the rotation arrow.

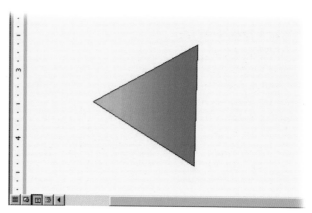

2 ROTATING BY 90 DEGREES

● Select the drawing object that you want to rotate, click on **Draw** on the **Drawing** toolbar and select **Rotate or Flip**.
● From the pop-up menu that appears, click on either the **Rotate Left** or the **Rotate Right** options.

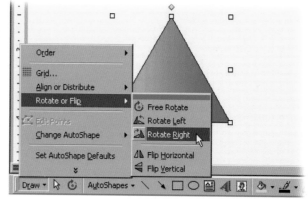

● The object is now turned through 90 degrees.

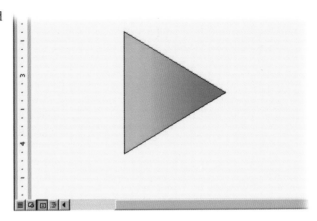

3 HORIZONTAL OR VERTICAL FLIP

● Select the object you want to flip, click on **Draw** on the **Drawing** toolbar, and select **Rotate or Flip**. Click on either **Flip Horizontal** or **Flip Vertical** on the submenu. The object is now turned through either its horizontal or vertical axis.

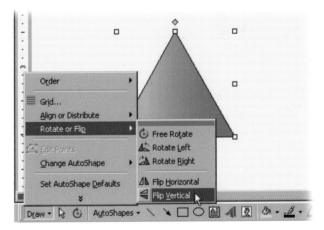

Rotate around a handle

You can rotate an object or set of objects around the handle opposite the one you have selected by holding down the Ctrl key as you move the **Free Rotate** tool.

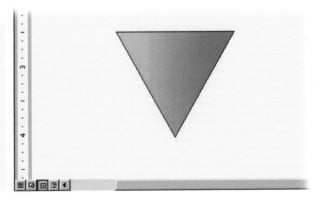

DRAWINGS AND TEXT

There are many ways to combine drawing objects with text in Word. Text can be made to wrap around drawing objects and can be placed within drawing objects by using text boxes.

TEXT BOXES

Using Word's text boxes could fill a chapter in its own right, but in relation to drawing objects, text boxes can be used to insert text into a drawing object precisely where you want it to be and can be formatted using all Word's features.

1 INSERTING A BANNER

● In this example, we'll use a banner from the **Auto Shapes** menu. Click on the **AutoShapes** button in the **Drawing** toolbar, move the cursor to **Stars and Banners,** and select a banner style from the pop-up menu.

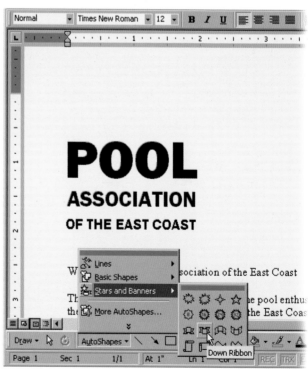

199 ❷⓿ **AutoShapes Menu**

- Position the crosshair in the document window where a corner of the banner is to appear, hold down the left mouse button and drag the mouse to draw the banner. Release the button when the banner is the size you want.

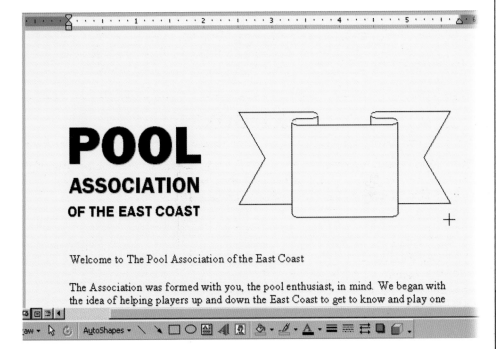

2 INSERTING A TEXT BOX

- Click on the Text Box button ⬜ on the **Drawing** toolbar.

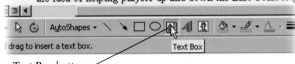

Text Box button •

25 Text Box

● Move the cursor, which is now a crosshair, onto the banner, hold down the left mouse button, and drag until the box is the required size. Release the mouse button and the text box appears with a blinking cursor ready for text to be typed in.

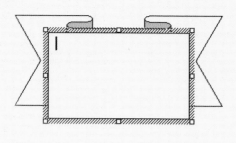

● Now simply type in your text.

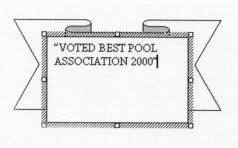

3 FORMATTING THE TEXT

● The text appears in the default font, usually Times New Roman, and is left-aligned, which isn't appropriate for banner text.
● To format the text, begin by highlighting it.

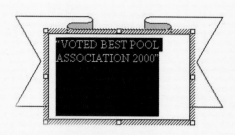

● Select a font from the **Font** drop-down menu in the **Formatting** toolbar. Here, **Gill Sans MT** is being selected.

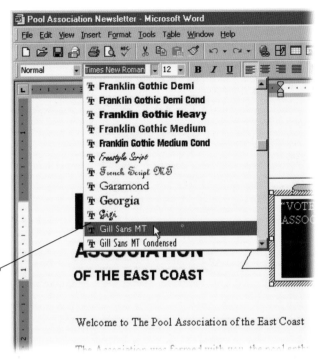

Font being selected ●

● The text now appears in the selected font, one that is more suitable for stand-alone text at the head of a document.

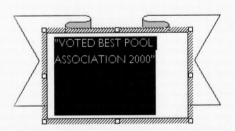

❷ Font Selector

198

- The next step is to center the text. With the text still selected, click on the **Center** button on the **Formatting** toolbar.

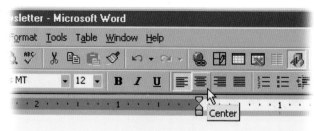

- The text is now centered, but the font size, usually the default size of 12pt, is too small for a banner.

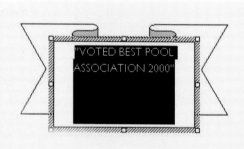

- The text should still be highlighted, so click on the down arrow to the right of the font size box and select a larger size. In this case **16pt** is selected.

Font size selection ●

❷❻ **Font Size Selector**

● The text in the box now repositions itself to accommodate the larger font size.

ciation of the East Coast

ed with you, the pool enthusiast, in mind. We began with up and down the East Coast to get to know and play one

● Once the formatting of the text is complete, click off the text box to view the results of the work so far.

ciation of the East Coast

ed with you, the pool enthusiast, in mind. We began with up and down the East Coast to get to know and play one

4 HIDING THE BORDER

● By default, text boxes have a black border. If you want to remove it, highlight the text box, click on **Format** in the Menu bar and select **Text Box**.

● Click on the **Colors and Lines** tab if it is not already displayed. Click on the arrow to the right of **Color** and select **No Line** from the drop-down menu.

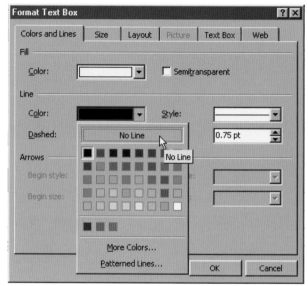

Another way to hide the border

Make the text box border color the same as the fill color of the drawing object by clicking on the **Line Color** button. If the object has no fill color, make the border white.

● Click on **OK**, and the text box no longer has a border.

5 CONCEALING THE TEXT BOX

● If the banner is given a fill color , as we have here, the box stands out from the banner because the text box has its own color. This color can be removed to completely conceal the presence of the text box . Select the text box by clicking on it.

● Click on the arrow to the right of the **Fill Color** button ⧉ on the **Drawing** toolbar and select **No Fill**.

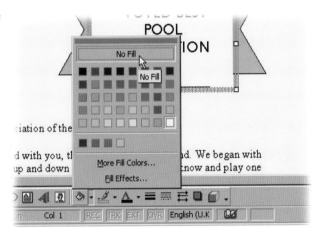

● The text box now becomes transparent and its presence is no longer apparent.

CLICK AND TYPE

You can type directly into a drawing object without inserting a text box by right-clicking inside the object and selecting **Add Text** from the pop-up menu. Each drawing object has a preselected location within it where text will appear. Also, it is possible to change the margins of the text. Using a text box superimposed on a drawing object gives you greater control over the precise positioning of your text because the box itself can be moved easily.

6 CHANGING THE MARGINS

● You can increase or decrease the distance between the borders of a text box and the text it contains. Select the text box by clicking in it and select **Text Box** from the **Format** menu.

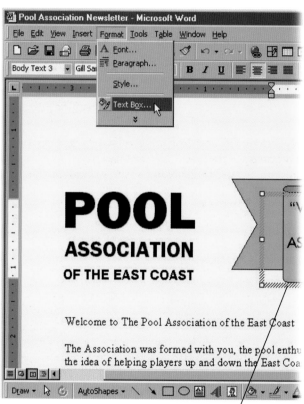

Text box selected ●

● The **Format Text Box**
dialog box opens. Click on
the **Text Box** tab and alter
the four margin options as
required.

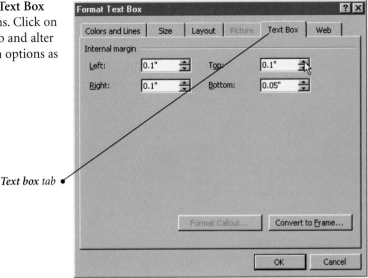

Text box tab ●

● Click on **OK** and the text
now occupies the new
position in the box that you

specified in the margin
settings.
● The **Format Text Box**

dialog box also allows you
to change other features
such as line style.

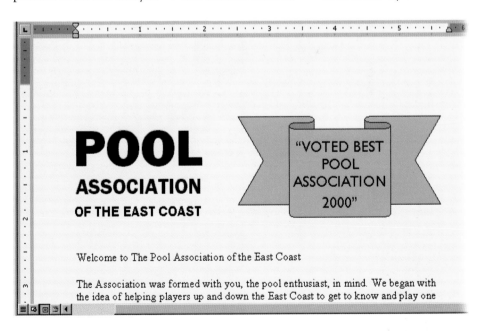

MAKING LOGO GRAPHICS

A number of techniques have been dealt with in the book, and it is now possible to combine them into a simple, but effective, logo. The examples shown here are intended to be purely illustrative and show the results rather than the steps.

1 INSERTING THE SHAPES

● The first step here is to insert a circle and a triangle into the current document. A circle can be created by selecting the **Oval** tool and holding down the ⇧ Shift key while drawing the object.

2 ADDING FILL COLORS

● The fills used here are two-color fills using white and the second color. The shading style chosen is **From center** .

3 INSERTING A THIRD ELEMENT

● A third element, a smaller circle, is inserted close to the existing objects for later use.

 206 Adding Ovals

 215 Colors as Gradients

4 INSERTING A TEXT BOX

● A text box is added to the document containing the figure 8, which has been formatted in **18pt Helvetica**, and centered. Its fill color has been removed so that it is transparent ⬜.

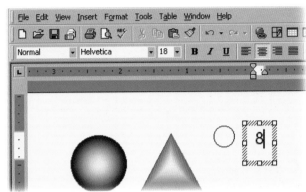

5 COMBINING THE ELEMENTS

● The separate elements are now being brought together. The small circle has been place over the black ball, and the text box is now being dragged across. The figure 8 will rejoin the box once it has been dropped into place.

6 THE COMPLETED LOGO

● With the separate elements combined, the logo is now finished.

TEXT WRAPPING

Any one of the drawing objects that can be created by using Word can be placed anywhere within a passage of text. The text itself can wrap around the drawing object in one of several ways, which are available via a menu. In addition, the margins between the text and the drawing object can be set very precisely.

1 WRAP TEXT AROUND OBJECT

● First place the drawing object over the text that is to wrap around it.

● Select the drawing object by clicking on it so that its handles are being shown.

● Select the **AutoShape** option from the **Format** menu. This option contains the majority of formatting commands you will need for drawing objects.

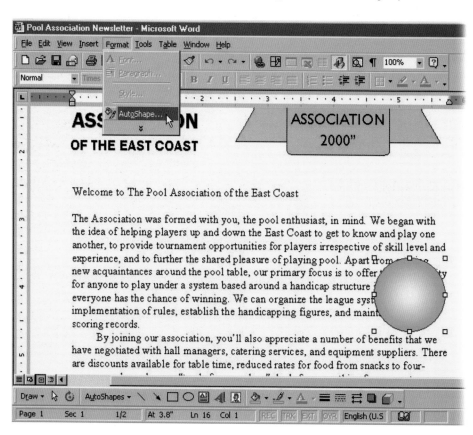

- The **Format AutoShape** dialog box opens. Click on the **Layout** tab.

Layout tab

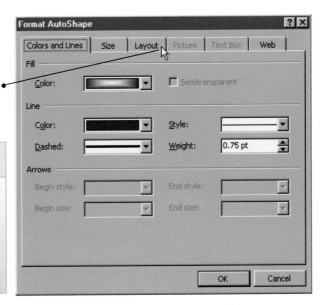

NUDGING AN OBJECT

A drawing object can be moved in small steps by selecting it and pressing the ← → ↑ ↓ keys on the keyboard to fine-tune its location.

- There are five possible options for relating the object to the text. In this case, we'll select the **Tight** option to illustrate how the text can flow around the object.
- With the **Tight** option selected, click on **OK**.

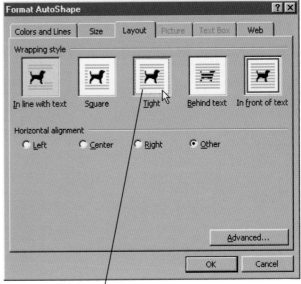

The Tight option

● The text flows around the drawing object by following its shape.

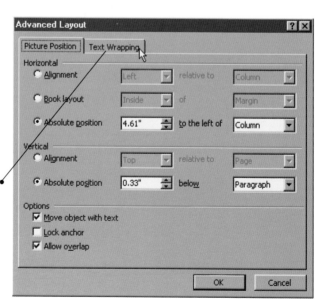

the East Coast

u, the pool enthusiast, in mind. We began with
wn the East Coast to get to know and play one
rtunities for players irrespective of skill level and
pleasure of playing pool. Apart
and the pool table, our primary
nyone to play under a system
which everyone has the
the league system, oversee
the handicapping figures, and

The text follows the • *shape of the object*

'll also appreciate a number of benefits that we
catering services, and equipment suppliers. There

2 CONTROLLING THE MARGINS

● It is also possible to use more advanced controls, such as adjusting the margins between an object and its surrounding text.

● Select the drawing object, select **AutoShape** from the **Format** menu, click the **Layout** tab in the **Format AutoShape** dialog box, click on the **Advanced** button, and click on the **Text Wrapping** tab.

Text Wrapping tab •

- Click on **Top and bottom** in the **Wrapping style** options.

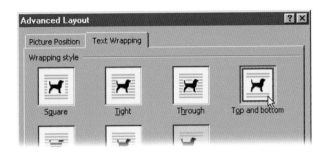

- Set the **Top** and **Bottom** margin settings by clicking on the spin buttons in the **Distance from text** section at bottom-left and click on **OK**.

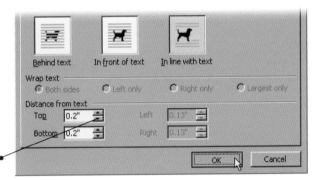

Margin settings spin buttons •

- The object is now separated from the text by the selected distances.

ON

OAST

Association of the East Coast

ormed with you, the pool enthusiast, in mind. We began with yers up and down the East Coast to get to know and play one

ASSOCIATION
2000"

USING TABLES

You can insert graphics into table cells ⌐ and insert text into adjacent cells to align with the graphic – either horizontally or vertically. You can increase or decrease the distance between text and graphics by changing the size of the table cells and the alignment of the text in the cells.

rnament opportunities for players irrespective of skill level and her the shared pleasure of playing pool. Apart from making

3 LAYERING TEXT AND DRAWINGS

● There may be occasions when you want to "layer" the text and the graphic associated with it. Begin by selecting the drawing object and select **AutoShape** from the **Formatting** menu to open the **Format AutoShape** dialog box.

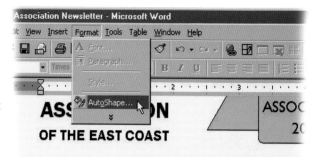

● In the **Format Auto-Shape** dialog box, click on the **Layout** tab and click on the **Behind text** rectangle.

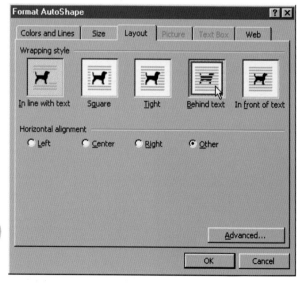

- Click on **OK**, and the text flows over the drawing object. Once you have seen the effect, it's apparent that the colors used with the text need to be chosen carefully. Dark colors cannot be used as they will make the text unreadable.

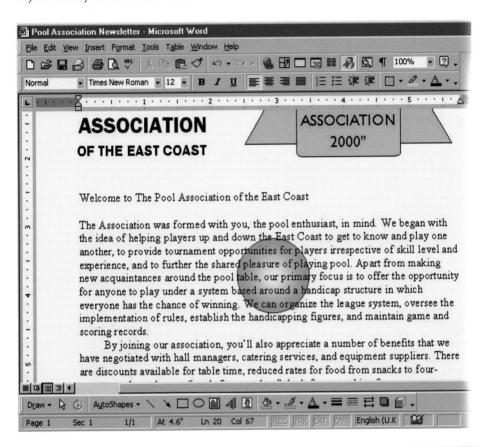

CAN'T SELECT IMAGE?

If the object that has been placed behind the text is completely covered by the text, you will not be able to select it again simply by clicking on it. To select the object, first click on another drawing object to select it (or create a temporary object if there are no others in your document and select it). Hold down the ⇧ Shift key and press the Tab⇆ key repeatedly to cycle through the objects until the object behind the text becomes highlighted. Then select **In front of text** in the **Layers** tab of the **Format AutoShape** dialog box. Once the object is in front, you can change the object as required.

ANCHORING TEXT AND DRAWING OBJECTS

Inserting a drawing object into text links it to the paragraph immediately preceding it. This link is indicated by an anchor icon in the left-hand margin, which you can see when you turn on the formatting marks. The anchor icon is at the start of the paragraph, and it is this paragraph to which you can permanently attach the object.

1 SELECTING THE OBJECT

● You may want a drawing object to move when the paragraph to which it is linked is moved. The paragraph may move position, for example, when text is inserted nearer the beginning of the document. First click on the object to select it.

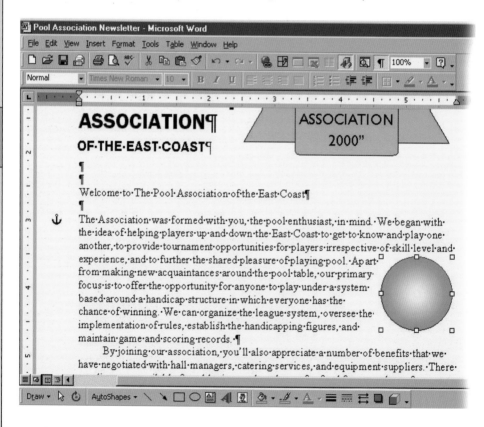

● Select **AutoShape** from the **Format** menu ⬚, click on the **Layout** tab at the top of the **Format Auto-Shape** dialog box, and click on the **Advanced** button to display the **Advanced Layout** dialog box.

● Click on the **Picture Position** tab at the top of the dialog box.

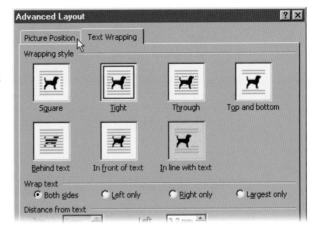

2 MOVE OBJECT WITH TEXT

● In the **Options** section, click in the **Move object with text** checkbox to insert a checkmark.

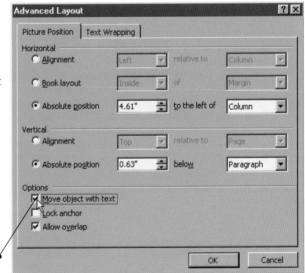

Move object with text •
check box

● Click on **OK** twice to close the dialog boxes. If the anchor icon is not visible, then click on **Show/hide** in the **Standard** toolbar.

┌───┐
│250│ **Layering Text**
└───┘ **and Drawings**

- The drawing object is now anchored to that paragraph.

- You can still move the object to any new location within the paragraph and

the text will continue to move to accommodate the object and flow around it.

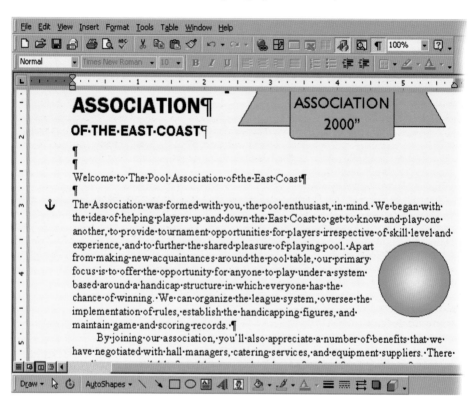

KEEPING TEXT AND OBJECTS ANCHORED

When you move a drawing object to another paragraph, the anchor icon disappears from that paragraph and reappears at the beginning of the paragraph that now contains the drawing object. In many cases, this may not present any difficulty, but there may be times when you want to move the object while making sure that it remains anchored to its original paragraph and will move with it. This is simply done by checking the **Lock anchor** checkbox in the **Options** section of the **Advanced** settings of the **Format AutoShape Layout** tab. Now, no matter how far you move the object within the document, it still moves with that paragraph.

● Now as the text is added to the first paragraph, the second paragraph moves down the page as usual, but now the drawing object attached to the paragraph also moves with it and retains its precise position within the paragraph.

OF·THE·EAST·COAST·|

¶
¶
Welcome·to·The·Pool·Association·of·the·East·Coast.·We·greatly·appreciate·your·
enquiry·and·hope·that·the·enclosed¶
¶
The·Association·was·formed·with·you,·the·pool·enthusiast,·in·mind.·We·began·with·
the·idea·of·helping·players·up·and·down·the·East·Coast·to·get·to·know·and·play·one·
another,·to·provide·tournament·opportunities·for·players·irrespective·of·skill·level·and·
experience,·and·to·further·the·shared·pleasure·of·playing·pool.·Apart·
from·making·new·acquaintances·around·the·pool·table,·our·primary·
focus·is·to·offer·the·opportunity·for·anyone·to·play·under·a·system·
based·around·a·handicap·structure·in·which·everyone·has·the·
chance·of·winning.·We·can·organize·the·league·system,·oversee·the·
implementation·of·rules,·establish·the·handicapping·figures,·and·
maintain·game·and·scoring·records.·¶
    By·joining·our·association,·you'll·also·appreciate·a·number·of·benefits·that·we·
have·negotiated·with·hall·managers,·catering·services,·and·equipment·suppliers.·There·

● The completed additional text has been accommodated at the start of the document and all the following text and graphics have moved down.

OF·THE·EAST·COAST¶   2000"¶

¶
¶
Welcome·to·The·Pool·Association·of·the·East·Coast.·We·greatly·appreciate·your·
enquiry·and·hope·that·the·enclosed·information·is·of·use·to·you.·If·you·have·any·
queries·whatsoever,·please·do·not·hesitate·to·contact·us.·We·would·like·to·take·the·
opportunity·of·pointing·out·that·our·membership·is·approaching·the·one-thousand·
mark,·and·that·the·first·five·members·to·join·once·we·have·passed·that·figure·will·be·
entitled·to·life-time·membership.¶
¶
The·Association·was·formed·with·you,·the·pool·enthusiast,·in·mind.·We·began·with·
the·idea·of·helping·players·up·and·down·the·East·Coast·to·get·to·know·and·play·one·
another,·to·provide·tournament·opportunities·for·players·irrespective·of·skill·level·and·
experience,·and·to·further·the·shared·pleasure·of·playing·pool.·Apart·
from·making·new·acquaintances·around·the·pool·table,·our·primary·
focus·is·to·offer·the·opportunity·for·anyone·to·play·under·a·system·
based·around·a·handicap·structure·in·which·everyone·has·the·
chance·of·winning.·We·can·organize·the·league·system,·oversee·the·

SHORTCUTS IN WORD

WORD CONTAINS A WIDE VARIETY OF methods for customizing the program to reflect the way in which you work. Everyone uses the Word program slightly differently, so this section will help you to build in your own preferences. These might include the look of the toolbars and screen, spelling preferences, or the many ways in which text that you use frequently can be made instantly available. There is also a comprehensive listing of those invaluable keyboard shortcuts that can save so much time and effort once you are used to them.

CUSTOMIZING TOOLBARS

Besides the default Standard and Formatting toolbars, Word offers many other useful toolbars. You can also create your own custom toolbar containing just the buttons you need.

SHOWING, MOVING, AND HIDING TOOLBARS

There is a range of available toolbars from which you can choose to view those that are most useful to the tasks that you are performing in Word. Making a toolbar visible is extremely simple, and you can then choose to place it in the most convenient position on the screen. When you have finished with a toolbar, it can again be hidden. In the example shown here, we will use the WordArt toolbar.

1 SHOWING TOOLBARS

● Position the mouse arrow anywhere on the Menu bar, the Standard toolbar, or the Formatting toolbar at the top of the Word window ⬚.

● Click on the right mouse button (right-click) and a list of all the available toolbars is displayed in a drop-down menu.

● You will see that the two default toolbars – Standard and Formatting – that are already shown on the screen are checked.

- To bring up the WordArt toolbar, drag the mouse arrow down the list until **WordArt** is highlighted.
- Now click on the left mouse button, and the WordArt toolbar appears on the screen.

- When a toolbar is shown onscreen, it may appear as a "floating" toolbar in the screen area, away from the edges, or as a "docked" toolbar, attached to an edge of the screen in the same way as the Standard and Formatting toolbars. In either case you can move it to your preferred position.

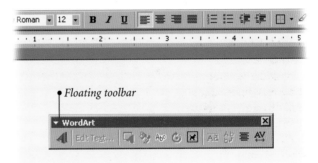

Floating toolbar

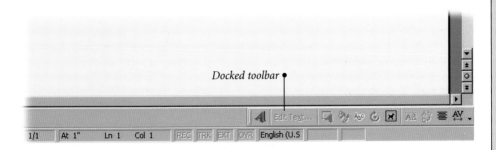

Docked toolbar

2 MOVING DOCKED TOOLBARS

● To move a docked toolbar to the top of the screen to join the Standard and Formatting toolbars, start by positioning the mouse arrow over the extreme left side of the toolbar, where you can see a vertical gray line.

● The arrow turns into a four-headed black arrow.

● Now click the left mouse button and hold it down.

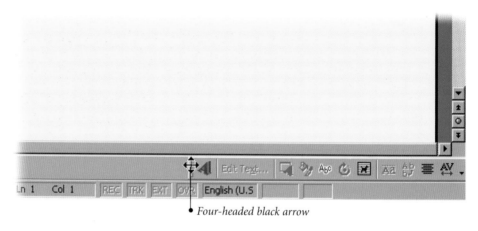

● *Four-headed black arrow*

● Drag the mouse upward and the docked WordArt toolbar changes into a floating toolbar 🗋.

● Drag the toolbar further up the screen until it is over any part of the Formatting toolbar 🗋.

● When it changes shape again and slots in at the top of the screen, release the mouse button.

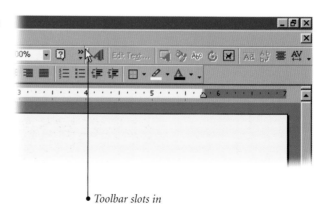

● *Toolbar slots in*

| 259 | **Showing Toolbars** | | 15 | **Formatting Toolbar** |

3 MOVING FLOATING TOOLBARS

● Click on the blue bar at the top of the toolbar next to the word **WordArt**, and then drag the toolbar over part of the Formatting toolbar at the top of the screen. When the WordArt toolbar changes shape again and slots in at the top of the screen, release the mouse button.

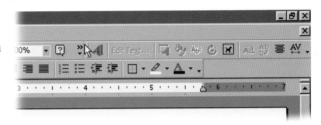

4 HIDING DOCKED TOOLBARS

To hide any docked toolbar, the operation is the reverse of making a toolbar visible.

● Position the mouse arrow anywhere on the menu or toolbars at the top of the screen, as before ⬜.

● Right-click the mouse button, and the list of all of the available toolbars is displayed.

● Click the **WordArt** entry to deselect it, and the WordArt toolbar disappears from the screen.

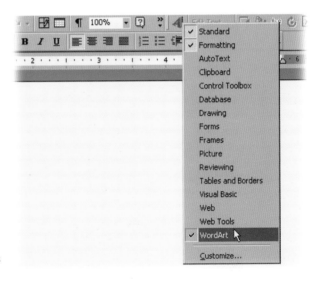

Instant hiding

To hide any floating toolbar quickly, just click on the X at the top right of the toolbar.

258 **Showing Toolbars**

ADDING AND REMOVING BUTTONS

There is a wide range of commonly used toolbar buttons available in Word that are not shown as standard. These can be found via the toolbars themselves, providing an easy way to customize your toolbars to suit the way you work.

1 VIEWING THE CHOICES

● Click on the down arrow at the right-hand end of the Standard toolbar. The **Add or Remove Buttons** panel appears.

● Hold the mouse over the **Add or Remove Buttons** button (or click on it) and the drop down list of available buttons appears. Using this list, you can decide which buttons you wish to appear on your Standard toolbar, and which you may wish to remove.

● As well as the **Print** icon on your toolbar, you will see that there is a second **Print** icon at the bottom of the list, under Microsoft Word Help. This one displays the **Print** dialog box, saving you from clicking on **File** and then **Print** each time you need to set up some print options. As an example, we are going to add this button to the Standard toolbar.

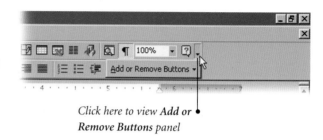

Click here to view Add or Remove Buttons panel

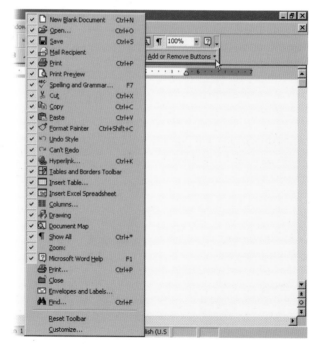

2 ADDING THE BUTTON

● To add the second Print option to the Standard toolbar, click on the icon.

● A checkmark appears in the checkbox next to the icon. Now click anywhere on the screen to close the list of buttons.

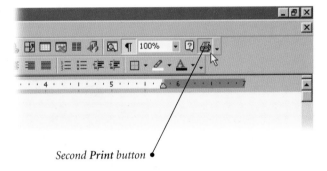

● The new **Print** icon now appears at the right-hand end of the toolbar.

● To test the button, click on the new **Print** button and the **Print** dialog box will appear.

*Second **Print** button* ●

● Click on **Cancel** at the bottom of the **Print** dialog box to close it.

Restore to Default

If you want to restore the toolbars to their default settings, open the list of available buttons as described above and click on **Reset Toolbar** at the bottom of the list.

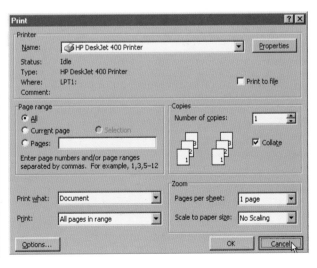

3 EDITING THE BUTTON IMAGE

● To distinguish between the new **Print** button and the original (which prints a single copy of the current document), we are going to color the new one blue.

● Click on **Tools** in the menu bar, and choose **Customize** from the drop-down menu.

● Leaving the **Customize** dialog box open, right-click the new **Print** icon on the toolbar. Another drop-down menu appears.

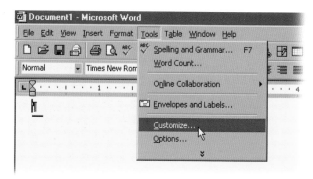

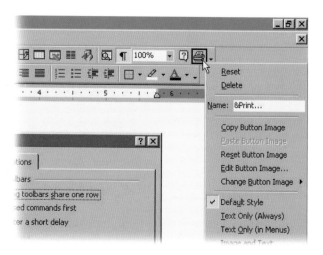

● Click on **Edit Button Image** and the **Button Editor** dialog box will be displayed.

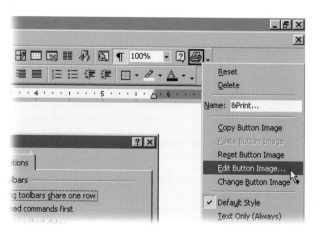

Unchangeable icons
Although you can edit the image of a **File** menu button, you cannot change it to a different icon.

● The **Button Editor** dialog
box displays the existing
Print icon image, in a
pixelated form, as well as a
color palette.

● Click on the blue block
in the palette (to select the
color that you want to use).

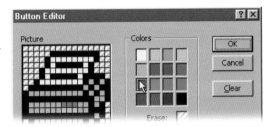

● When the **Print** icon in
the **Picture** box is as you
want it, click on **OK**.

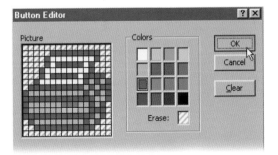

- The **Print** icon on the toolbar is now blue.
- Click on **Close** in the **Customize** dialog box.
- We now have two printer icons. One will just print out a single copy of a document, and the other will automatically display the **Print** dialog box.

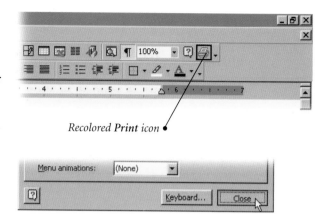

*Recolored **Print** icon* •

4 REPOSITIONING THE BUTTON

- The two **Print** icons should be next to each other, so we are going to move the new one.
- Holding down the Alt key on the keyboard (to the left of the spacebar), click on the **Print** icon to be moved and hold down the mouse button.
- Now drag the blue **Print** button, in the form of a small rectangular block, to its new location and release the mouse button.
- The two printer icons are now next to each other.

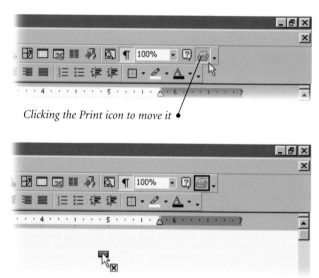

Clicking the Print icon to move it •

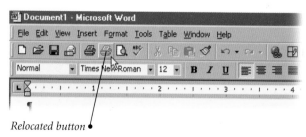

Relocated button •

5 CHANGING BUTTON STYLE

If, for example, you confuse the icon for **Format Painter** (the paintbrush) with the **Paste** button next to it, you can change the **Format Painter** icon to a picture of your choice.

● Click on **Tools** in the menu bar, and choose **Customize** from the drop-down menu.

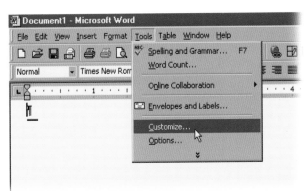

● Leaving the **Customize** dialog box open, right-click the **Format Painter** icon on the Standard toolbar and another drop-down menu is displayed, with **Format Painter** displayed in the **Name:** panel.

● Select **Change Button Image** and a panel of different icons is displayed. We are going to choose the icon that shows two identical pages – showing that one page has the same format as the other.

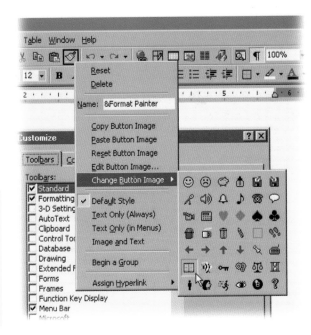

Copying a Button

To copy a toolbar button, follow the steps to move a button, but hold down the [Ctrl] and [Alt] keyboard keys, simultaneously.

- Click on the new icon, and this will now be displayed as the **Format Painter** button on the Standard toolbar. Click on **Close** in the **Customize** dialog box.

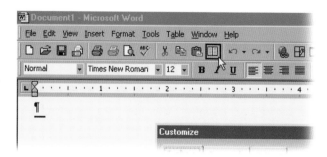

6 DELETING BUTTONS

- To delete a button from a toolbar, click on **Tools** in the menu bar and choose **Customize** from the drop-down menu.

- Now right-click on the toolbar button to be deleted (in this case the Format Painter icon that we have just changed). Another drop-down menu appears.

- Click on **Delete** in the drop-down menu, and the button is deleted from the toolbar.

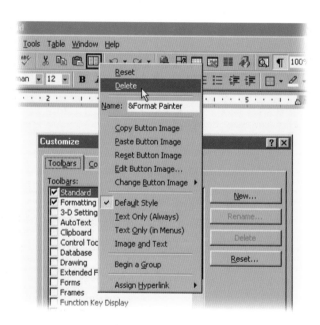

The button is deleted ●

CREATING NEW BUTTONS

Using the **Customize** option in the **Tools** menu, it is also possible to add useful buttons to the existing toolbars, add icons to the buttons, remove a button from a toolbar, or change the button's appearance and create your own personalized toolbar.

1 ADDING A NEW BUTTON

In this example, we are going to add a button to the Standard toolbar to take us directly to the **Save As** window, rather than having to use **File** in the menu bar.

● Click on the **Tools** menu, then on **Customize**.

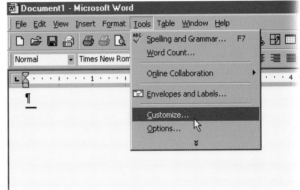

● The **Customize** dialog box is displayed.
● Click on the **Commands** tab at the top of the box to bring it to the front.

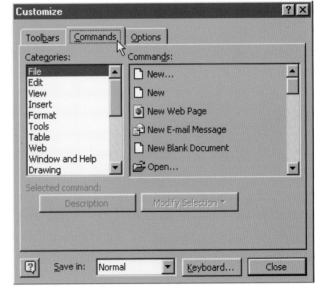

● The category we are interested in is **File**, since the **Save As** option is found in the **File** drop-down menu, so click on **File** in the **Categories:** list, if it is not already highlighted.

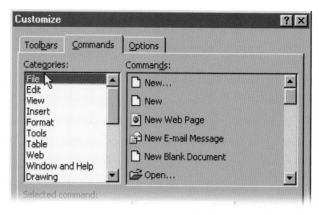

● Scroll down the **Commands:** panel to the right of the **Categories:** list and highlight **Save As....**
● Click on **Save As...** and drag it to the place in the Standard toolbar where you want the new button to be.
● Release the mouse button, and the words **Save As** now appear on the Standard toolbar.

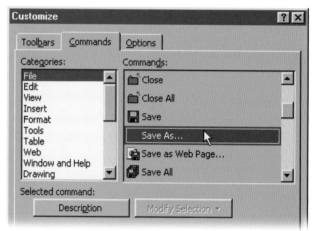

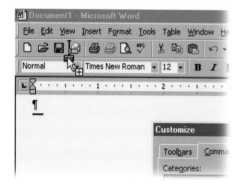

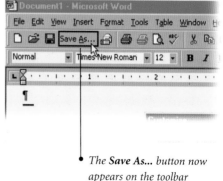

● *The Save As... button now appears on the toolbar*

2 ADDING A BUTTON ICON

Although we have **Save As...** on the toolbar, it would be better if it also had an icon as well, so let's add an appropriate icon to the text.

● Leaving the **Customized** box open on the screen, right-click the **Save As** text on the toolbar.

● From the drop-down menu, hold the mouse arrow over **Change Button Image**.

● On the drop-down menu, click on an icon that you feel is appropriate for **Save As**. In our example, we have chosen the "Arrow into disk" icon.

● This icon now appears as a button on the toolbar next to the **Save As...** text.

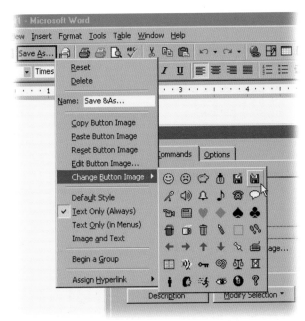

*Newly created **Save As** button*

● Click on **Close** on the **Customize** window.

● To test the new button, simply click on it and check that the **Save As** window appears, and click on **Cancel** at the bottom of the screen to close the window.

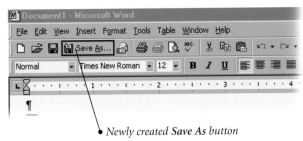

CREATING YOUR OWN CUSTOM TOOLBAR

You might want to create a toolbar that reflects the kind of work that you do and the tasks that you use within Word 2000 on a regular basis. This can save a great deal of time and effort, and it is easy to set up your own customized toolbar.

1 OPENING A NEW TOOLBAR

● Click on **Tools** in the menu bar, and choose **Customize** from the drop-down menu.

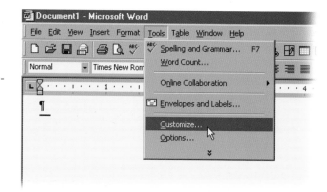

● Click on the **Toolbars** tab at the top of the **Customize** dialog box to bring it to the front.

● Click on the **New** button at the top of the right-hand side of the window, and the **New Toolbar** dialog box is displayed.

● The **Toolbar name:** field is highlighted. This is where you should enter the name of your new toolbar. In our example we are going to call it **Daily Working**.

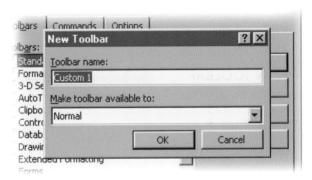

● Leave the text in the **Make toolbar available to:** field as **Normal**. This means that the toolbar will be available to you from now on whenever you open a new document based on the normal template.

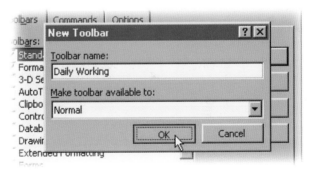

● Click on **OK** at the bottom of the window, and a small "floating" toolbar appears on the screen.

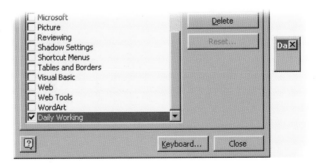

274 · SHORTCUTS IN WORD

2 ADDING BUTTONS TO THE TOOLBAR

● Now that we have our
new toolbar, we need to
select the commands that
we want to have on it. We
will start by adding the
Undo button to the new
toolbar.

● In the **Customize**
dialog box, click on the
Commands tab to bring it
to the front.

● Under the **Categories:**
list, click on **Edit**, and then
select the command **Undo**
from the **Commands:** list.

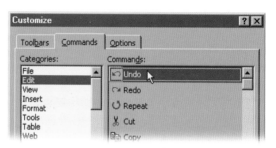

● Holding down the
mouse button, drag and
drop the **Undo** button onto
the new toolbar.

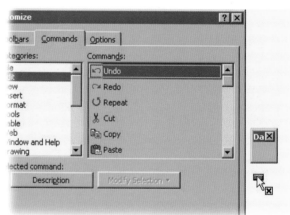

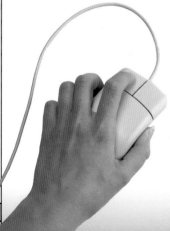

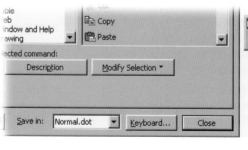

- To add more command buttons to the new toolbar, repeat these steps for the **Redo**, **Repeat**, **Clear**, and **Select All** commands, all of which are to be found in the **Edit** category.
- Click on **Close** at the bottom of the **Customize** window and the newly created toolbar is complete.
- This customized floating toolbar can be "docked" at the top of the screen like any other toolbar.

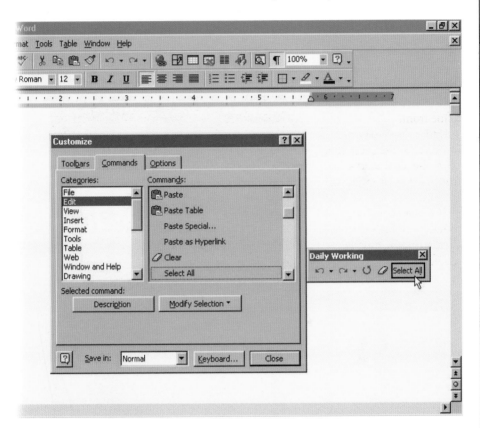

DELETING YOUR OWN TOOLBAR

To delete a custom toolbar, click on **Tools** in the Menu bar, select **Customize** from the drop-down menu, and click on the **Toolbar** tab to bring it to the front of the **Customize** dialog box. Click on the toolbar you wish to delete and then click **Delete**. The toolbar is deleted.

It is not possible to delete a built-in toolbar.

261 **Moving Floating Toolbars**

CUSTOMIZING WORD

There are three text correction features that you can customize to suit your needs. The spell checker, AutoText, and AutoCorrect can all be tailored to handle your own unique words and text.

WORD'S SPELLING OPTIONS

Word recognizes that people want their documents checked in different ways, and that many documents will contain unique spellings that, although unrecognized by Word, are nonetheless correct. Here you will learn how to control Word's spell checking, and how to tell Word that your own, unrecognized, spellings are correct.

1 CONTROLLING THE SPELL CHECK

● The principal tools for controlling how Word spell checks a document are contained in the **Spelling & Grammar** tab of the **Options** dialog box.

● To open this tab, begin by clicking on **Options** in the **Tools** menu.

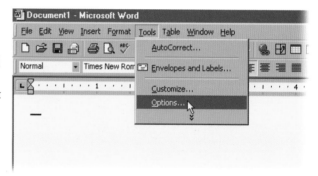

SKIP TEXT IN A SPELL CHECK

If there is a section of text that you don't want Word to check, begin by highlighting that piece of text. Select **Language** from the **Tools** menu and click on **Set Language**. In the dialog box, make sure there is a checkmark in the **Do not check spelling or grammar** check box. That text will be ignored.

● The **Options** dialog
box opens. Click on the
Spelling & Grammar tab.

● The various ways in
which you can control the
way that Word checks your

documents are shown in
the annotated **Options**
dialog box shown below.

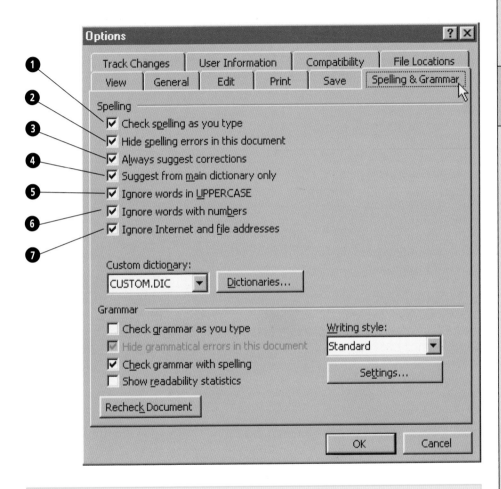

SPELLING OPTIONS

❶ With this box checked,
Word places a wavy line
beneath unknown words.
❷ Spelling errors, in this
file only, will be hidden.

❸ Spelling suggestions are
omitted in a spell check.
❹ Custom dictionary
entries are ignored.
❺ This prevents unknown

acronyms being checked.
❻ Codes, such as model
numbers, are ignored.
❼ Word recognizes a web
address and can ignore it.

2 CUSTOMIZING A DICTIONARY

● The principal way to tell Word that the spelling of a unique word is correct is to add it to a custom dictionary. Once you have done so, Word will no longer question this word.

● There are two ways to add a word to your Custom dictionary: first, when Word questions the spelling; and second, when you carry out a spell check.

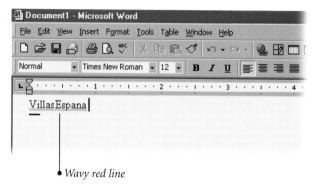

Wavy red line

QUESTIONING A SPELLING

● If you have Word set up to check the spelling as you type, a red wavy line appears below any word that Word does not know.

● Place the insertion point over the questioned word and right-click with the mouse button. A pop-up panel appears.

● Click on **Add** to add the word to your Custom dictionary.

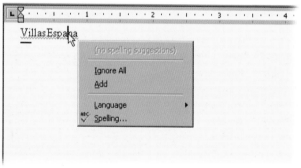

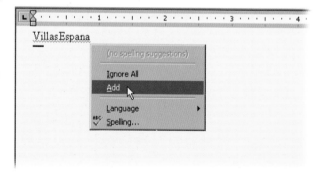

● The red wavy line disappears and the word will not be questioned again.

WHEN CARRYING OUT A SPELL CHECK

● This time the word **VillasItalia** has been typed in, and it is questioned during a spell check. The **Spelling & Grammar** dialog box contains an **Add** button. Click on the **Add** button and the word is added to the Custom dictionary.

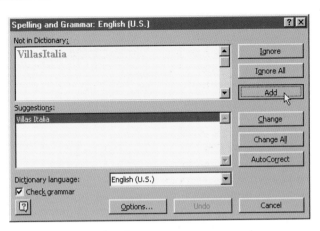

3 EDITING THE DICTIONARY

● You may have added a misspelled word to your dictionary in error, or you may wish to delete a word. These can be corrected easily. Begin by opening the **Spelling & Grammar** tab ⌐. Click on the **Dictionaries...** button.

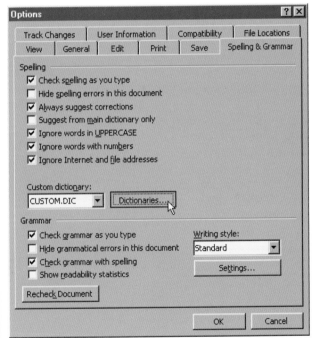

Correct language?
If you find that the **Add** option is grayed out, click on **Language** on the pop-up panel and make sure the correct language is selected.

● The **Custom Dictionaries** dialog box opens. Make sure that the dictionary checkbox **CUSTOM.DIC** is checked. Click on **Edit** at the foot of the dialog box.

● Word displays an alert panel telling you that automatic spell checking stops when you edit a dictionary, and what to do. Click on **OK**.

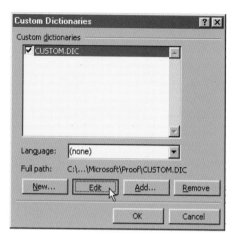

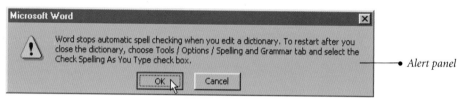

● Alert panel

● The contents of the Custom dictionary are listed on the screen as a Word document, named **CUSTOM.DIC**, which can be edited.

DELETING WORDS

If you wish to delete words from your dictionary, follow the steps shown here for editing, and delete the word as you would in any Word document.

- Let's assume that we should have left a space between **Villas** and **Italia**. Insert the space and click on the **Save** button on the Standard toolbar.
- Close the document and you are returned to your original document. Remember to open the **Spelling & Grammar** window and click on the **Check spelling as you type** checkbox before continuing with your document.

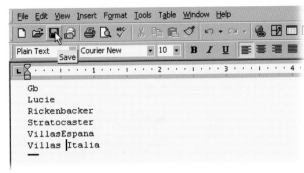

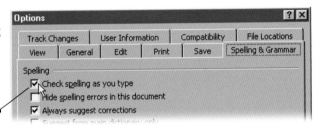

After editing the dictionary, turn on the spell check again

USING AUTOTEXT

AutoText is a very useful feature in Word that stores your own text and graphics. These can then be inserted into your documents whenever they are required.

Each AutoText entry has a unique name, chosen by you, and when this is keyed in AutoText automatically inserts the text or graphics you have linked to the name.

1 CREATING AN AUTOTEXT ENTRY

- Let's assume that you want to hold your business address in AutoText. Enter the address and set it as right-aligned text.

Align right button

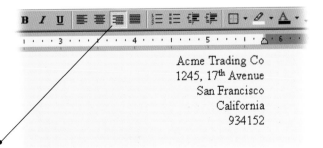

Acme Trading Co
1245, 17th Avenue
San Francisco
California
934152

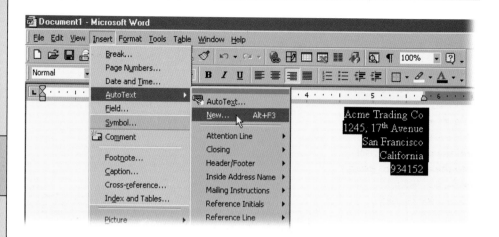

- Highlight the complete address, click on **Insert** on the Menu bar, followed by **AutoText,** and then **New**.
- The **Create AutoText** dialog box opens.
- Word suggests a name for the AutoText, but it can be made shorter so that there is less to enter. However, the name must be at least four characters long, and any AutoText entry itself must be at least five characters. Edit the name to **Acme** as the AutoText name and click on **OK**.

AUTOTEXT ALTERNATIVE

Once you have set up an AutoText entry, you can also insert it into your document by clicking on **Insert,** then **AutoText,** and then on **Normal**. A submenu of all AutoText entries is displayed. Click on the one you require and its associated text or graphic is inserted into your document.

No to AutoText
If you do not want to insert the AutoText entry, simply continue typing and it disappears.

2 INSERTING AN AUTOTEXT ENTRY

● Open a new document and type **Acme**. The AutoText containing the first part of the address is displayed above the name.
● Press the [Enter ↵] key and the address is inserted into the document exactly where you want it to be placed on the page.

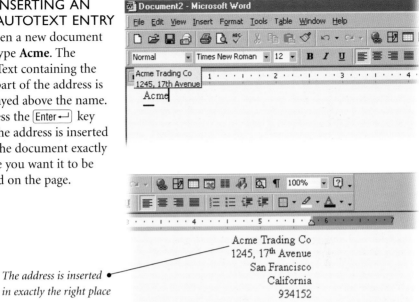

The address is inserted in exactly the right place

USING AUTOCORRECT

The AutoCorrect feature allows you to set up the automatic correction of words that you often misspell or mistype. Many common errors are already set up in AutoCorrect, but you can easily add your own. You can also use it to capitalize words, such as days of the week, and to insert symbols such as © by entering (**c**).

1 AUTOCORRECT: ADDING WORDS

● As an example, we'll use the common misspelling: **decieve** for **deceive**.
● Click on **Tools** on the Menu bar and then on **AutoCorrect...** .

● The **AutoCorrect** dialog box opens. Click on the **AutoCorrect** tab to bring it to the front. In the **Replace:** text box, enter the incorrect spelling: **decieve**. In the **With:** text box, enter the correct spelling: **decieve**. Then click on **Add**.

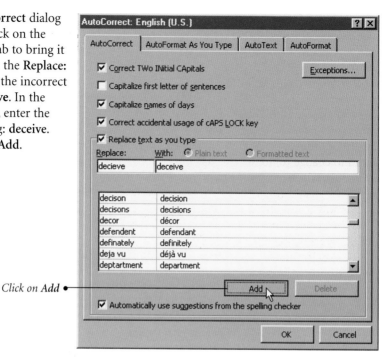

Click on Add

● The AutoCorrect entry that you have just made is now displayed in the list of AutoCorrect entries. Click on **Close**, and each time that you now type **decieve**, it will be replaced automatically with the correct spelling.

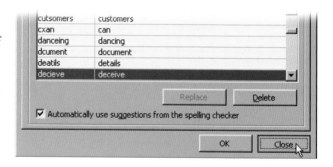

RESETTING AUTOCORRECT

If you wish to reset AutoCorrect so that entering (c) will always change to © again, use the steps outlined above to add a new entry to the list – in the **Replace:** box enter (c) and in the **With:** box type Ctrl + Alt + C to insert the symbol ©.

2 AUTOCORRECT: DELETING ITEMS

● There may be an AutoCorrect entry set up either by you or Word that is no longer required. For example, if you are listing points in a document as: (a) (b) (c), you do not want Word to change (c) to the symbol ©, which is already included in AutoCorrect.

● To remove this entry, begin by opening the **AutoCorrect** dialog box.

● Click on the line of AutoCorrect entries that contains (c) to be replaced by ©, and click on **Delete**.

● In the **Replace:** text box, (c) appears, and in the **With:** text box, © appears. If you were to click on **Add** at this point, the AutoCorrect entry would be reinstated, but simply click on **OK**. Now when you type (c) in a document, it will not automatically change to ©.

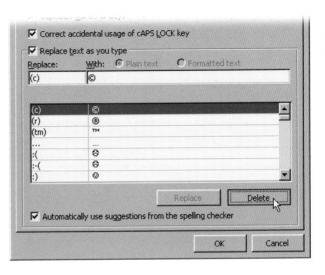

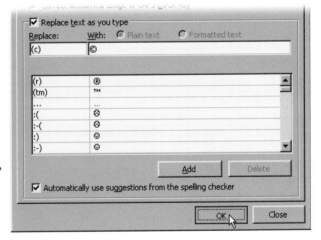

CUSTOMIZING AUTOCORRECT

In the **AutoCorrect** dialog box there are checkboxes that you can use to set up AutoCorrect to correct errors such as a sequence of two initial capital letters or beginning a sentence with a lower-case letter. As these corrections are controlled by checkboxes, you can disable them if required.

283 **AutoCorrect: Adding Words**

USING TEMPLATES

A template is a document that Word uses to build other documents. It contains settings that include the font, font size, page layout, and any special formatting features and text.

CUSTOMIZING THE NORMAL TEMPLATE

By default, all new documents are based on the settings in the Normal template unless you specifically open a new document by using an alternative template. If there are settings in the Normal template that you have to change each time you open a new document, you can change these settings in the Normal template itself, and you will not have to reset them again.

1 CHANGING FONT AND INDENT

● The default font in the Normal template is Times New Roman, but perhaps you prefer to use Arial. In addition, you may need a wider left indent.

● The first step is to locate the Normal template. Click on **Tools** on the Menu bar, followed by **Options**, and then click on the **File Locations** tab in the **Options** dialog box.

● Click on **User templates** and click on **Modify...** .

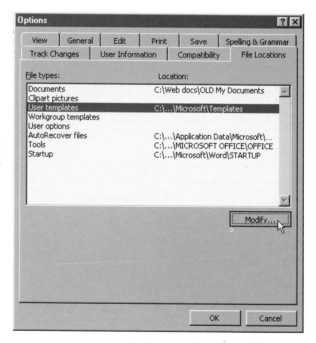

● The **Modify Location** dialog box opens. The location of the folder containing the User Templates is shown in the **Folder name:** text box. In the example, the full path is **C:\WINDOWS\ Application Data\ Microsoft\Templates**. Make a note of this path as you will need it to access the **Normal** template.

● Click on **OK** in this dialog box and click on **Close** at the foot of the **Options** dialog box.

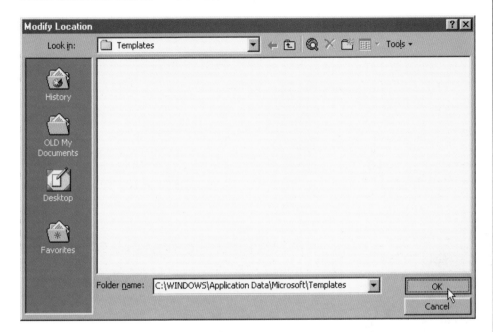

● As you cannot amend a file while it is in use, the current document window must be closed, so click on **Close** in the **File** menu.

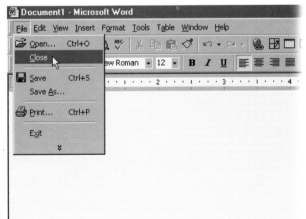

FILE EXTENSIONS

All files that are templates have a file extension of **.dot** (e.g. **Normal.dot**). Ordinary documents have an extension of **.doc**.

2 OPEN NORMAL TEMPLATE

● Click on **Open** button on the Standard toolbar.

● The **Open** dialog box appears. To find the **Normal** template, double-click on the following sequence of folders: **C:**; **Windows**; **Application Data**; **Microsoft**; and finally the **Templates** folder where the **Normal** template file is located.

● Click on **Normal** and click on **Open**.

● The template file, **Normal**, opens and can be edited as any other Word document. Begin to make the changes by clicking on the down arrow next to the font selection box and select the font **Arial**.

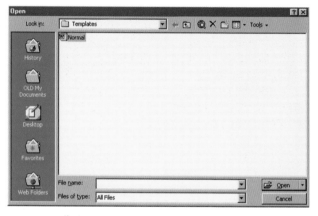

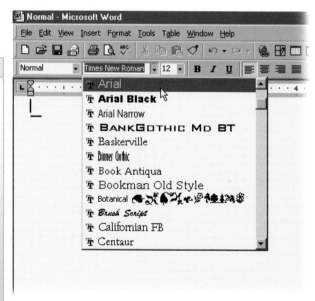

UPDATING FILES

When a template is edited, existing documents based on that template are not affected. If you want an existing file to adopt the new settings, click on **Templates and Add-Ins** in the **Tools** menu and click in the **Automatically update document styles** checkbox before you open the document.

● Place the cursor over the lower rectangle at the left of the ruler until the **Left Indent** ScreenTip appears.

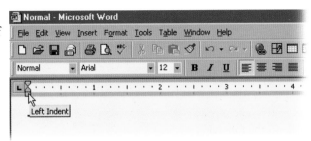

● Hold down the mouse button and drag the left indent to the half-inch position on the ruler.
● Release the mouse button and the new, wider indent is set.

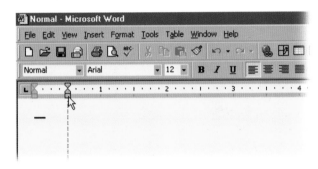

● Now click on **Save** in the **File** menu.
● The edited template cannot be used until you close Word and relaunch it. Close Word by clicking on **Exit** in the **File** menu.

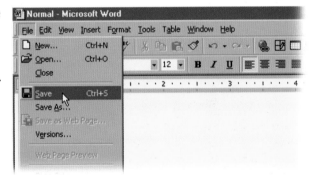

● Relaunch Word, and **Document1** appears onscreen as usual, but the font is now Arial and the left indent appears at the half-inch position. Each time you launch Word, the initial document will have these settings.

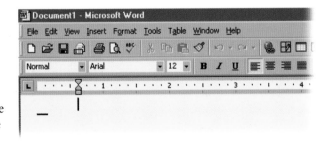

CREATING A NEW TEMPLATE

Templates can be created to contain any text and graphics that you require. These can include, for example, your business logo, your name and address, and any text that you need to be included in a series of documents. Once you have created the template, each document that you base on it will contain all those elements.

1 A TEMPLATE FROM A DOCUMENT

The easiest way to create a new template is to set up a document with the required formatting and save it as a template. We will set up a template for an agenda, with a logo, title, heading, and a date.

● Open a document based on the new **Normal** template, click on **Insert** on the Menu bar, and select **Symbol...** .

● In the **Symbol** dialog box, click on the down arrow next to the **Subset:** box and choose **Letterlike Symbols**.

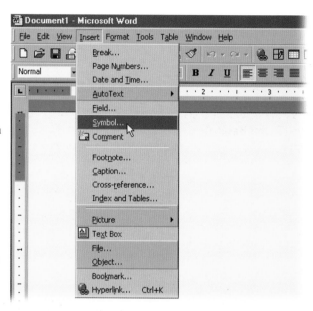

Other symbols

You can view the symbols that are available in other fonts by clicking on the down arrow next to the **Font** selection box and clicking on a font in the drop-down menu.

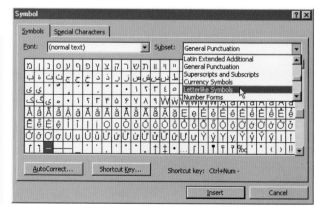

● Click on the Ω (omega) character and then on **Insert** at the foot of the dialog box. Then click on **Close** at the foot of the **Symbol** dialog box.

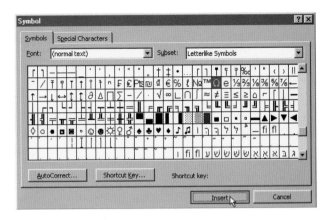

● Press ⌷Enter↵⌷ twice to create two line spaces below the Ω character and then enter: **Dallas Baseball Club**.

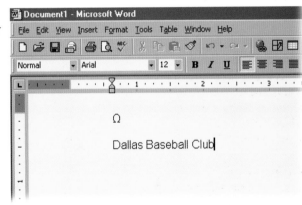

● Leave another two lines and enter: **AGENDA**.

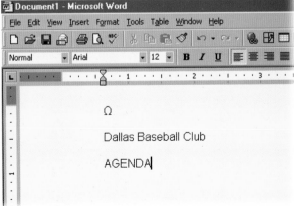

● Highlight all three lines and:

(1) Click on the **Bold** button.

(2) Click on the **Underline** button.

(3) Click on the **Center** button.

(4) Make the font size **14**.

● Place the insertion point at the end of AGENDA and press Enter↵.

● Click the **Align Left** button and deselect the **Underline** setting by clicking the button again. Leave two more line spaces and enter **Attendees**.

● Use the Tab⇆ key to move to the 4-inch ruler position and type **Date** followed by a space.

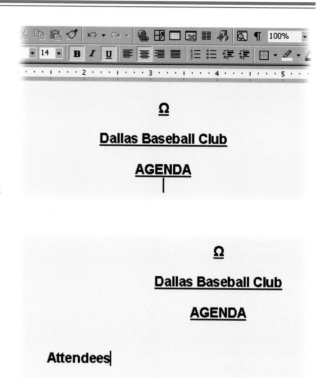

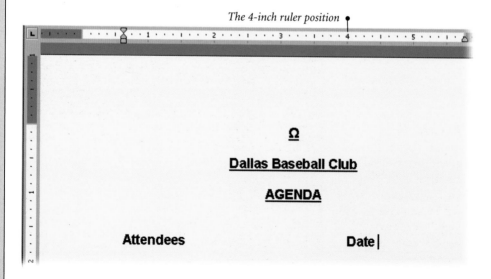

The 4-inch ruler position ●

● Click on **Insert** on the Menu bar and then choose **Date and Time...** .

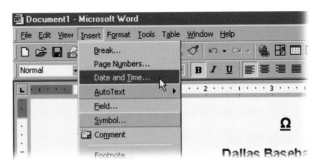

● The **Date and Time** dialog box opens. In our example, we have chosen the format: **29-Sep-00**. Click on **OK**.

● Now the agenda can be saved as a template, which can be used as the basis for all club agendas in the future. Click on **File** on the Menu bar and then click on **Save As**.

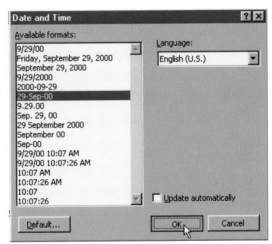

Updated date
If you click in the **Update automatically** checkbox in the **Date and Time** dialog box, then each time you open the document, the date will show the current date.

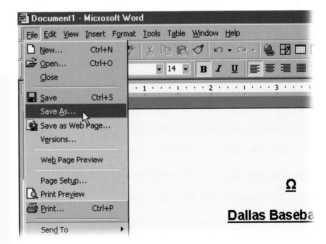

● The **Save As** dialog box opens. If the **Templates** folder is not shown in the **Save in:** text box, navigate to it as we did earlier 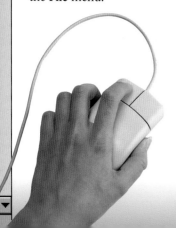. You can see in the **File name:** box that Word has suggested the file name: **Dallas Baseball Club**.

● Click on the down arrow next to the **Save as type:** text box and select **Document Template** (*****.dot**).

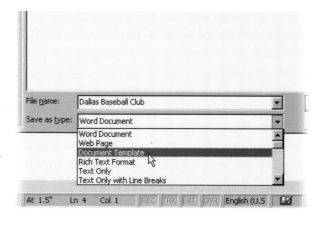

● Now the file type has changed to a template file. Click on **Save**.

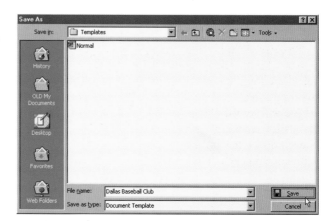

● Close the new template file by selecting **Close** from the **File** menu.

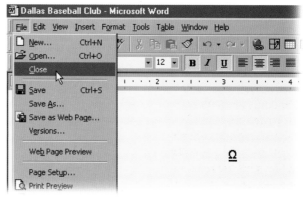

USING THE NEW TEMPLATE

The more that you use a template that you have created, the sooner you will discover how useful and time-saving they are. And now that you have found out how easy they are to create, don't be surprised if eventually you find yourself creating more templates and using them more often than the default templates provided by Word.

USING THE NEW TEMPLATE

● To write an agenda using the new template, begin by clicking on **New...** in the **File** menu.

● The **New** dialog box opens. Click on the **General** tab at the top if its contents are not visible.

● You will see the **Dallas Baseball Club** template in the window. Click on the template and click on **OK**.

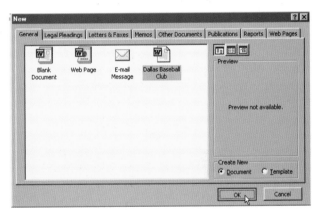

● A new document opens containing the text and formatting that was entered into the **Dallas Baseball Club** template. You can now write a new agenda and save it as a document with its own file name. The original template remains intact and ready for you to use again.

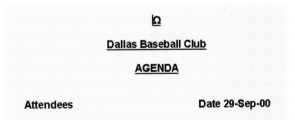

DOCUMENT SHORTCUTS

Word has many timesaving ways of dealing with documents. You can view different parts of a document simultaneously, merge documents, and use Undo, Redo, and Find and Replace.

VIEWING, MERGING, AND FINDING

Formatting a document and entering the text are central to word processing. However, Word contains many features that make it easy to deal with documents. These include methods of viewing one or more documents.

1 SPLITTING THE SCREEN

● When working with long documents, it can be useful to split the document onscreen to view different parts of it at the same time. This reduces having to scroll down the document.

● With the document open, position the cursor over the split box at the top of the vertical scroll bar. The cursor changes into two short horizontal bars with a vertical two-way arrow, sometimes called the split-screen cursor.

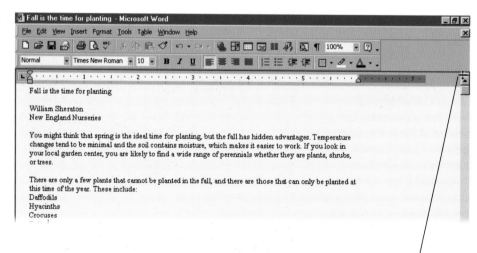

The split-screen cursor ●

● Hold down the left mouse button and drag the split-screen cursor downward. A horizontal line appears across the screen showing where the split will occur.

● Release the mouse button and the document is displayed in two panes, which you can click on, scroll through, and make changes to the document.

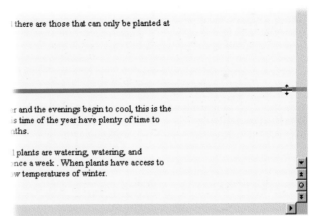

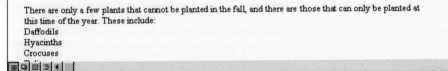

or trees.

There are only a few plants that cannot be planted in the fall, and there are those that can only be planted at this time of the year. These include:
Daffodils
Hyacinths
Crocuses

Planting tips
Once the summer sun has passed its peak and the days are shorter and the evenings begin to cool, this is the time to get digging. The plants that you put in your garden at this time of the year have plenty of time to develop a sound root system to serve them during the winter months.

The three most important activities you can carry out for new fall plants are watering, watering, and watering, which means giving the roots a thoro soaking at least once a week . When plants have access to

2 MULTIPLE DOCUMENTS

● If you are working on related documents, it can be useful to view them onscreen simultaneously.

● Open the two documents that you wish to view, click on **Windows** on the Menu bar and select **Arrange All**.

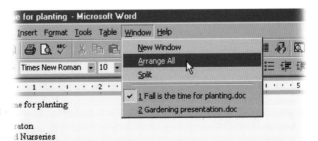

● Two half-screens appear. To edit either document, click in the half-screen and continue with the word processing as usual. The title bar at the top of the half-screen is blue when it is the active window.

● To revert to a single window again, click on the Maximize or Restore button of the document that you wish to see in full.

The active half-screen ●————

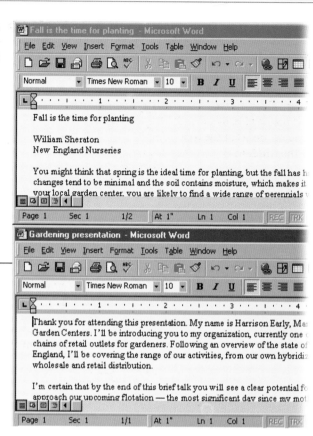

3 MERGING DOCUMENTS

● If you have written several documents that you wish to merge, you can do this by using **Insert**.

● Open the main document and place the insertion point where the second file is to be inserted. Click on **Insert** on the Menu bar and select **File...** .

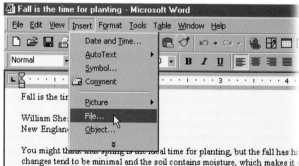

● The **Insert File** dialog box appears. You can use the **Look in:** box to navigate to the location of the file that you want to insert. Click on the document's file name and click on **Insert** at the foot of the window.

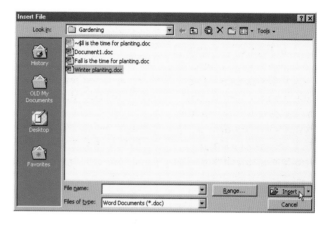

● The file is now merged with the main document. You can use the **Insert** command to merge as many documents into one as you need.

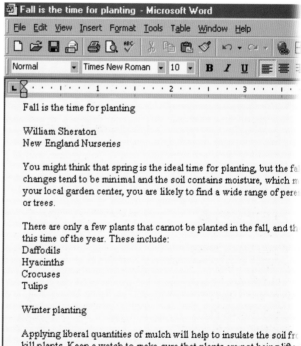

Removing the split screen
To revert to only having one document window after you have split the screen, position the cursor over the split bar until it turns into the two-way arrow, then double-click on the left mouse button.

4 UNDO & REDO COMMANDS

● As you type in or move text, Word maintains a record of your actions, which you can undo, and then redo if necessary, by using the **Undo** and **Redo** buttons on the Standard toolbar.

● To see how they work, open a new document and type in: **A demonstration of the Undo and Redo commands.** Use the Tab⇆ key to move the text to the right-hand side of the page.

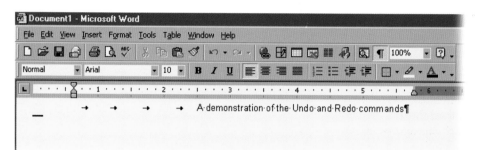

● Click on the **Undo** button on the Standard toolbar.

● The highlighted text is moved back to the left by one tab position.

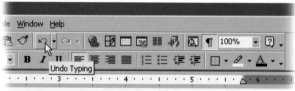

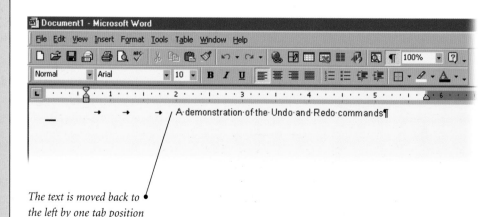

The text is moved back to the left by one tab position

● Continue clicking on the **Undo** button until you have undone all actions. This includes the sample sentence that you typed in, which will be removed from the document.

● The actions that were first carried out can now be redone by using the **Redo** button. Click on the **Redo** button next to the **Undo** button. For each click you will see the text and tab positions reinstated.

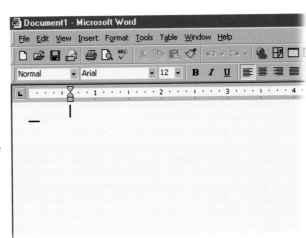

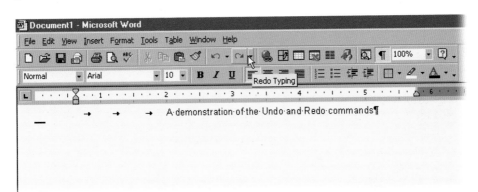

THE UNDO MENU

Word keeps an extensive list of the actions that you can undo and redo. To see the lists of actions, click on the down arrow next to the **Undo** and **Redo** buttons. From the drop-down menu you can select, for example, the last six actions to undo. Don't worry if you make a mistake – you can always redo them again. The drop-down menu displays six actions at a time. To see the previous actions, you can use the scroll bar to the right.

5 FIND AND REPLACE

● When creating documents, you may discover that you have misspelled a word or name throughout the document, or you may want to use a different word, such as **disc** instead of **disk**. Using the **Find and Replace** command, you only need enter the word to find, and enter the replacement word, and Word replaces the error when you instruct it to do so.

● An outline schedule for a two-day sales executives' training course might contain entries as shown in the example at right.

● Due to circumstances beyond the organizers' control, the first day of the course has to be brought forward by one day. Select **Replace...** from the **Edit** menu.

● The **Find and Replace** dialog box opens. Enter **Tuesday** in the **Find what:** box, enter **Monday** in the **Replace with:** box, and click on **Replace All**.

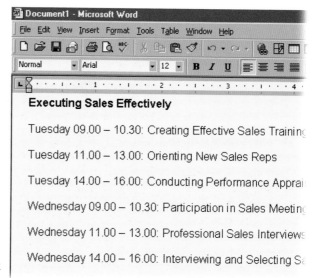

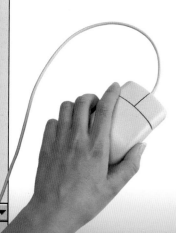

● A message is displayed that three replacements have been made. Click on **OK**.

● Click on **Close** at the foot of the dialog box.

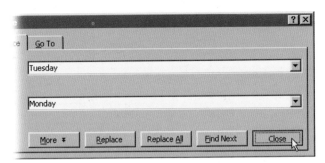

● The schedule now shows the course taking place on Monday and Wednesday.
● By using the **Replace...** button rather than **Replace All**, you can replace each instance of a word for another, one at a time. This is useful if you do not need to replace all occurrences of a word. If you use the **Find Next** button, Word highlights each occurrence of the word without replacing it. If you then decide to replace it, click on the **Replace...** button.

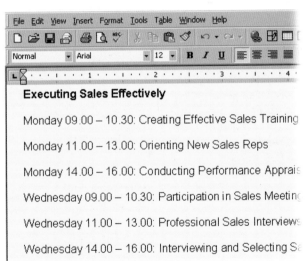

FINDING WITHOUT REPLACING

If you need to find a word in your document without replacing it, click on **Edit** on the Menu bar and then on **Find**. With a click on the **Find Next** button, the next instance of the word is displayed and highlighted. At the end of the document, a message box will appear, offering options or stating that the search is finished. To cancel a word search while it is in progress, press the [Esc] key.

KEYBOARD SHORTCUTS

In Microsoft Word 2000, a large number of tasks can be achieved using keyboard shortcuts. A basic knowledge of these can save you time and effort when producing a document.

USING THE KEYS

This section of the book provides lists of the most commonly used keyboard shortcuts. The section begins by showing how it's possible to work through a piece of unformatted text and apply formats and styles using only keyboard shortcuts. Many of these involve using letter keys together with Ctrl, Alt, and ⇧ Shift.

Key combinations

When two keys are used, one is held down while the other is pressed. For example, the shortcut Ctrl + **O** means hold down Ctrl and press **O** (to open a document). More complex commands use three keys, two of which are held down while the third is pressed. For example, to change to small capitals, use Ctrl + ⇧ Shift + **K**, meaning hold down Ctrl and ⇧ Shift, and then press **K**. The text must first be highlighted.

⇧ Shift   ⇧ Shift

Ctrl

Windows key   Alt   Alt   Windows key   Ctrl

OPENING A NEW DOCUMENT

- Ctrl + N

Pressing these two keys opens a new blank document.

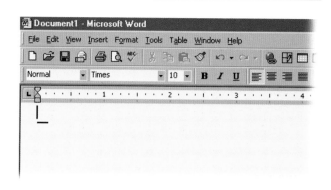

- The illustration on the right shows the basic document that will be used to show how and when keyboard shortcuts are used. If you wish to work through the example, key in the text on which to work.

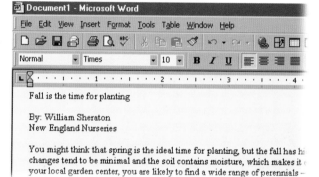

SELECTING ALL

- Ctrl + A

This combination selects all the text in the document so that you can, for example, change the font for the whole document.

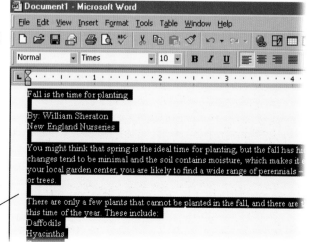

All the text in the document is selected

SELECTING TEXT TO THE END OF A LINE

● ⬆Shift + End

Place the cursor at the beginning of the text. Press these keys to highlight the text to the end of the line.

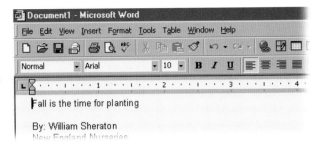

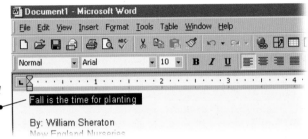

The text is highlighted to the end of the line ●

CENTERING THE TEXT

● Ctrl + E

With the text selected, press these keys to center the text.

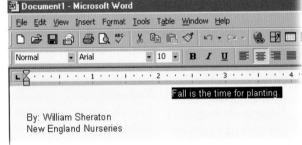

CHANGING THE FONT SIZE

● Ctrl + ⇧ Shift + >
The font size of any highlighted text can be increased by using these keys. Each press of the combination increases the font size by one point.
● To reduce the font size, press Ctrl + ⇧ Shift + <

DOUBLE UNDERLINING TEXT

● Ctrl + ⇧ Shift + **D**
Any highlighted text can be double underlined with these keys.

The text is double underlined ●

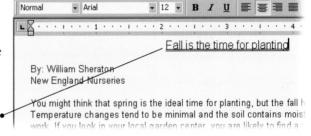

INDENTING TEXT

● Ctrl + **M**
Highlighted text can be indented using these keys. Press the combination once for each half-inch indent.

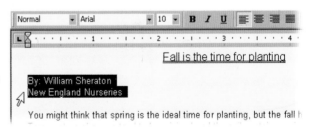

The text is indented ●

● To decrease the indent in half-inch steps, press Ctrl + ⇧ Shift + **M**.

SELECTING A WORD AT A TIME

● [Ctrl] + [⇧ Shift] + [→]

This combination selects one word to the right of the cursor.

Place the cursor at the beginning of the word ●

One word to the right of the cursor is selected ●

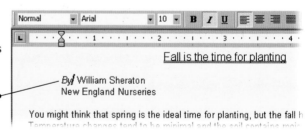

MAKING TEXT ITALIC

● [Ctrl] + **I**

Pressing these keys italicizes the highlighted text.

The italicized text ●

MAKING TEXT BOLD

● [Ctrl] + **B**

This combination of keys emboldens the highlighted text.

Emboldened text ●

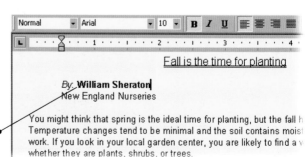

CHANGING TO SMALL CAPITALS

● Ctrl + ⇧ Shift + **K**
This key combination changes the highlighted text to an initial capital followed by small capitals.

Small caps ●

Normal ▾ Arial ▾ 10 ▾ **B** *I* <u>U</u>

<u>Fall is the time for planting</u>

By: **William Sheraton**
NEW ENGLAND NURSERIES

You might think that spring is the ideal time for planting, but the fall h
Temperature changes tend to be minimal and the soil contains mois
work. If you look in your local garden center, you are likely to find a v
whether they are plants, shrubs, or trees.

JUSTIFYING A PARAGRAPH

● Ctrl + **J**

To make both ends of the lines of a paragraph align vertically (called *justified* text), highlight the paragraph and use this combination of keys.

<u>Fall is the time for planting</u>

By: **William Sheraton**
NEW ENGLAND NURSERIES

You might think that spring is the ideal time for planting, but the fall has hidden advantages. Temperature changes tend to be minimal and the soil contains moisture, which makes it easier to work. If you look in your local garden center, you are likely to find a wide range of perennials – whether they are plants, shrubs, or trees.

There are only a few plants that cannot be planted in the fall, and there are those that can only be planted at this time of the year. These include:
Daffodils
Hyacinths
Crocuses

Justified text ●

OPERATIONS ON THE DOCUMENT

SAVING A DOCUMENT

● Ctrl + **S**
This combination of keys is one of the most useful for saving your work both while it is in progress and when you have finished.

PRINTING A DOCUMENT

● Ctrl + **P**
This key combination opens the **Print** dialog box where you are prompted to answer questions in preparation for printing.

CLOSING A DOCUMENT

● Ctrl + **W**
Pressing these keys closes the active document. If the document has not been saved, you will be prompted to save it.

SHORTCUT GLOSSARY

There are something in the neighborhood of 300 keyboard shortcuts available in Word 2000. This chapter consists of a glossary of the most useful and commonly used shortcuts.

LEARNING SHORTCUTS

Learning shortcuts is probably the most avoided activity in word processing. Everyone acknowledges their usefulness, but at any particular point it seems easier and faster to use the the menu options, for example, rather than spend a few seconds to learn and remember key combinations that will eventually save you a lot of time. Here a selection is presented to help you begin to learn Word's shortcuts.

WORKING WITH DOCUMENTS

A range of keyboard shortcuts allows you to carry out operations that affect the whole of the document. Several of these will open a dialog box.

For example, Ctrl + O (to open a document) will bring up a dialog box prompting you to choose the Word document that you want to open.

Pressing the F12 key, (above), has the effect of opening the Save As dialog box.

To Open a document .... Ctrl + O
To Save a document .... Ctrl + S
To Save a document as
(giving the document a
new name) F12
To Close a document .... Ctrl + W
To Print a document .... Ctrl + P
To Create a new
document in the same
style as the most recent .... Ctrl + N
To View document as
Print Layout .... Ctrl + Alt + P
To View document as
Normal .... Ctrl + Alt + N

POSITIONING THE INSERTION POINT IN THE TEXT AND THE DOCUMENT

These shortcuts enable you to move the insertion point on a page or between pages without using the mouse. Many require the use of the keyboard cursor arrows and of the Page Up `PgUp`, Page Down `PgDn`, and Home `Home` keys.

To Move the Insertion point:

One character to the left .... ⟵

One character to the right .... ⟶

One word to the left .... `Ctrl` + ⟵

One word to the right .... `Ctrl` + ⟶

One paragraph up .... `Ctrl` + ↑

One paragraph down .... `Ctrl` + ↓

One line up .... ↑

One line down .... ↓

To the end of the current line of text .... `End`

To the beginning of the current
line of text .... `Home`

To the top of the current
document window .... `Ctrl` + `Alt` + `PgUp`

To the bottom of the current
document window .... `Ctrl` + `Alt` + `PgDn`

Up one screen (scrolling through
document) .... `PgUp`

Down one screen
(scrolling through document) .... `PgDn`

To the top of the next document page .... `Ctrl` + `PgDn`

To the top of the previous document page .... `Ctrl` + `PgUp`

To the end of the document .... `Ctrl` + `End`

To the beginning of the document .... `Ctrl` + `Home`

Used in combination with the `Ctrl` *key, the keyboard cursor keys will move the insertion point back and forth along a line a word at a time, or up and down the page a paragraph at a time.*

SELECTING TEXT

Select one character to the right	Shift + →
Select one character to the left	Shift + ←
Select one word to the right	Ctrl, Shift + →
Select one word to the left	Ctrl, Shift + ←
Select text to end of line	Shift + End
Select text to beginning of line	Shift + Home
Select text of current line and then each line downward	Shift + ↓
Select text of current line and then each line upward	Shift + ↑
Select text to the end of the current paragraph	Ctrl + Shift + ↓
Select text to the beginning of the current paragraph	Ctrl + Shift + ↑
Select text to the beginning of the document	Ctrl + Shift + Home
Select text to the end of the document	Ctrl + Shift + End
Undo an action	Ctrl + Z
Redo an action	Ctrl + Y

DELETING TEXT

There is a difference between deleting text and cutting it, in that deleted text cannot be pasted back onto the page (see Copying and Pasting Text at right).

Delete one character to the left	← Bksp
Delete one word to the left	Ctrl + ← Bksp
Delete one character to the right	Del
Delete one word to the right	Ctrl + Del
Cut selected text to the Clipboard	Ctrl + X

The illustration shows the key combination to delete one word to the right of the cursor position: Ctrl + Del.

COPYING AND PASTING TEXT

These two keyboard shortcuts are probably the most widely used of all. They can be used not only in Word but in most Microsoft® programs and many others, too.

Copy selected text to the Clipboard . . . . [Ctrl] + C
Paste copied text into a document . . . . [Ctrl] + V

Copying and pasting using the keyboard can save a great deal of time once you are used to this easy option.

EDITING TEXT

The editing keyboard shortcuts will only apply to text that has been highlighted. Select your text using the shortcuts outlined above or by using the mouse if it is more convenient. Note that these shortcuts are "toggles" – that is they "switch" on and off the editing functions. Thus, for example, to make text bold select the text, hold down the [Ctrl] key, and press the letter **B** key. To revert to normal text, you use the same [Ctrl] and letter **B** keys.

Make text bold . . . . [Ctrl] + B
Make text italics . . . . [Ctrl] + I
Make text underlined . . . . [Ctrl] + U
Make words only underlined . . . . [Ctrl] + [Shift] + W
Make text double underlined . . . . [Ctrl] + [Shift] + D
Make text all capital letters . . . . [Ctrl] + [Shift] + A
Allow changes to the font style . . . . [Ctrl] + [Shift] + F
Allow changes to the font size . . . . [Ctrl] + [Shift] + P
Increase font size . . . . [Ctrl] + [Shift] + >
Decrease font size . . . . [Ctrl] + [Shift] + <
Format the text as small capital letters . . . . [Ctrl] + [Shift] + K

The font size of any selected text can be quickly decreased by using the key combination:
[Ctrl] + [Shift] + <

SETTING UP LINE SPACING IN A DOCUMENT

Select the text in which you wish to alter the line spacing and press the keys detailed below. These keys are not toggle keys and if, for example, you have altered the line spacing for some text to be double and then want the spacing to be single again, you have to reselect the text and enter Ctrl and 1.

Make text single line spacing............................ Ctrl + 1
Make text double line spacing........................... Ctrl + 2
Make text 1.5 line spacing.............................. Ctrl + 5

INSERTING BREAKS IN A DOCUMENT

To insert a break in a document, position the insertion point where you want the page break or line break and then press the appropriate keys.

Insert a page break............. Ctrl + Enter ↵
Insert a line break............. Enter ↵

You can determine yourself where a page ends by placing the cursor at that point and pressing Ctrl + Enter ↵ .

ALIGNING PARAGRAPHS IN A DOCUMENT

To change the alignment of a paragraph (which may be just a single line), select the paragraphs you wish to align and then enter the keys detailed below.

Center a paragraph .... Ctrl + E
Right align a paragraph............................... Ctrl + R
Justify a paragraph.................................. Ctrl + J
Left align a paragraph .... Ctrl + L
Indent a paragraph on the left .... Ctrl + M
Remove an indent from a paragraph
on the left... Ctrl + Shift + M
Create a hanging indent .... Ctrl + T
Reduce a hanging indent.............................. Ctrl + Shift + T
Remove paragraph formatting .... Ctrl + Q

WORKING WITH DOCUMENT WINDOWS

The Function keys (or F keys as they are also known) used in the shortcut tables below are shown as F1 through to F12. The keys can be found in the top row above the main part of the keyboard area.

Display the Clipboard . . . . `Ctrl` + C, `Ctrl` + C
Maximize the document window . . . . `Ctrl` + F10
Minimize the document window . . . . `Ctrl` + F5
Split the document window . . . . `Ctrl` + `Alt` + W
Close the document window . . . . `Ctrl` + W
Quit the Word program . . . . `Alt` + F4
Display the Start menu . . . . Windows key

Some newer keyboards now incorporate a Windows key that displays the Start Menu.

WORKING WITH MENUS VIA THE FUNCTION KEYS

Some of the actions available in the drop-down menus are also available via the function keys at the top of the keyboard. As well as simple operations such as **Save As** (carried out by pressing F12), these actions also include several of the more complex functions in Word, such as checking Spelling and Grammar, getting Microsoft Office Assistant Help, and opening the Thesaurus.

Microsoft Office Assistant Help F1
Print Preview. . . . . `Ctrl` + F2
Find and Replace dialog box. F5
Spelling and Grammar dialog box F7
Thesaurus . . . . `Shift` + F7

To see on screen how the printed version of your document will appear, hold down the `Ctrl` key and press F2 to change to Print Preview.

GLOSSARY

ALIGNMENT
In word processing, this refers to the edge of the text aligned in a straight vertical line along one side (for instance, left-aligned text is straight on the left edge and the line endings are ragged on the right). With drawing objects, this refers to the edges of objects aligned vertically or horizontally with each other or with the edges of the page.

ANCHOR ICON
The anchor icon sits alongside the paragraph to which a drawing object is linked.

AUTOCORRECT
A feature that can either correct errors you make frequently, or translate a few keystrokes into previously defined text.

AUTOSHAPES
A collection of shapes and drawing tools used to create drawing objects in a document.

AUTOTEXT
Allows you to specify text, which is inserted when a sequence of characters linked to the specified text is entered.

BLOCK (OF TEXT)
A selected portion of the text, highlighted in white letters on a black "block" on the screen.

CELL
The smallest unit in a table, and the location for data.

CENTERED TEXT
One or more lines laid out on the page centered around the midpoint of the page.

COLUMN
A vertical line of cells from the top of a table to the bottom.

COLUMN BREAK
A manually inserted break to end one column and force the text to start at the beginning of the next column.

CROSSHAIR CURSOR
When a drawing tool has been selected and the cursor is moved onto the document, it changes to a crosshair to indicate where a line or shape will be positioned.

CUSTOM DICTIONARY
A dictionary separate from the main dictionary, which can contain spellings defined by the user.

DATA SERIES
A group of related points in a chart – usually linked by belonging to the same category.

DATA SOURCE
In a mail merge, the list containing the data that will fill in the blanks in the main document.

DATASHEET
A table that is always linked to a chart or a graph. Data represented in the chart or graph is entered, stored, and edited in the datasheet.

DEFAULT SETTINGS
These are settings that may include, for example, layouts, formats, or fonts that Word is programmed to use unless instructed to do otherwise by the user.

DOCKED TOOLBAR
A toolbar that is locked in position at one of the edges of the document window.

DRAWING OBJECT
Any graphic or drawn shape that has been placed on a page.

DROP CAP (CAPITAL)
An initial letter of a paragraph that is larger than the rest of the text of the paragraph and drops down two or more lines.

EDIT POINTS
Points at which a curve or a freeform changes direction on the page. More commonly referred to as vertexes.

FIELD
In a mail merge, a variable part of the text, e.g. the name in "Dear <<Name>>."

FLIPPING
Changing the orientation of a drawing object by rotating it around either its vertical or horizontal axis.

FLOATING TOOLBAR
When a toolbar is selected for display, it may appear in the document window unattached to any of the edges of the window, this is known as "floating" and is the opposite of "docked."

FONT EFFECT
Effects that can be applied to areas of text, and that are in addition to the type of font and its size.

FONT
The typeface in which text

appears onscreen and when it
is printed out.

FORMAT PAINTER
A method of applying an
existing character and
paragraph format to other
text in the document.

FREEFORM
A drawing tool used to create
both straight and curved lines.

GRADIENT
The shading of one color into
another in a drawing object.

INDENT
Any part of the text that is inset
from the left margin.

INSERTION POINT
A blinking upright line on the
screen. As you type, text appears
at the insertion point.

JUSTIFIED TEXT
Text where both the left and
right edges are straight.

LINE STYLE
Alternative thicknesses or
"weight" of lines around a
drawing object.

MAIL MERGE
A way of combining a list of
data for different people with a
set letter; to send a single letter
to many people at once.

MAIN DOCUMENT
In a mail merge, the master
document is the bulk of the
text with blanks (fields) to be
filled with records from the
data source.

MARGIN
The space between the text or a
drawing object and the edge of
the paper. The four margins are:
top, bottom, left, and right.

PASTE
To place text that has been "cut"
or "copied" into the document
at the insertion point.

PLOT AREA
The area of a chart, usually in
the center, where the data is
calculated and laid out.

PRINT LAYOUT VIEW
This view displays the
document and its contents in
exactly the same way as it will
appear when printed.

PRINT PREVIEW
An on-screen view of exactly
how a page will appear when
printed.

RADIO BUTTON
A small circle next to an option
in a dialog box, which is either
empty or contains a small black
circle to indicate that the option
has been selected.

RECORD
In a mail merge, a record is one
entry for a certain field, such as
"John" in the "Name" field.

RESIZING
Dragging one of the handles
surrounding a drawing object
to change its shape.

ROW
A horizontal line of cells
extending from one edge
of a table to the other.

RULERS
Indicators at the top and left of
the screen, with intervals
marked in inches or centi-
meters. Rulers also show the
indents and margins of the text.

SCROLL BARS
Bars at the foot and the right of
the screen that can be used to

display different parts of
the document.

SHADING
Also known as a "fill," this effect
applies a background color or
shade to a section of text.

STYLE SHEET
A collection of formatting
instructions that can all be
applied simultaneously to a
selected area of text.

TAB LEADERS
A sequence of periods or
hyphens leading from the end
of a section of text to the text
at the next tab position.

TABS
Preset or customized positions
along one or more lines of text.
Text is aligned down the page
against these positions when the
tab position is reached after
pressing the tab key.

TEMPLATE
A file containing styles that will
be applied to every document
that is based on it.

TEXT WRAPPING
The flow of text around an
object embedded in the text.

VERTEX
A point at which a curved line
or a freeform changes direction.
Vertexes can be added and
deleted, and can be used to
alter the degree to which a
line curves.

X-AXIS
Usually the horizontal axis in a
graph, which contains
categories.

Y-AXIS
Usually the vertical axis in a
graph, which contains values.

INDEX

J
justified text 38, 87, 89

K
keyboard shortcuts 26–7, 304–15

L
launching
 style sheets 117
 Word 11
layering 226–7, 250
layout 34–9
 charts 162
 tables 144–51
 text and images 246–51
leaders, tab stops 111
letter spacing 82
letters 16–18
lines 200–5
 drawing 221–2
 spacing 44–5
lists 100–15
logos 244–5

M
mail merge 66–73
margins 52
 text boxes 242–3
 wrapping text 248–9
merging 72–3, 298–9
mouse, selecting text 28–30
moving
 around document 26–7
 buttons 266
 text 31–3
 toolbars 260–1
multiple
 columns 112–15
 documents 297–8
 line spacing 45
 styles 131–2

N
nudging 247

O
offsets, shadows 220–1
options
 charts 173
 spell check 277
ovals 206

P
page setup 52
pagination 23
paragraphs 22–3, 86–99
 indenting 36–7
 style sheets 120–1
patterns, charts 192
plot areas 186–7
positions, tab stops 106
printing 50–3
 letters 25
 merged mail 72–3
proportions, AutoShapes 210–11

R
records 68–70
rectangles 207
redo 300–1
resizing borders 95
right tabs 110
rotating, objects 231–3
rows 139, 145–6, 150–1
 charts 178–9
rulers
 columns 149
 tab stops 108–11

S
sample charts 168
saving files 24, 47, 49, 294
selecting text 28–30
semitransparent shadows 219
shading tables 155–7
shadows 197, 218–21
shift key 304
size
 AutoShapes 208–11
 charts 165, 170–1
 columns 148–9
 fonts 41, 79–80, 119
 rows 150–1
 table cells 147
 text boxes 238–9
sorting data 142–3, 151
spaces
 between paragraphs 90–1
 style sheets 120
spell check 54–5, 58–60
 customizing 276–81
splitting the screen 296–7
start menu 11

storing letters 46–7
style
 borders 94
 buttons 267
 fonts 42–3, 80
 lines 222
 sheets 116–33

T
tabbed lists 105–11
tables 136–57, 249
 convert to chart 159–60
templates 61–2
 customizing 286–95
text
 boxes 45, 234–43
 editing charts 180–2
 style sheets 124–5, 132–3
 tables 140–1
 wrapping 246–51
texture, charts 191
thesaurus 57–8
titles
 charts 174–5
 toolbars 273
toolbars 12–15, 197–9
 customizing 258–75
types, charts 163–7, 171–2, 182

U
underline 43, 85
undo 300–1
updating template files 288–9
using templates 29

V
vertical lines 115
viewing documents 296–303

W
weight, charts 188
window 12–13
wizards 63–5
WordArt toolbar 259
wrapping text 246–51

ACKNOWLEDGMENTS

PUBLISHER'S ACKNOWLEDGMENTS
Dorling Kindersley would like to thank the following:

Indexing Specialists, Hove.

Paul Mattock of APM, Brighton, England, for commissioned photography.

Microsoft Corporation for permission to reproduce screens
from within Microsoft® Word 2000.

Every effort has been made to trace the copyright holders.
The publisher apologizes for any unintentional omissions and would be pleased,
in such cases, to place an acknowledgment in future editions of this book.

Microsoft® is a registered trademark of Microsoft Corporation
in the United States and/or other countries.